Series Editors:
Alan Ware (University of Oxford) and
Vincent Hoffmann–Martinot (Sciences Po Bordeaux)

political conflict and political preferences

communicative interaction between facts, norms and interests

Claudia Landwehr

First published by the ECPR Press in 2009

The ECPR Press is the publishing imprint of the European Consortium for Political Research (ECPR), an independent, scholarly association, which supports and encourages the training, research and cross–national cooperation of political scientists in institutions throughout Europe and beyond. The ECPR's Central Services are located at the University of Essex, Wivenhoe Park, Colchester, CO4 3SQ, UK

Typeset in Times 10pt by the ECPR Press
Printed and bound by Lightning Source

British Library Cataloguing in Publication Data
A catalogue record for this book is available from the British Library

ISBN 13: 978–0–9558203–0–4

The ECPR Monographs series is published by the ECPR Press, the publishing imprint of the European Consortium for Political Research (ECPR).

The ECPR is an independent, scholarly association, established in 1970. It supports and encourages the training, research and cross-national co-operation of political scientists throughout Europe and beyond. The ECPR currently has nearly 350 European institutional members and associate members in over 40 countries, from as far afield as New Zealand and Japan. These members together form a network of thousands of individual political scientists, international relations and European studies specialists.

The ECPR Monographs series publishes major new research in all sub-disciplines of political science and includes work from both senior and younger members of the profession and translations of important new research not yet published in English.

To Martin

contents

list of tables and figures

acknowledgements

This book is a revised version of my doctoral thesis, which was written between 2004 and 2007, while I was a doctoral student and junior research fellow at the University of Hamburg. I thank my supervisors, Katharina Holzinger and Michael Th. Greven, for their frequent encouragement and for their constructive criticism and suggestions. Manfred J. Holler and his group have commented on the project in the Adam Smith seminar on Tuesday evenings and have corrected some (but surely not all!) of my misunderstandings of economic theory. In 2007, I had the opportunity to spend two months at the Australian National University in Canberra, where I found not only beautiful weather, but also an atmosphere of lively and inspiring discussions in seminars as well as over lunch, coffee and wine. Bob Goodin has kindly agreed to be a member of my examination board and has given valuable comments and advice. I also want to thank all of those who have discussed this project with me at several conferences, in workshops and in seminars. Some points which I initially did not see I was able to take up later and I am sure they have improved this book.

I thank the Max-Delbrück-Centre for allowing me to use the excellent transcripts of the citizen conference on stem cell research which they organised, together with the Forschungszentrum Jülich, in Berlin in 2003. I also thank all my interview partners for patiently answering my questions on what happened before, during and after the Bundestag's decision on stem cell import. Ingrid Schneider in particular has spent two long nights with me, providing me with inside information and discussing my outside interpretation of what happened. Surely, this interpretation remains subjective and may partly be driven by my theoretical interests and perspective, so that some of those who were directly involved may think it biased or even entirely mistaken. I want them to know that I have greatly valued their information and have done my best to take it seriously and to provide a fair and accurate account of the German stem cell conflict.

My friends and colleagues at the University of Hamburg have been part of a friendly and enjoyable work environment. Not only their encouragement and advice, but also the distraction they offered have greatly helped me write this book. I miss them and will always think back to the great time I had in Hamburg.

Finally, I want to thank my parents for bringing me up to enjoy books and theories and for giving me the confidence to pursue my own projects, and my brother and sister for the early training in different modes of communicative interaction (successful to differing degrees).

Most dearly, however, I thank my husband Martin to whom this book is dedicated. Without his love and support, I might not have embarked on the project and would not have completed it with so few moments of frustration. His ideas have both inspired my work and taken my attention to other important topics at the right times.

introduction

Modern societies are characterised by conflicts between incommensurable values and norms, clashing interests, and competing acceptances about the state of the world and causal mechanisms within it. The diversity of different possible positions and opinions also means that actors are confronted with a deep uncertainty about what is true and right. Under these conditions, the success of deliberative theories of democracy is hardly surprising. In a nutshell, deliberative democracy promises to replace – by means of a power-free discourse – conflict and uncertainty with consensus and truth.

This is a book about political conflict and political preferences and about the role of communicative interaction in politics. It is also a book about deliberative democracy that addresses not so much the promise of deliberation and how it is going to be fulfilled but rather the fundamental empirical and analytical assumptions upon which it is based. These assumptions concern rationality, political preferences and the effects of communicative interaction on preferences. My goal is to propose a positive theory that takes a step towards filling what are, in my eyes, important gaps in the theory of deliberative democracy: the lack of an adequate model of preference-transformation and the lack of a theory of the effects of distinct institutional properties on interaction and actor preferences.

The 'deliberative turn' (Bohman & Rehg 1997) in democratic theory began in the early 1990s.[1] The idea of deliberation is now immensely popular, not only in academic settings but also in public debates. It is advocated as a means of overcoming conflicts between seemingly irreconcilable interests and opinions and as a way of promoting the common good by tracking sensible solutions to intricate problems.

However, the early deliberative democrats developed their theories at a highly abstract level, formulating desiderata for inclusive government and just decisions. Although deliberative theory is eventually based on positive assumptions, empirical research that tests them is a rather new development. As a result, the empirical foundations of deliberative democracy have long remained contestable and still require more underpinning. Moreover, deliberative democracy's first advocates were, apart from a general affirmation of liberal democracy, comparatively reluctant to make explicit proposals as to how deliberative institutions should be constructed. This meant that the theory of deliberative democracy could be criticised for lacking criteria to assess the deliberative qualities of *existing* institutions and practices as well as an account of how these could become more deliberative (cf. Fung 2005: 398).

In reaction to such criticism, a large body of empirical literature on deliberative democracy has emerged in the last few years.[2] The early pioneer in empirical research on deliberation was James Fishkin, who invented the method of deliberative polling (Fishkin 1991). Since the early 1990s, Fishkin and his students have organised and analysed numerous public consultation procedures, most famously in New England. Deliberative polls, consensus conferences and other examples of citizen participation have provided researchers with valuable quasi-experimental evidence on the feasibility and effects of deliberative democracy in practice.[3]

Others have focused on communicative interaction itself in order to assess its qualities and derive desiderata for effective communication. On the one hand, there is an influential debate on the respective merits of arguing and bargaining as modes of interaction, especially within the discipline of international relations (see Gallhofer & Saris 1996, Risse 2000). On the other hand, a group of researchers around Jürg Steiner have developed a 'discourse quality index' that measures properties such as mutual respect among interlocutors and the sophistication of arguments (Spörndli 2004, Bächtiger 2005, Steiner *et al.* 2005).

On the effects of communicative interaction on individual motivation, and specifically on the issue of preference transformation, some new monographs must be mentioned. Simon Niemeyer fruitfully uses the Q-method to illustrate dynamics of preference change in a citizen conference that dealt with a conflict on environmental policy (Niemeyer 2002). Kasper Hansen employs survey methods to analyse the effects of deliberation on participants in a Danish national consensus conference on the introduction of the European currency, the Euro (Hansen 2004). Another recent and interesting contribution comes from Diana Mutz, who sounds a critical note by pointing out empirically that involvement in deliberative processes can undermine the motivation for political activism (Mutz 2006).

Finally, the contexts in which interaction takes place and the possibility of institutionalising deliberative democracy have come into view. Deliberative democracy has been connected with theories of consociational democracy and advocated for divided societies (O'Flynn 2006) and in the transformation to democracy (Leib & Baogang 2006). These considerations are also relevant in the context of international negotiations (Risse 2000) and European integration (Eriksen 2007).

While deliberative democracy becomes increasingly dominant in democratic theory, practice seems to be overtaking theory. The parliament, which most democratic theories regard as the primary deliberative forum, is often better described as a place for public contestation and justification of decisions than as one for dialogical exchange of arguments. But decisions are typically made *before* parliamentary debates on a given topic take place. Around the world, the number of new, mandated forums that prepare and implement decisions 'at arm's length' from the government and outside the elected legislature keeps growing (van Thiel 2004: 175). In the institutional design and public justification of these new forums, deliberative democracy is often explicitly referred to. Given its proponents' reluctance to deal with matters of institutionalisation, however, important institutional properties, such as the composition, task and decision-rule of a forum, rarely seem to be deliberately chosen.

In practice, deliberative democracy's goals of consensus and epistemic progress have commonly been translated into distinct institutional structures. Interest-bargaining rounds will, if they succeed, yield consensus on particular courses of action to be taken. Actors stick to their interests and preferences but trade concessions on some points for greater benefits in other areas. Expert commissions, by contrast, are not supposed to take decisions but rather to produce information and recommendations with regard to a given goal. Contrary to the expectations of deliberative democrats, however, such commissions rarely achieve consensus.

I think that one of the reasons for deliberative democracy's remaining deficits in theory and research on how distinct institutional properties affect outcomes is that it so far lacks an explicit model of preference-transformation as well as a model that specifies and explains the effects of different modes of interaction on actor preferences. Accordingly, the plan of this book is to derive such models from the theory's most basic assumptions.

The first of these fundamental assumptions concerns rationality and preferences. Whereas economic theories typically apply a narrow conception of rationality that concerns only the choice of means, theories of deliberative democracy adopt a wider understanding that extends beyond instrumental rationality to the choice of ends, values – and preferences. This more far-reaching conception of rationality has an empirical as well as an analytical aspect. The empirical one is the assumption that actors seek to adopt rational goals and preferences and base their selection on reasons. The analytical one is the assumption that these reasons are, in principle, accessible to the observer and that actions and decisions can be accounted for by reference to these reasons.

The second fundamental assumption on which theories of deliberative democracy are based is the idea that communicative interaction promotes and encourages both epistemic progress and consensus. The relationship between communication and consensus or *Verständigung* (reaching understanding) through the convergence of actor preferences is apparently regarded as one of necessity. As Habermas puts it: 'reaching understanding is the inherent *telos* of human speech' (1984: 287). There are assumed to be constitutive rules of communicative interaction that induce some kind of co-ordination wherever people engage in it. The relationship between communication and truth, by contrast, must clearly be a more contingent one. Exclusion and power imbalances can lead to manipulation and polarisation instead of democratic deliberation – Habermas himself has pointed out the dangers of 'systematically distorted communication' (Habermas 1976).

The conception of preference that takes centre stage here is not necessarily a central element in theories of deliberative democracy. David Estlund has famously argued that 'preference models' of democracy fail the challenge of Kenneth Arrow's impossibility theorem (Estlund 1990). In his article 'Democracy Without Preference', he argues for a model of democracy in which common-interest statements instead of actors' preferences become the input to democratic decisions.

Kasper Hansen claims that 'preference' is simply the economic term used to refer to individual motivations where psychologists speak of 'attitudes' and political scientists of 'opinions' (Hansen 2007). However, as I will argue in chapter one, both the concept of attitude and that of opinion (or belief, or statement) lack a central element that is implicit in the concept of preference: that of *comparative evaluation*. This element is central where political conflicts and decisions are concerned, as it implies both the freedom and the necessity to choose. Robert E. Goodin points out the importance of the preference, belief and value elements of democracy and highlights the legitimacy of the preference element as constitutive for the preservation of individual autonomy (Goodin 2003).

Many deliberative democrats therefore use the concept of preference, and with good reason. Besides the conceptual advantages, the use of a common concept with economic theories of democracy makes it easier to clarify empirical and normative differences. The first monographs on deliberative democracy in the early 1990s set out this model of democracy in clear opposition to economic models. Economic models typically treat preferences as exogenous to their models and thus assume that they are stable and universally homogeneous. Taking a normative turn from these analytical assumptions, authors in the tradition of Robert Nozick (1974) and William Riker (1982) have argued that preferences must be respected in political decisions and that interference with them is necessarily manipulative. What most deliberative democrats highlight, in contrast to this, is not so much that preferences are empirically irrelevant in politics (they clearly aren't) or that their role is not legitimate, but that they are *endogenous* to decision-making, that they are formed and transformed in processes of communicative interaction.

Cass Sunstein was probably the first to discuss the phenomenon of endogenous preference in a political context, arguing that

> ...preferences are not fixed and stable, but are instead adaptive to a wide range of factors – including the context in which preference is expressed, the existing legal rules, past consumption choices, and culture in general (Sunstein 1990: 5).

He criticises the economic model of what he terms 'subjective welfarism', which assumes that the only legitimate input to democratic decisions is the subjective conceptions of welfare citizens have. Instead, Sunstein points out that one goal of democracy is 'to ensure autonomy not merely in the satisfaction of preferences, but also, and more fundamentally, in the processes of preference formation.' (Sunstein 1990: 12)

What is important to theorists of deliberative democracy, therefore, is the conditions under which political preferences are formed and transformed in processes of communicative interaction. The origins of such transformation can, as the next chapter will show, be both of a cognitive kind (seeing that my original preference is not instrumental to my goals) and of a volitive kind (seeing that my original goals are not worth pursuing). While the former kind is highly relevant to democratic theory, it is the latter that marks off deliberative democracy from economic models of democracy (see Sunstein 1993 and the comment by Ferejohn 1993).

At the same time, it is important to remember that preference-transformation is not *per se* a good thing but that its desirability depends, like its probability, on the communicative contexts in which preferences are expressed and formed. Preference-formation is influenced not only by the mode of interaction (such as bargaining or arguing) but also by the composition of the communicating group, the power structures within and outside the group and the dynamics of interaction. 'Group think' can induce polarisation and one-sided information and lead to endogenous preferences which are, from a normative point of view, less desirable than the original ones and more likely to spark than to accommodate conflicts (Sunstein 2003).

I consider the concept of preference to be not only of analytical value but also central to normative democratic theory and to the justification of liberal rights and institutions, positive and negative rights are based on the assumption that citizens' interests and values motivate their decisions and that there exists a systematic relation between utility and action: children, for example, are denied some of these rights because it is assumed that their actions and decisions do not always promote their own utility. The relation between utility and action is made up by rational preferences. The book therefore focuses on actor preferences and the role institutional factors play in their co-ordination and transformation through different modes of interaction. It is based on an understanding of politics that assumes that social conflict can rarely be resolved but often accommodated by political decisions. This does not mean that the instrumental and co-ordinative qualities of decisions cannot be assessed. However, the concern is not with truth but with the rational selection of premises for decisions.

I argue that a closer look at the premises of preferences and the reasons on which they are based allows the observer to better understand the various dimensions of political conflicts. In political practice, communicative interaction can serve to make these premises explicit, to assess and co-ordinate preferences, and to disentangle the factual, moral and interest dimensions of a conflict. However, different modes of interaction can be expected to have different effects on actors' preferences and their premises, and to play different roles in the decision-making process. My goal in the first part of the book is to develop a theoretical framework that allows me to identify such different modes of interaction, to describe their preconditions and properties and to outline possible institutionalisations of them.

The second part of the book applies this theoretical framework to the political conflict in Germany over whether to allow the importation of embryonic stem cells. The case is typical in that the conflict entailed factual and moral dimensions as well as competing interests; it is also exceptional in that a number of different forums were concerned with this conflict, some of which enjoyed a high public profile. The result of the decision-making process was a political compromise that, at least temporarily, served to accommodate a conflict that was morally irresolvable and, in terms of interest, irreducible. This raises questions about the role and necessity of compromises in politics and particularly in potentially divisive and polarising bioethical conflicts.

At the same time, the application of the theoretical framework to a political conflict and decision enables inferences on how, when and why specific institutional contexts promote or prevent the rational transformation and co-ordination of preferences. Such inferences are of value to deliberative theory in that they contribute to the resolution of the question of how deliberation can best be institutionalised. They are of value to democratic theory in general in that they show what contribution different types of forums, in particular ones outside the elected legislature, can make to the accommodation of conflict and to the justification of decisions.

OUTLINE OF THE BOOK

The first chapter addresses the central concepts of rationality and preferences. It looks at existing concepts in the literature and advocates a wider understanding of both rationality and preferences than is typically applied in economic and rational-choice approaches. A wider understanding of rationality, which includes the choice of both ends and means, is endorsed. An adequate concept of political preference, in turn, is argued to have both a volitive component (ends, desires) and a cognitive one (acceptances about the world and causal mechanisms within it). I try to show that every political conflict and decision requires the formation and transformation of preferences over policy options and programmes. Accordingly, political preferences must be assumed to be endogenous to the discursive processes that precede and accompany a decision. Engaging in communicative interaction in order to assess the premises of one's preferences is described as a requirement of rationality.

Chapter two moves from the challenges of individual decision- and preference-formation to those of collective decision-making and points out the importance of communicative interaction for both. The link between the two levels, I argue, is the requirement for justification. Drawing on speech-act theory and theories of discursive commitment, I argue that justification and reciprocity, as constitutive rules of communication, also drive the assessment and co-ordination of preferences in political discourses. I look at the reasons why people enter discourses and the conditions under which co-ordination can be successful. Thus, while chapter one deals with deliberative democracy's fundamental assumptions about the rationality and transformability of preferences, this chapter addresses its assumptions about the origins of rational preference-transformation in communicative interaction.

Chapter three puts the theoretical framework together. Using the results of the first two chapters, it seeks to develop a typology of modes of political interaction. The discursiveness and the co-ordinativeness of institutional settings are pointed out to be the central factors that determine the mode of interaction and probability of preference-transformation within them. On the basis of these parameters, the modes of discussion, deliberation, bargaining and debate are distinguished as ideal-types. Each of the ideal-typical modes of interaction, with its respective properties, is discussed in some detail, and possible institutionalisations are pointed out by reference to empirical examples. In so far as a mode of interaction is successfully realised in a forum, testable hypotheses can be derived on whether and how actors' preferences are going to be transformed.

Chapters four and five are devoted to the empirical case study of forums, interaction and preference-formation in the decision whether to allow embryonic stem cells to be imported into Germany. Chapter four sets out the problems political actors were confronted with when the topic first appeared on the agenda. It outlines the various controversial questions and thus the different dimensions of conflict and gives a brief overview of events, stages of decision-making and central actors. In addition to this, it provides information on the kind of data that were available and describes the methods used for their analysis. The methods of speech-act analysis and argumentation analysis are shown to be particularly suitable for the application of the theoretical framework and for an assessment of the hypotheses derived from it.

Chapter five analyses the different forums concerned with the conflict over importing stem cells: two expert commissions, the parliamentary plenum, an informal bargaining round and a citizen conference. Interaction in each of the forums is compared to the respective ideal-type mode and analysed with regard to its discursive and co-ordinative qualities. The aggregation of reasons and processing of the conflict in each of the forums is described, and occurrence and direction of preference-transformation are assessed.

While this comparatively small number of observations does not allow for a satisfactory test of hypotheses, the value of the theoretical framework is illustrated and a number of inferences on the contribution of different types of forums to the decision-making process and accommodation of conflict are derived. Despite the fact that the main goal of the case study is to apply the theoretical framework and illustrate its use, rich chronological description is also intended to provide insights into a political conflict and compromise that is, in many ways, exemplary for the challenges of political decision-making under conditions of diversity, complexity and uncertainty.

NOTES

1. Probably the first to use the term 'deliberative democracy' was J.M. Bessette (1980). For recent accounts of deliberative democracy, see, for example, Gutmann & Thompson (1996),

Bohman (1996), Dryzek (2000) and Goodin (2003), as well as collections by Bohman & Rehg (1997), Elster (1998), Macedo (1999) and Fishkin & Laslett (2003).

2. See, for example, the special issue of *Acta Politica* (Vol. 40, No. 1+2).
3. See Niemeyer (2003), Hansen (2004) or the collections by Joss & Durant (1995) and Gastil & Levine (2005). A particularly famous example is the consultations in connection with the Oregon health plan (see, for example, Fleck 1994 and Daniels 1996).

chapter one | preference and decision

What does it mean for an actor to be rational? Why do social scientists seek to 'rationalise' behaviour? What are standards for the rationality of collective decisions? This first chapter seeks to clarify the concepts of rationality and preference, which are considered central to political theory (sections 1 and 2). A concept of political preference is distinguished from the typical economic concept of preference. While the latter refers only to volitive aspects of motivation (wants and desires), the former should include cognitive aspects as well. It is argued that both the cognitive and the volitive premises of political preferences can be modelled and rationalised (sections 3 and 4). The rational decision as to what to do or which political options to support, so the argument goes, requires decisions about what to accept as true and about what to want, i.e. what goals to pursue and rules to abide by (section 5). The final section (6) points out that the formation and transformation of political preferences through communication is a requirement of rationality.

A model for the rational formation and transformation of preferences at the individual level is necessary in order to develop a theory about the effects of communicative interaction on actor preferences and decisions at the aggregate level, which is attempted in chapter two. With regard to empirical analysis, it helps to point out how and why single important actors changed their position.

1. RATIONALITY

The demand for a general rule to guide action is first of all an epistemological rather than an ontological one (Searle 2001: 145): the observer seeks to organise the world through categorisations and generalisations, while the actor herself does not depend on general rules to act and decide. An obvious candidate for a general theory of human action appears to be a theory of human rationality. Rationality may be understood either as a property of the decision-making processes by which actions are selected on the basis of volitive and cognitive attitudes, or as a property of the results of actions. Accounts of rationality as a property of results of actions are known as 'externalist' accounts of 'objective' rationality, while accounts of rationality as a property of decision-making processes are known as 'internalist' accounts of 'subjective' rationality.

Externalist accounts are less interested in explaining particular decisions but rather use rationality as an 'as-if' assumption to predict the behaviour of large numbers of people. Their focus is on the macro rather than the micro level (see Green & Shapiro 1994: 20–23). Proponents often refer to the 'law of great numbers', which is thought 'somehow to reconcile the indeterminism in the behaviour of the individual with determinism in the behaviour of the collectivity'. In addition, many tend to apply evolutionist arguments in order to justify the rationality assumption. The idea is that evolution favours individuals who successfully choose the appropriate means for their ends (cf. Nozick 1993: 181). This implies, among other things, a capacity to form true beliefs. Evolution, moreover, would favour individuals with strong incentives for survival and reproduction as those who lack these incentives would simply die out. The latter argument entails a 'thick' concept of rationality that, besides the rationality assumption, contains presuppositions about the kind of preferences actors pursue. According to the evolutionist argument, actors should be expected to have preferences for instrumental goods such as money and status as well as for anything that increases their chances of survival and reproduction.

The 'thick' evolutionist reading of rationality also helps to justify the 'homogeneity assumption', claiming that 'models apply equally to all persons under study' (Green & Shapiro 1994: 17), which otherwise could only be defended as theoretical parsimony. One case in which the evolutionist argument is commonly applied is the behaviour of companies (as collective actors) in the free-market economy. Market pressures can plausibly be compared to evolutionary ones, in that companies that do not maximise profit simply are not going to survive.[1] However, the attempt to explain human action by 'laws of nature' that is entailed in externalist approaches must be abandoned where models fail to yield true predictions (Green & Shapiro 1994.: 23, 31). Only where rules sufficiently general to make non-trivial (and true!) predictions could, in fact, be established, could social theory justly claim to meet the requirements of a (natural) science by discovering laws of nature. As the ability to define such 'laws' appears so far limited to some exceptional cases in economics, and because predicting an action still would not be the same as explaining it, it seems more reasonable to look for an alternative to the externalist concept of objective rationality: action, as Scharpf points out, 'cannot be explained without reference to the subjective "meaning" that this action has for the actor in question' (1997: 19).

The internalist alternative aims to adopt the perspective of the observed subject and tries to understand the agent's beliefs and motives in a given situation in order to rationalise decisions as conditional on these. From an internalist perspective, rational action is action for reasons, where a rational choice is a solution derived from these reasons (or premises) according to certain rules. An actor's choice can be rationalised by an observer if the observer can point out premises and rules from which this very choice can be derived as a solution. An internalist account expects actions to be subjectively rather than objectively rational, i.e., in a situation where the relevant information is not available to the actor, the actor is expected to take decisions that are sub-optimal or even detrimental for the fulfilment of his ends. As Coleman points out, the internalist perspective of subjective rationality thus entails elements of 'understanding':

> Since social scientists take as their purpose the understanding of social organization that is derivative from actions of individuals and since understanding an individual's action ordinarily means seeing the reasons behind that action, then the theoretical aim of social science must be to conceive of that action in a way that makes it rational from the point of view of the actor (Coleman 1990: 17–18).

The problem with 'understanding' approaches, however, is that they necessarily imply assumptions about unobservable mental states. These are difficult to back up empirically but, at the same time, can hardly be contested (cf. Friedman 1996: 14). Moreover, where the aim of social theorising is to develop general hypotheses and explanations rather than to account for unique events, the gap between understanding unique individual actions and proposing general explanations for behaviour somehow needs to be bridged. The problem with this gap appears to be the freedom of the human will and the resulting indeterminacy of individual decisions. Reinhard Zintl argues that the appropriate strategy to deal with this indeterminacy is to analyse situations with regard to their objective properties, such as high interdependence and dominant actor strategies which constrain subjective idiosyncrasies (Zintl 2006). The focus, that is, should be on constraints (how-possibly) rather than motivation.

Even if we permit space for a free will, any plausible account of rationality will require it to be a general feature that human beings have. So how do we justify a general assumption of rationality if not as a 'law of nature'? Gerald Gaus points out that, to achieve anything like intersubjective intelligibility, there must be rules of thought which are to some extent universal (1996: 48). He concludes that following the laws of logic cannot be merely an art but must be understood as an ability all human beings have the capacity to develop. As pointed out above, the requirement for rationality is first of all one of the observer, not of the observed actor. The observer, however, need not be a social scientist. Journalists, politicians or judges will similarly have an interest in developing accounts of the rationality of behaviour. In fact, it is common for all of us to seek to identify regularities in the behaviour of other individual or collective actors.

Alfred Schütz, seeking to combine the works of Max Weber (1985 [1922]) and Edmund Husserl (1980 [1920]), provided an account of the role of ideal types in the social sciences (Schütz 1993), which, I think, is instructive with regard to the choice of a concept of rationality. According to Schütz, actors frequently use ideal types in their everyday lives in order to structure and make sense of the vast amount of information facing them. The ideal types used by social scientists must hence be 'ideal types of a second order', they 'must build upon or be derived from other ideal types that the social actors themselves have formed in order to act in the social world' (Knudsen 2004). A concept of rationality is likely to feature among the ideal types people use in their everyday lives. The degree of abstraction of an ideal type, or, as Schütz terms it, its anonymity, will depend on the purposes of the person who applies it, in particular on the number of actors it is supposed to cover. Nonetheless, all ideal types fulfil the same function: they serve to make other actors' behaviour understandable and predictable, which facilitates our own decisions under conditions of fundamental interdependence and uncertainty.

The ideal types to be utilised by social scientists may, quite analogously, vary in their degree of abstraction or generality. The ideal type of rationality, too, can assume differing degrees of abstraction. The minimal, 'thin' concept of rationality may reduce the general assumption so far that all that can be asserted about human behaviour is that actors will, when confronted with a number of options, choose the one that, for whatever reasons, appears to them, at that moment, optimal. This is not much more than entailed in the definition of action itself, which only requires behaviour to be intentional. The use of a minimal concept of rationality as a general theory of action therefore ends in tautology: actors can be said to carry out actions because they have intentions, and any specific action is carried out because the respective actor had an intention to carry out this action.

Thicker concepts of rationality, hence, entail further assumptions within the rationality assumption itself. The 'weak requirements' commonly regarded as obligatory include the impossibility of contradictory beliefs and preferences as well as the impossibility of intransitive preferences.[2] To these, George Tsebelis adds the requirement that actors use a correct probability calculus (1990: 26). He goes on to propose some stronger requirements for rationality, among them the ones that beliefs should approximate reality and that subjective probabilities should approximate objective probabilities (Tsebilis 1990: 29–30). Both the weak and the strong requirements appear to be instrumental for the successful pursuit of any kind of goal. If action, as is most plausible to assume, is guided by more fundamental motives than the ones that turn actions into ends in themselves (e.g. scratching one's nose for the purpose of having one's nose scratched), then certain properties will be instrumental for the pursuit of any of them. The absence of contradictions from one's belief system and preferences, as well as the acquisition of certain types of beliefs, count among those instrumental properties. However, the beliefs that are instrumental for the fulfilment of goals and desires, or, in other words, pragmatically appropriate, need (contrary to Tsebelis' argument) not necessarily be true: one can choose the optimal option for the wrong reasons. In particular where beliefs concern social rather than physical reality, the truth of a proposition will in a sense depend on whether it is socially accepted as true.

If rational decision-making is understood to consist in the rule-based derivation of a solution from premises, generality assumptions so far concern only the rules, not the premises to which they are applied. Rational-choice theorists maintain that decision-making is to be conceived of as a matter of finding the appropriate means for given ends and that a general theory of action therefore needs to be based on means–ends rationality. Models that regard premises for decision-making as given and stable (and hence exogenous to analysis) are known as 'closed' models, while models considering the evolution of premises have been described as 'open' ones (cf. Kirsch 1977: 26). Closed models thus imply a narrow instrumental concept of rationality that excludes reasoning about the ends of action.

It may be useful, in the context of instrumental rationality, to evoke the classical distinction between practical and theoretical reason. Practical reason is supposed to tell us what to do, while theoretical reason is supposed to tell us what to believe. Instrumental reason seems to have its place somewhere between the two: 'It cannot tell us where to go; at best it can tell us how to get there. It is a gun for hire that can be employed in the service of any goals we have, good or bad.'[3] In order to tell us how to get somewhere, instrumental rationality must have a theoretical aspect: whether one option is more serviceable than another is an empirical fact, about which one can have true or false beliefs. As only true beliefs will enable instrumentally rational selection, theoretical reason is commonly treated as a component of instrumental rationality. By telling us 'how to get there', however, instrumental reason also tells us what to do in order to achieve a given goal. By recommending certain actions rather than others, instrumental reason obviously has a practical aspect to it. What it nonetheless excludes is the part of human decision-making that is not concerned with optimality and instrumentality but with what is 'right' and what is 'wrong' to want and to want to do. Robert Nozick therefore rightly notes that classical instrumental decision-theory is 'a theory of best action, not of rational action' (1993: 65).

Closed models of decision-making that treat premises (in particular, goals) of decisions as given are nevertheless so dominant within political theory that the term 'rationality' has come to be used as synonymous with 'means–ends rationality'. Nozick dismisses a theory of practical reason as follows:

A fully specified theory of substantive rationality opens the door to despotic requirements, externally imposed. To be sure, the lack of such a theory allows some objectionable desires, including some unethical ones, but it is a substantive theory of ethics that should deal with these – despite philosophers' persistent attempts to subsume ethics within rationality. Instrumental rationality leaves us the room to pursue our own goals autonomously (1993: 176).

However, quite apart from the question of whether there are 'moral truths' out there to be tracked by practical reasoning,[4] it seems that the description of decisions solely as procedures of finding optimal means for given ends is empirically inadequate. To address the important question of how actors choose their goals does not necessarily imply a normative evaluation of these. Rather, the issue of practical reason has both a normative and a positive aspect to it. Even if one sees no point in seeking moral truth and believes that scholarship should be concerned only with 'empirical reality', this does not serve to deny the salience of morality and rationalisation of aims for the empirical actors one observes.[5] Moreover, although Nozick is certainly correct in pointing out the dangers of a theory marking certain goals as rational and others as irrational, it is far from clear that a theory of instrumental rationality rules out instrumentation and despotism.

Like goals, actions and beliefs must be regarded as a product of the individual's decisions. If particular actions and beliefs are branded as irrational by a theory of rationality, that may constitute as much of an exercise of paternalism in relation to individual decisions as the corresponding verdict over individual goals. In fact, concepts of rationality that are both narrow and 'thick' are sometimes used to justify a moral reductionism that treats actors as generally self-interested and opportunistic. Opening up the model of decision-making to consider the premises of decisions not only as independent, but also as dependent variables, may then also be a way to challenge assumptions about these premises that have become prescriptive and despotic. Descriptively, it would do justice to Searle's observation that classical (rational-choice) decision-theory only applies after the hard part of the decision, namely to decide what your aims are, has already been made (Searle 2001: 125).[6]

The discussion about open and closed models of decision-making is closely related to that about *descriptive* or *prescriptive* theories of action. Kirsch points out that open models of decision-making relate decision-theory to more empirical and descriptively accurate disciplines, such as social and cognitive psychology (1977: 26). It should be noted, however, that prescription is not necessarily a procedure whereby certain people impose their own norms upon others, or the same as the expression of intersubjectively binding rules. The researcher trying to establish rules of rationality need not want to influence the behaviour of the actors she analyses. Where she does, this aim is obviously a political rather than a scholarly one. What she employs, instead, will be either ideal types or useful generalisations, which she expects to help her understand and predict behaviour.

To establish her own ideal type of rational action, the analyst may refer to introspection. From subjective ideal types she may derive an idealised abstraction, in Schütz' sense, a 'second-order ideal type' of rational choice. She might, for instance, turn his personal commonsense maxim to 'choose whichever option seems best' into 'maximise expected utility'. The resulting abstraction is likely to entail complex prescriptions for how to form expectations (e.g. by Bayesian belief updating) or for how not to have contradictory beliefs and preferences. The point in this abstraction, apparently, is to establish axioms from which further assumptions can be derived by means of logic. As unambiguous quantitative statements and predictions are to many theorists desiderata of modelling, axioms will be such as to enable formalisation and mathematical calculation. The maximisation principle that is central to dominant concepts of rationality and rational choice hence constitutes, above other things, a requirement for formalisation.[7] Where the applied concept of rationality is tantamount to such an 'idealised ideal type', discussion of assumptions in modelling will be predominantly immanent, i.e. it will concern contradictions, possibilities and impossibilities rather than the questioning of the premises of the ideal type. The fact that, in this procedure, basic assumptions are based on introspection rather than observation also accounts for the assertion of their 'self-evident truth' which, derived from classical economics, is still common, although rarely made explicit (cf. Friedman 1996: 9).

Generalisations derived from observation, which constitute the alternative, differ essentially from ideal types. Ideal types, as abstractions from reality, cannot be observed, but serve as a point of reference for different realisations. Counter-examples and contradicting evidence cannot serve to deny the validity of an ideal type; they can only question its pragmatic usefulness – assumptions are valid by definition. Generalisations based on observation, by contrast, explicitly claim truth. They assert to describe adequately – if with concessions and conditionalities – any empirical token the type of which they refer to. Generalisations can thus, in principle, be falsified, although falsification of probabilistic assertions can be difficult or even impossible. Nonetheless, empirical counter-examples question the validity of generalisations. While generalisations are the aim and tool of all 'natural' sciences, ideal types have, since Max Weber, been regarded as the appropriate corresponding tool for the social sciences.

Where rationality is concerned, social psychologists have for many years been questioning the formal ideal-type 'as-if' models developed by economists and offered generalisations to replace them. The most important approaches in this respect are those of 'bounded rationality' (see Simon 1983; Gigerenzer & Selten 2002; Selten 2002) and 'framing' (see Kahnemann & Tversky 2000), which overlap in some respects. The difference between the two is mainly one of focus: while scholars in the tradition of Kahnemann and Tversky indicate the numerous ways in which human beings fail to adhere to prescriptive norms of rationality, the 'bounded rationality' approach seeks to answer the question how, in the face of uncertainty, we succeed in making reasonable decisions *at all*.

In a famous 1974 article, Tversky and Kahnemann presented evidence that, contrary to traditional economic assumptions, human beings are in fact poor statisticians. Among other things, participants in their experiments misjudged the effects of sample size, used inadequate information to form predictions and failed to understand the principle of regression towards the mean (Tversky & Kahnemann 1974). Their early findings have since been extended to form a wider framework and research programme that challenges all of the premises of formal decision-theory. Apparently, people make more effort to avert losses than to achieve further benefits and tend to value things they already have more than things they could have, regardless of both objective value and preferences previously expressed (this effect is known as the 'endowment effect'). Most importantly, however, choice seems to depend on the framing (i.e. mental representation) of the choice situation itself rather than on exogenous wants and expected utilities, leading Tversky and Kahnemann to conclude that:

> Because framing effects and the associated features of invariance are ubiquitous, no adequate descriptive theory can ignore these phenomena. On the other

hand, because invariance (or extensionality) is normatively [i.e. prescriptively, C.L.] indispensable, no adequate prescriptive theory should permit its violation. Consequently, the dream of constructing a theory that is acceptable both descriptively and normatively appears unrealizable (2000: 220).

In particular, the phenomenon of framing violates the 'invariance' requirement that *'the preference between options should be independent of their description'* (Tversky & Kahnemann 2000: 211). Where the description of a situation alone determines the plans and desires of actors, rational selection of options is replaced by a determinism between situation and action. Any theoretical account seeking to comprise the phenomenon of framing with all its implications will apparently need to give up the notions of a free will and a situation-independent identity. Giving up the assumption of invariance is, therefore, tantamount to abandoning prescriptive models of rationality altogether.[8] Moreover, the framing effect diminishes hopes that rational-choice models can provide explanations and predictions of empirical events. The 'revealed preference' hypothesis, claiming that decisions in future situations can be predicted by entering observed choices as preferences into utility functions, is refuted if an option that is preferred in one situation is rejected in another although no superior alternative was added. However, where no empirical information to specify the content of utility functions is available, model-building loses its practical relevance and is turned into an end in itself. In these cases results, although true by definition, will in some sense be meaningless.

The 'bounded rationality' approach, by contrast, is based on contradictions that are immanent to the model of perfect rationality itself. Even for skilled statisticians with enormous cognitive capacities, these contradictions make it impossible to determine adequate rules of choice and to select optimally. The problem is essentially one of infinite regression: in order to choose among alternative options, we require, on a meta-level, a method for choosing optimally. But how are we to establish this method without a method for finding optimal methods? This sequence can be continued infinitely, with the actor at each meta-level k seeking a method for level $k-1$ (Selten 2002: 17). In slightly different terms, the same point has been made by Jon Elster, who draws attention to the fact that actors cannot possibly know at which point to stop seeking information on which to base a decision. After all, we cannot judge the value of information before we actually obtain it (Elster 1986).

Proponents of 'bounded rationality' have pointed out that the refusal to maximise and fully exploit cognitive capacities and skills is by no means irrational but can, rather, yield objectively rational outcomes. They call particular attention to the fact that, with decision-problems, superficial analysis or even intuition can deliver outcomes superior to full analysis. Accordingly, they stress the importance of qualitative compared to quantitative reasoning (cf. Selten 2002). As time and energy are scarce in most real-life situations, people are expected to employ 'fast and frugal heuristics' rather costly mechanisms like Bayesian updating (see Todd 2002). Where 'bounded rationality' is described as 'a form of ecological rationality rather than of consistency and coherence' (Gigerenzer & Selten 2002: 9), though, it becomes apparent that the approach is essentially an externalist one, dealing with objective rather than subjective rationality. It will therefore reveal little about the first-order ideal type of rationality actors base their decisions on. The use of 'fast and frugal heuristics' is, while intentional, not an example of the conscious application of rules of rationality.

The respective essence of these alternative accounts of rationality appears to be the following: 'bounded rationality' shows that, in not trying to be fully rational, people are effectively even *more* rational than otherwise. Work on 'framing', on the other hand, has indicated that, for whatever reasons, people simply do not behave as the prevailing prescriptive theory of rationality expects them to.

How can the alleged incompatibility between prescription and description be overcome? I believe that a possible answer lies in Schütz's observation about first- and second-order ideal types and in considering the pragmatic use of the concept of rationality as a norm to guide action. This distinction enables the rules of rationality to be used by the analyst to be viewed as ideal types and generalisations at the same time. Where 'second-order ideal types' are based on observation of 'first-order ideal types' and constitute both abstractions from and generalisations about them, they can be prescriptive and descriptive at the same time. In a defence of the universal character of rationalist theories, Ferejohn and Satz make a very similar point (although without reference to Schütz):

> We claim, first, that in everyday life, human agents must and do make use of intentionalist interpretation in order to make attributions about mental states. Second, we claim that this form of intentionalism must satisfy a pragmatic test – it must allow its holders to make good predictions as to how others will behave in a wide variety of settings – so that it is 'generative,' and cannot consist of mere tautologies. In order to satisfy these requirements, we claim that this 'folk intentionalism' must be describable in universalistic terms. Finally, we claim that successful intentional scientific accounts must 'track' folk intentionalism, and therefore inherit its universalistic features (1996: 79).

Ferejohn and Satz, however, fail to note (or at least to make explicit) the most important implication of their 'folk intentionalism'. People not only rationalise others' behaviour by means of intentional explanation but are likely also to apply the very same rules they presuppose in others in the making of their own decisions. That is, on the individual level, the rules that explain behaviour will in everyday life be the same as the ones that guide behaviour. In this sense prescriptive (or normative) and descriptive rationality may be said to presuppose one another. De Sousa goes as far as to claim that 'every normative model is *identical* with a descriptive model: the difference merely depends on the context of use' (1998: 120). The need for rationalisation seems closely related to the problem of the construction of individual identity. Behaviour that cannot be properly rationalised is commonly regarded not only as 'irrational' but even as 'insane', the latter signifying the idea that a person has in a way lost part of her identity. As soon as we come across a suitable rationalisation, the impression of insanity vanishes and identity is restored. The construction of a convincing rationale for one's own action might, hence, correspond to the construction of individual identity.

In order to accommodate some of the challenging findings from social psychologists in the tradition of Tversky and Kahnemann, it would be necessary to open up the model of decision-making and devote more attention to how premises for decisions evolve. Homogeneity in the rules guiding individual action may be particularly common where rules concern the choice of ends rather than of means, or, in other words, the sphere of practical rather than theoretical reason. The selection of ends makes up an integral part of both individual and collective decision-processes. In some cases, the first part of the decision-process will already have been completed, enabling the application of traditional decision-theory, which deals solely with the process of finding adequate means. In other cases, where ends have not yet been established, formal decision-theory is bound to fail. The decision to apply open or closed models should thus be justified methodologically rather than normatively. The model proposed in the following sections represents an attempt to open up the model of decision-making by reconstructing the formation of premises for decisions as a reason-based decision itself. Such an open model, I maintain, is required where the evolution of political goals and preferences is to be analysed.

2. CONCEPTS OF PREFERENCE

The concept of preference is a central one in both decision-theory and political theory, as well as in everyday reasoning about politics. Politics, it seems, is not about fulfilling desires but about deciding between *alternative* goals and options for action. The kind of decisions that are correctly described as political decisions are collective decisions, i.e. decisions that are binding on all their addressees. In democracies, the means of arriving at joint decisions is by aggregation of individual preferences. In modern liberal democracies, aggregation is supplemented by representation: it is not preferences concerning particular issues that are aggregated but preferences for political programmes, or sets of decisions, that are represented by political actors and parties. Representatives are elected to represent the preferences of those people who voted for their respective programme but are also expected to pursue the 'common good' of the whole society.

Political decisions are consequential decisions. They are normally meant to produce specific consequences – and where this is not the case, decisions are derogatively labelled 'gesture politics' or 'merely symbolic'. Representatives are held accountable not so much for their decisions as such as for the consequences of these decisions. Responsibility for unfavourable consequences can only be assigned, though, where alternative options that would have led to superior results can be indicated. Without alternatives, there can be neither choice nor responsibility.

Both citizens and representatives choose between alternatives on the basis of preference. The alternatives representatives choose from are policy options, while the alternatives citizens choose from are persons, parties and programmes. Preferences over parties and candidates are then motivated by preferences over the policy options they have chosen and intend to choose.

In order to conceptualise the formation of political preferences, the understanding of preference itself needs to be clarified in a first step. Despite its central role in social theory, the concept of preference is rarely satisfactorily explicated. All that seems to be agreed upon is that preferences are a type of mental attitude that motivate and hence explain actions. As such, they create a link between the internal subjective and the external objective world. Even such more or less consensual assumptions are not usually made explicit, but implicitly presupposed to be shared. For instance, all that Allan Feldman, in his introduction to welfare economics (1980), has to say on the topic of preference is the following:

> We suppose that there is a set of states, or alternatives, or bundles of goods, or 'things' in the world. ... The first fundamental assumption we make is that people know what they like: they know their preferences among the set of things (Feldman 1980: 9).

His circumscription entails two central assumptions of economic theory and classical decision-theory: those of comparison and completeness. Comparison, or comparative evaluation, results from the fact that preference is the basis of choice between alternatives. Even in everyday usage an utterance like 'I prefer an ice-cream' would very likely trigger the response 'to what?', as the English word 'prefer' is a transitive verb requiring two objects (direct and indirect object). This grammatical property of the word mirrors an aspect of the concept it refers to and is one of the characteristics that makes it useful for the analysis of decisions. In order to have a preference for one thing, there must be at least one other thing available for choice that the first is compared with.

For a situation to be one of choice and thus one to which preferences are relevant, two conditions must obtain. First, external constraints may not entirely determine the selection of an option – otherwise, it could not count as the result of a decision. Second, the choice of one option should, in some sense, reduce access to the alternatives – otherwise, a decision would not be necessary. The aspect of comparison thus distinguishes the notion of preference from other concepts used to describe motivation for actions, such as desires, goals or needs. Preference is a relation between objects constitutive for preference orders with several elements (the 'set' in Feldman's definition).

In order for a preference order to be complete, it is required that, for a given set of options (choice set), binary preference relations are defined over all possible subsets.[9] That is, if a choice set consists of options x, y and z, preference relations between x and y, y and z, and x and z must be defined. The axiom of completeness is, in Feldman's quote, circumscribed as the assumption that 'people know what they like'. Only complete preference orders can serve as a basis of rational choice and motivate action. As long as preference relations between options are lacking, the actor is stuck in a situation of indecision. The story of Buridan's ass, who is to choose between two haystacks and eventually starves due to its inability to choose one, is one of incomplete preference orders.

Incompleteness must be distinguished from indifference, which is just one possible way in which objects within a preference order can be related and poses no difficulty to rational choice. The assumption of complete preference orders is typically entailed in formal models for analytical purposes. Empirically, it makes little sense to assume that people hold complete preference orders over all conceivable choice sets. Rather, a preference order needs to be formed whenever a new choice set becomes available. As the goal of the present project is to conceptualise processes of preference-formation and transformation, stability and completeness of preference orders will need to be questioned. The analytical value of these axioms for many other purposes, however, need not be challenged.

What remains entirely open in Feldman's quote above is the nature of the objects to which preferences refer. What are the 'things' people have preferences over? Apparently, preferences can be defined either over alternative options for action or over states of the world resulting from actions.[10] The standard assumption in economic theory is the latter: people have fixed preferences over outcomes of action. On the basis of these, and under consideration of relevant beliefs (in the form of probability assignments), an expected utility for each of the available options for action is calculated. The option with the highest expected utility is then selected more or less automatically.[11]

However, this does not solve the problem that preferences enter the theory in two separate functions: they 'come in as determinants of behaviour and they also come in as the basis of welfare judgments' (Sen 1982: 66). Hence, even if preferences are not conceived of as preferences for actions as such, they are still relevant as constituting intentions for action. If I have a preference for one state of the world over another, this must entail a disposition to choose actions bringing about that outcome – otherwise, the preference could not serve to explain actions. If one intends to change the behaviour of another person, one will have to change either her constraints (i.e. the available options) or her intentions (i.e. preferences). To change those preferences is to change the actor's welfare judgments, which are the basis for beliefs about how much 'good' the possible actions will bring about, as well as about what actually constitutes 'good'.

Classical decision-theory is a theory of utility-maximisation. Actors are assumed to possess utility functions with a specific content and structure. The content of utility functions represents actors' preferences: actors maximise the extent to which the actual state of affairs matches the one they wish to come true. Decision-theory is usually more concerned with the structure than with the content of utility functions – it is in this respect that it applies the term 'rational preference'. In order to qualify as a structurally rational preference, a utility function is commonly expected to fulfil the requirements of cancellation, separability, transitivity, dominance and invariance. These structural properties of preference orders can again be discussed on different levels, concerning either their analytical value or empirical accuracy.

The *cancellation* criterion requires that the preference between options should depend only on states in which they yield different outcomes. If, for instance, A is preferred to B, then the prospect of winning A if it rains tomorrow should be preferred to winning B if it rains tomorrow (cf. Tversky & Kahnemann 2000: 210). Related to the cancellation criterion is that of *separability*. It demands that 'what happens in one state of nature can be evaluated independently of what happens in any other' (Broome 1991: 140). Broome illustrates the relevance of the separability criterion with the following examples: 1. Can what one person gets be assessed without regard to what others get? Is it, for instance, better to increase overall wealth or to increase equality? The former would require preferences (for wealth) to be separable. 2. Can what one person gets at one time in her life be assessed independently of what the same person gets at other (later) times in her life? 3. Can what happens if one option is chosen be assessed independently of what would have happened if another option had been chosen? (Broome 1991: 140–1) Where the utility of an option depends not on its effects on the chooser herself alone but also on the effects it has on other actors, at other times or on the effects that other options would have produced, separability does not obtain. Examples of inseparable preferences would concern phenomena such as hostility, regret or *Schadenfreude*.[12]

The axiom of *transitivity* claims that, if an actor prefers A to B and B to C, then she should not prefer C to A. The argument goes that actors with intransitive preference orderings could be induced to pay money to exchange A for B, then B for C and, in the end, C for A. Finally, they will end up with what they initially held, only poorer – they will have been exploited as 'money pumps'. The principle of *dominance* simply demands that if an option is better than another in one respect and at least as good in all other respects, this option should be chosen (Tversky & Kahnemann 2000: 211). While the dominance principle appears to be both an obvious requirement of rationality and one that is easy to fulfil in real-life situations, the principle of *invariance* has been heavily challenged. Invariance demands that the preference between options should be independent of their description. The 'framing effect' pointed out by Tversky & Kahnemann (1974, 2002) indicates that, at least in many experimental situations, the requirement of invariance is not met.

The problem of invariance and context-dependence is connected to two further questions. The first of these is the question of whether rational preferences are stable. It is one that can be, and in fact is, denied by most decision theorists. There is nothing irrational about changing one's preferences over time. In some cases, such changes may even be spontaneous and arbitrary, as when one prefers chocolate ice cream today and vanilla tomorrow. If all changes in preferences were in fact entirely spontaneous and arbitrary, however, there would be no possibility of gaining useful information about actors' preferences. This concerns the second important question: what can we possibly know about the content of preferences? As mentioned before, such knowledge is indispensable for any analysis of empirical decisions.

Empirical information about the content and structure of preferences is available from two sources. In face of the fact that preferences have their place inside the actors' heads, the analyst can either ask for them directly, by means of questionnaires or interviews, or she can try to infer preferences from actors' behaviour. The latter approach, labelled the 'revealed preference' approach, was first advocated by Paul Samuelson (1938). The idea of revealed preference has strong behaviourist credentials, with many adherents claiming to do away with the 'metaphysics' of fundamental values as well as with the difficulties of introspection and communication as methods of obtaining information about individuals. Although still popular in mainstream economic theory, the revealed preference approach has been heavily challenged.

Probably the most distinguished campaigner against revealed preference is Amartya Sen (Sen 1982: 55–7). To begin with, Sen contradicts the notion that the approach manages to avoid considerations about underlying preferences by treating preferences as nothing more than dispositions to choose. Revelation, he points out, is an essential feature of 'revealed preference', as it is only a common underlying preference that can make choices inconsistent – everything else would result in tautology. Revelation of underlying preferences through choices, however, causes further problems: in the example of the prisoner's dilemma, each prisoner's choice would obviously reveal a preference for a longer prison sentence over a shorter one (Sen 1982: 64). In so far as we assume people's welfare to be higher in freedom than in custody (otherwise there would be no dilemma), choices in the dilemma therefore cannot be regarded as reflecting welfare judgments or underlying preferences. Sen concludes that

> [p]reference can be defined in such a way as to preserve its correspondence with choice, or defined so as to keep it in line with welfare as seen by the person in question, but it is not in general possible to guarantee both simultaneously. Something has to give place to the other (1982: 73).

Where the alternatives are either to give up the notion of preferences as dispositions to choose or to renounce the relation between preference and individual welfare, Sen opts for the former. This decision is an obvious requirement for normative democratic theory: there is little point in aggregating individual dispositions for action if these are unrelated to the welfare of individuals. However, it cannot mean to discard the relationship between welfare and action altogether, as this constitutes the essence of individual autonomy. Whatever it is that we take as a measure of our personal welfare is the same as that which motivates our actions. The notion of preference is a reasonable way to conceptualise it. Moreover, where explanation and understanding of empirical decisions, i.e. a positive theory of decision-making, are goals of research, reasons and thus causes for action are what is sought. I therefore think that a viable solution is to retain preferences as motivators of choice but to give up on the idea that choices alone can provide all the necessary information.

This implies the methodological consequence of referring to communication rather than mere observation for information about preferences. Insights from communication, however, cannot only be obtained in form of targeted social research by means of interviews. Particularly in the case of political actors, information about preferences is available from a number of sources, including press releases and interviews or party programmes (cf. Zintl 1994). After all, verbal behaviour, including both speaking and writing, is still behaviour that is open to interpretation. As Sen puts it, '[m]uch of economic theory seems to be concerned with strong, silent men who never speak' (Sen 1982: 9). Actors may of course intentionally mislead observers about their preferences and fake preferences they do not truly hold. However, the same problems of indeterminacy and misrepresentation are encountered by the behaviourist 'revealed preference' approach, which has numerous other disadvantages (for a defence of revealed preference, see Dowding 2002).

One of the problems in inferring preferences from behaviour lies with the conditionality of preferences over options for action. Preferences for options are always conditional on the belief that these options will actually lead to the outcomes associated with them. Hence, if we observe the choice of an option, we can only conclude that the actor prefers the state of the world that this option brings about if we have full information on his beliefs about the consequences of the decision. However, to derive information about someone's beliefs (or, in the terminology of classical decision-theory, about subjective probabilities) from their actions, one would need to know their preferences over possible states of the world. To put it briefly: one can infer beliefs from behaviour only if desires are known and one can infer desires only if beliefs are known (cf. Von Kutschera 1973: 110–13).

If we regard preferences as kinds of mental attitudes, their function – both analytically and empirically – is to provide a link between an actor's mind and the world he has to decide and act in. Preferences, in other words, relate the subjective and the objective world. There are, however, at least two different types of connections between subject and object, both of which are entailed in the classical model of rational action, as shown in Figure 1.1.

Figure 1.1: Desires, Beliefs and Actions (Elster 1989: 31)

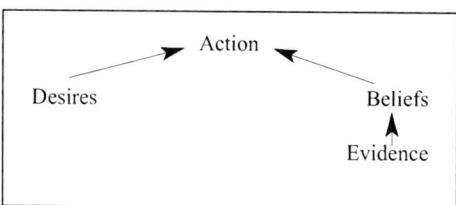

'Desires' constitute a volitive relation between subjective and objective world, whereas 'beliefs' create a cognitive relation. John Searle (1983) has characterised these two types of links by their 'direction of fit'. In analogy to assertive speech acts (claims), he defines beliefs by their 'mind-to-world' direction of fit. Beliefs aim to create an isomorphism between mind and world by adapting the subjective representation to an objective reality. Desires, by contrast, are, in analogy to directive speech acts (demands), defined by a 'world-to-mind' relation of fit. They aim at changing real states of the world so as to match imagined (and desired) ones.

Figure 1.2: Relations between subjective and objective world

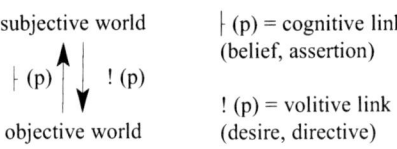

subjective world $\vdash$ (p) = cognitive link
                             (belief, assertion)

$\vdash$ (p)   ! (p)

                              ! (p) = volitive link
objective world   (desire, directive)

If one chooses to employ the concept of preference within the frame provided by the classical model of rational action, the question remains whether the concept should cover both or only one of these links between mind and world. Looking at the model, preference could be inserted either in place of desires, or it could be understood as the joint product of beliefs and desires, an attitude formed on their basis and immediately motivating action.[13]

The standard notion of preference in economics and classical decision-theory is a purely volitive one. Preference is here conceptualised as a measure for welfare that is independent of beliefs and changes in beliefs (see, for instance, Kirchgässner 2000: 41). Many misunderstandings between economists and political scientists, and economic and deliberative theorists of democracy in particular, result from the fact that political scientists typically employ a notion of preference that entails both a cognitive and a volitive component but fail to recognise or point out the difference to the economic concept. This is because the preferences motivating a citizen to vote for a specific party or a parliamentarian to vote for new law are preferences over political programmes and strategies rather than preferences over states of the world.

Cass Sunstein, arguing that political preferences are endogenous to the collective decision-making process and transformable in response to new arguments and evidence, has highlighted the problems of non-autonomous preference-formation (Sunstein 1990, 1993). In a similar line of argument, Robert Goodin (1986) has pointed out that 'malinformed' preferences require discursive laundering before they constitute a respectable input to democratic decisions. Christian Rostbøll shares these concerns about the autonomy of preference-formation and claims that what makes preferences autonomous is that they have survived a deliberative process: 'My preference is autonomous if I still find reasons to hold it after I have heard the relevant arguments and considered the relevant information.' (Rostbøll 2005: 377).

John Harsanyi (1955: 315) seemed to have had something similar in mind when he distinguished 'subjective' from 'ethical' preferences. While the former are preferences in the classical economic sense, referring only to subjective utility, the latter represent 'individual social welfare functions'. These are motivated by information about the utilities of other members of the community. The volitive aspect of 'ethical preferences' is thus reduced to one's own utility in the social welfare function while the cognitive aspect becomes central. According to Harsanyi, political decisions – at least normatively – require actors to force 'a special impartial and impersonal attitude' upon themselves (Harsanyi 1995: 315) and to base their choice on ethical rather than subjective preferences.

In the somewhat different context of constitutional economics, Vanberg and Buchanan (1994) differentiate between an 'interest' and a 'theory' component of preferences, which again come close to the volitive and cognitive links between mind and world described above. In constitution-making, they argue, actors' theories about, for example, the benefits from different decision-rules, are equally important as subjective interests (i.e. preferences in the economic understanding). In a response to Sunstein (1993), John Ferejohn (1993) draws a distinction between 'genuine' and 'induced' preferences and argues that political preferences are naturally of the latter kind. Genuine preferences, he points out, concern 'real' fundamental goods. These are the type of preferences economists usually refer to. Induced preferences, by contrast, are preferences over socially constructed entities. As party programmes and policy options are obviously constructed entities rather than fundamental goods, he points out, political preferences cannot be 'genuine'.

Fehige and Wessels (1998: *xxv*) use a distinction that is similar to Ferejohn's but better grasps the connection between the two types of preferences: they differentiate between 'intrinsic' and 'extrinsic' preferences. Intrinsic preferences are equivalent to preferences in the standard economic understanding or 'genuine' preferences. Extrinsic preferences are derived from these and entail a cognitive element besides the volitive one. They refer to concrete strategies, goals or programmes rather than states of the world. Focusing on extrinsic rather than intrinsic preferences appears a sound choice for political scientists because the causal relationships between the choice of a specific policy and its actual outcome are subject to deep uncertainties. Policy preferences therefore seem to have more explanatory potential for the analysis of political decisions than 'genuine', intrinsic preferences over bundles of fundamental goods.

Assuming (and normatively demanding) political decisions to be consequentialist decisions, it nonetheless remains important to regard intrinsic preferences over states of the world as the origin of political preferences. Otherwise, discursive preference-formation and political decision-making would end up as ends in themselves and the goal of generating welfare would be lost to democracy. At the same time, granting a sufficient degree of autonomy in the formation of political preferences, thus conceiving of them as choices, is also of great normative importance. As Sen notes:

Regarding preferences not as choices, but as desires for outcomes, would also open the door to an illiberal interpretation of choice: if actors fail to choose actions which bring about their preferred outcomes, then it should be permissible to have choices paternalistically made for them while if we regard preferences as choices, freedom of choice forbids this (2002: 315).

In what follows, preferences will accordingly be understood as extrinsic ones and thus as choices on the basis of cognitive and volitive premises. Referring back to the classical model of rational action, they are thus treated as the joint product of 'beliefs' and 'desires'. However, the very notions of belief and desire as motivators for action will be challenged, in that the cognitive and volitive components of preference, too, will be considered as the result of rational choice.

3. DECIDING WHAT TO WANT

The decision what to want, i.e. the selection of goals or ends for action, does not belong among the classical topics of decision-theory. Standard economic and rational-choice theory are concerned solely with instrumental rationality, with finding appropriate means for given ends. Although Nozick's concern about the 'despotic requirements' of a theory of substantive rationality is in many respects justified, the reduction of rationality to instrumentality leaves essential aspects of human decision-making unaccounted for. As Searle observes,

> Most of the difficulty with rational deliberation is to decide what you really want, and what you really want to do. You cannot assume that the set of wants is well-ordered prior to deliberation. …The really hard part of practical reason is to figure out what the ends are in the first place (Searle 2001: 125–6).

This claim is an empirical rather than a normative one. While it is true that a prescriptive theory aiming to provide actors with guidelines for rational action and decision might obtain a despotic quality once it tells actors not only what to do to achieve their goals, but also what goals to pursue, this does not hold for descriptive theories. Theories seeking to rationalise and predict action on the basis of observation should take all empirically relevant aspects of decision-making into consideration, unless a restriction promises insights on its own merit.

Dealing with the volitional aspect of preference-formation and hence with the question of how actors come to hold certain values, desires and goals, two questions stand out as central. First, one may ask how far actors are actually free to chose what they want. Is volition the result of free choice or of more or less unconscious mental or physical factors beyond our control? If there is reason to assume that actors are indeed free to choose what they want, the second question arising must be whether or not this decision can and should be guided by rules of rationality. Can the adoption of values, desires and goals be made rationally comprehensible, can it be rationalised?

Turning to the first question, there are obviously widely accepted arguments against freedom of choice. A very common claim, entailed in 'thick' concepts of rationality, is that evolution favours and produces actors with a certain set of desires, which, by itself, enhances the probability of survival. It seems hardly disputable that basic physical needs for food, drink and shelter are innate to all living creatures. But even the desire (or instinct) for reproduction seems to be less than universal, just like wants for company, power, wealth and status. Still, that desires (wants, needs) are not universal does not yet mean that they are freely chosen. They could involuntarily be determined by internal and external processes, be they social, cultural, mental or physical. In fact, the basis on which goals should be chosen seems questionable in the absence of any basic wants given prior to choice itself.

Wants and goals are a defining aspect of (individual and collective) actors' identities, although one need not go as far as Duncan MacIntosh, who claims that personal identity is impossible without rationally chosen goals and ends (1998: 294). MacIntosh, it seems to me, takes the point about freedom of choice of ends somewhat too far. According to him, the totality of volitions can be rationally chosen and revised. Choice of first ends, he claims, (can and) should be guided by something like Kant's categorical imperative: 'choose only those ends that you can rationally want everyone else to have', thus ruling out altruistic and malevolent ends.[14]

However, the common observation that people frequently have desires which they wish they did not have, e.g. for drugs, provides forceful empirical evidence against the assumption that human actors can freely choose all of their wants. At the same time, the claim that people have no control whatsoever over their wants is frequently used to reject appeals to moral and community-spirited action as unrealistic. The idea that in any action, the actor pursues selfish goals (wealth, power, status), even if she is not aware of it or would not 'admit' to it herself, is known as moral reductionism. Combined, these ideas serve as justification for social and political orders based on market mechanisms and individualistic pursuit of goals.

A distinction that is in my eyes central to the conceptualisation of human volition has been drawn by Keith Lehrer and, independently and in less detail, by L. Jonathan Cohen.[15] Lehrer and Cohen distinguish between mental states that arise in us involuntarily as results of processes beyond our control, and mental states that are the result of decisions. They thus refer to 'beliefs' and 'desires' on the one hand and 'acceptances' and 'goals' on the other. Only the latter are the result of conscious decisions: Lehrer points out the existence of a second-order evaluation system, a 'metamind', that evaluates first-order states such as belief and desire. This evaluation system is part of what is otherwise referred to as 'consciousness'. Without a metamental system of consciousness, Lehrer observes, we could not possibly know anything about our beliefs and desires; we would be blind to their existence (1997: 89–90).

Being aware of our first-order mental states enables us to evaluate them and to accept or refuse them as premises for action. A mental state like a desire does not normally determine action unless the actor chooses to have her actions and decisions guided by it. Once it is given metamental assent, a desire is turned into a premise for action. It is then no longer a first-order state of mind but an evaluated second-order one. The evaluation of first-order states of mind is itself an action and produces decisions, for which actors can be held accountable. Beliefs and desires, by contrast, cannot justly be subjected to external sanctioning, as they are products of processes beyond our control. Unless they are accepted as premises for action, first-order states of mind remain private; it is the actor's own responsibility to assess and reject them as premises if appropriate. Only the output of metamental processes can be subjected to ethical or moral judgments by others.

The introduction of a 'metamind' into decision-theory enables a better understanding of how people succeed in making plans and pursuing their goals at all. If choice were actually *determined* by desires (and beliefs), problems like akrasia (weakness of will) and myopia (short-term thinking) would be not exceptional but the general rule. In fact, one might question why actors should desire anything beyond immediate satisfaction:

> If the Utilitarian has to answer the question, 'Why should I sacrifice my own happiness for the greater happiness of another?' it must surely be admissible to ask the Egoist, 'Why should I sacrifice my present pleasure for one in the future? Why should I concern myself about my own future any more than about the feelings of other persons?' …Grant that the Ego is merely a system of coherent phenomena, that the permanent identical 'I' is not a fact but a fiction, as Hume and his followers maintain; why, then, should one part of the series of feelings into which the Ego is resolved be concerned with another part of the same series, any more than with any other series? (Sidgwick 1907 [1874]: 418–19, quoted in Sen 1982: 105).

The adoption of long-term goals is already an achievement of a metamental evaluation system. Only in so far as actors adopt goals do akrasia and myopia constitute problems at all. Once adopted, goals function as principles that guide the formation of preferences relating between goals and choice sets in the real world. A goal constitutes a particularly powerful *reason* for choices of preference and action. In the process of being translated into extrinsic preferences over options for action, a goal generates a number of secondary, or motivated, other goals standing in a means-end relationship to the primary goal.

To speak of akrasia or weakness of will is justified only where choice is determined by premises that are not freely adopted or in cases of self-deception. Lehrer points out that mere satisfaction of desires (e.g. craving for cigarettes when one has quit smoking) is the 'default mode' of decision-making (1997: 92). Strong physical or mental wants may cause actors to 'lose control' over their actions and decisions, which may be rationalised in a self-deceptive manner ('goal x is not really desirable after all').[16] To abandon a goal in favour of better reasons for action is by no means a failure of individual will-power but rather an expression of its strength. The ability to adopt and abandon goals voluntarily and consciously on the basis of reasoned evaluation enables actors to adapt flexibly to changing environments. It also helps them to escape the apparent paradoxes of 'self-binding' and 'precommitment'.

The famous example of Ulysses, who demanded to be bound to the mast in order to prevent him from succumbing to the temptation of the Sirens' song is commonly used to illustrate this. As Jon Elster observes, unforeseen events may lead Ulysses to wish he had not blocked out certain opportunities:

> Ideally, Ulysses would want to be loosely bound to the mast – with ties strong enough to keep him from acting against his own better judgment, but not so strong as to prevent him from intervening in emergency. Unfortunately, one can rarely have it both ways (Elster 1989: 49).

The adoption of goals seems to be the best possible way to bind the will loosely enough to enable both self-control and flexibility. The premises produced by metamental assent are at once stable enough to allow for long-term pursuit of ends and provisional enough to allow for revision in the light of new circumstances, reasons and evidence.

Having argued that volitional attitudes can be, and in fact normally are, subjected to the will, i.e. that we are free to choose our goals and reasons, I will now turn to the second question: whether goal-adoption is a rational process. Following Sen's understanding of rationality as 'the discipline of subjecting one's choices – of actions as well as objectives, values and priorities – to reasoned scrutiny', it seems appropriate to broaden the narrow concept of instrumental rationality and consider the adoption of practical reasons for action as rational choice. To observe that the choice of goals and reasons is driven by rational deliberation, however, is not the same as to advocate certain goals as more rational than others.

There are, I think, four aspects with regard to which the rationality of ends can be discussed: instrumentality, feasibility, identity and moral justification.

Instrumentality
In rational-choice theory, a common view on rational goals and preferences is that entailed in 'thick' concepts of rationality. Dealing with rationality on purely instrumental terms, rational-choice theorists point out the rationality and ubiquity of preferences for instrumental goods such as money, power or status. The goal of maximising instrumental goods need not be directly derived from specific higher-order goals. Rather, these goods serve most kinds of goals and are therefore sought for their own sake. For example, politicians seek power in order to be in a position to realise policy preferences and to attain goals, even if they do not yet fully know what these preferences and goals are going to be in the future.

Feasibility

Similarly common are arguments about the feasibility of goals. Where instrumental rationality asks which means best serve given ends, rational goal-adoption could ask which goals are most likely to be achieved given existing opportunities. In the extreme case, this strategy would be one of pure, and therefore pointless, opportunism. Nozick admits feasibility of goals as the only measure for the rationality of preferences: 'A person will not have a goal for which he knows that there is no feasible route, however long, from his current situation to the achievement of the goal' (1993: 146). Although the requirement of feasible goals may seem innocent, I doubt that it can escape the dangers of despotism with which Nozick is concerned. Is a terminally ill person irrational in sticking with the goal of recovery? Is a disadvantaged child irrational in aiming for a university degree? There is, of course, the concession that an actor has to 'know' that there is no feasible route in order for his goal to be irrational – maybe the terminally ill and the disadvantaged child do not know about (or rather do not accept) the futility of their goals. This qualification, however, is easily removed with arguments about what one 'should know', given experience and available evidence.

Identity

The importance of goals for individual and collective identity has already been mentioned. Without goals, MacIntosh (1998) claims, actors possess no such thing as a distinct identity. This claim is in many respects too strong, as it neglects the impact that factors beyond our control – such as the social and cultural background and family one is born into, as well as specific talents, wants and constraints, which are to some extent innate – have upon our identity. Gary Becker (1996) proposes to conceptualise such constraints as individual capital (e.g. experience of earlier choices) and social capital (e.g. the individual's network of family and friends). Becker assumes that people actively invest in their capital stocks in order to increase future utility. For instance, it would be rational in this understanding to invest in becoming a punctual person in order to have better job opportunities in the future. At this point, the wilful formation of identity by means of goal-adoption becomes purely instrumental. However, coherence and consistency of goals and actions are apparently sought without being instrumental for present or future utility. Accordingly, actors might rule out goals that are in conflict with what they regard as their identity as irrational, regardless of whether they conceive of this identity positively or negatively.

Moral justification

David Gauthier's (1986) famous attempt to account for morality in terms of rationality opens the way for MacIntosh (1998) to pursue the reverse strategy of acknowledging goals as rational only if they fulfil a Kantian requirement of 'categorical rationality'. For him, goals are rational only if the person who holds them can rationally want everyone else to share them, which excludes both altruistic and malevolent goals. This normative assessment of goals can be taken even further in order to exclude illiberal, undemocratic or simply extremely selfish goals, depending on what moral and ethical values one holds.

To describe those who do not share their own values as irrational, however, is both misleading and in Nozick's sense 'despotic'. Amy Gutmann and Dennis Thompson (1996) have drawn attention to the possibility of reasonable disagreement as well as to the necessity to accept it as rational. Even if one can point out good reasons why a goal is morally unacceptable, it is difficult to prove that use of reason should lead its holder to abandon it. Elijah Millgram makes a weaker claim than MacIntosh when he points out that, in order to motivate actions effectively, goals must be inferentially justified (1998: 16). This is in keeping with the acknowledgement that there can be sound moral arguments both for and against a goal but that there is likely to be something wrong with a goal for which no reasons at all can be given (much more so if the goal is a political one).

Empirically, people obviously do employ moral reasons in deciding whether to adopt something as a goal or not. This explains why, in the aftermath of the September 11 terrorist attacks, many people were surprised that the terrorists had pursued their goal with considerable instrumental rationality, given that the goal itself was seen as entirely irrational. These people obviously took rationality to be a property one either has or does not have, so that people who (instrumentally) rationally pursue their goals should also have rational goals. The measure by which the terrorists' goals were deemed to be irrational was at least partly a moral one; apparently the one that those who assessed it applied to their own goals as well.

All four, instrumentality, feasibility, identity and moral justification are, I believe, aspects in the light of which goals can be assessed and may generate reasons for their adoption or rejection. The task of evaluating whether or not a goal fulfils the requirements of each is clearly a cognitive one, requiring the resort to reasons and to rationality. Before it can feature as a reason in a decision, a goal itself requires reasons in order to be rationally adopted.

However, a rationally adopted goal will not be sufficient to produce a complete preference order over every possible choice set. Actors may be expected to adopt a number of goals which, even if they are not incommensurable at a more abstract level, result in conflict when choices between concrete options need to be made. For example, the goals to reduce national debt and to equip children from all social backgrounds with a good education are not contradictory as such but the political strategies derived from them are likely to conflict. Even where an actor pursues only a single primary goal, the secondary goals derived from it can constitute incompatible ends if the actor is faced with constraints: with a limited budget for education, primary schools will compete for support with secondary schools and universities.

In addition to this, it is important to keep in mind that there are reasons other than goals that can motivate choice, including values, needs, commitments, sympathy or social conventions. Sen has drawn attention to a bias of classical decision-theory towards 'goal priority', i.e. to the assumptions that '[e]ach player pursues his or her goal subject to feasibility considerations, without being restrained by any other values' (Sen 2002: 208) and that 'each act of choice of a person is guided immediately by the pursuit of one's own goal' (Sen 2002: 214). All of the above (values, commitments, sympathy or conventions) might constitute strong reasons for choice without being goals themselves.[17]

Assuming that the volitive component of preferences concerns possible states of the world, it must be properties of these possible states that motivate the intention to realise them (Pettit 1991). Properties of states are relevant for choices insofar as they can actually be affected by decisions (the law of gravity, for instance, cannot be changed by actor choices) and insofar as they are related to practical reasons such as goals, values and conventions. Properties of states of the world, that is, *are* reasons to choose them. Even if states of the world were defined by only four relevant properties, 64 different combinations of these (i.e. states of the world) are logically possible. Consider the following example, where the properties p, q, r and s all constitute reasons to choose states of the world.

Table 1.3: Alternative worlds and their properties

Worlds	Properties/reasons			
w_1	p	q	r	s
w_2	$\neg p$	q	r	s
w_3	p	$\neg q$	$\neg r$	$\neg s$
w_4	p	$\neg q$	$\neg r$	s
w_5	p	q	$\neg r$	$\neg s$
w_6	$\neg p$	$\neg q$	$\neg r$	$\neg s$

A preference for w_1, the perfect world, over all other worlds can clearly be established, as can preferences for all worlds over w_6, which would be a 'worst-case scenario'. However, where the choice lies between any of the other worlds (such as w_2-w_5) reasons conflict: for each of them, there are reasons for and against its selection. The challenge now is that of aggregating conflicting practical reasons into a complete and transitive preference order over available worlds.

Ian Steedman and Ulrich Krause (1986) have discussed this problem as an 'internal Arrow' problem. They draw an analogy between the interpersonal aggregation of preferences into a social-welfare function (discussed by Arrow 1963) and the intrapersonal aggregation of practical reasons.[18] They conclude that Arrow's theorem about the impossibility of aggregating individual preferences into a transitive and complete social preference order can be transferred to the individual level, where reasons have to be aggregated into a preference order over states of the world. I believe that Steedman and Krause's model not only demonstrates the challenges of 'deciding what to want' but also provides an approach to the rationalisation of this decision, which is why it will be discussed in some detail.

At least four of Arrow's five conditions appear compelling for the internal aggregation conflict as well. The *non-dictatorship* criterion requires that there may not exist a single reason which determines all choices. Formally, if such an internal dictator did exist, the actor would not be confronted with the necessity to aggregate reasons at all. Normatively, he might be discarded as a unidimensional fanatic (Steedman & Krause 1986: 208). The *citizen sovereignty* criterion would, translated to the intrapersonal level, require decisions not to be determined by an entity other than the decision-maker herself. It thus demands nothing more than individual autonomy. The *Pareto consistency* condition prevents decisions that would seem plainly irrational at the intrapersonal level, such as the choice of an alternative which is inferior to equally available ones with regard to all reasons. The *unrestricted domain* criterion ensures that actors can flexibly react to newly arising or newly discovered reasons.[19]

The escape route to the internal aggregation problem must therefore lie in dropping the *independence of irrelevant alternatives* (IIA) condition, which in Arrow's model prevents inconsistent choices and rules out weighing and interpersonal comparison of preferences. Comparison and weighing of practical reasons seems to be an important, if not *the* most important, feature of internal deliberation (and of external deliberation as well, as will be argued in the following chapter). Reconsidering the example in Table 1.3 above, it appears obvious that in order to reach a complete preference order over worlds w_2-w_5, reasons p, q, r and s need to need to be weighed against one another.

To begin with, the decision-maker might decide whether one of the reasons involved is an absolute or categorical reason to choose worlds with that particular property over worlds without it. Moral reasons are likely to be of this categorical kind, while goals and interests tend to motivate only 'ceteris-paribus preferences' (Grüne 2005). For example, the prohibition of the death penalty (say, p) might function as such an absolute or categorical reason. The actor for whom human rights take priority over anything else might apply the prohibition of the death penalty as an absolute reason and prefer all worlds w_i^p over all worlds $w_i^{\neg p}$. Accordingly, w_3 would be chosen over w_4 although all other reasons speak against it. A *ceteris-paribus* reason, by contrast, could only motivate preferences 'all other things being the same'. For example, one might prefer a state of the world with a lower crime rate over one with a higher one, but not at any cost. Assuming that q, r and s are such *ceteris-paribus* reasons, a preference for w_4 and w_5 over w_3 could thus be derived from them. Still, w_4 and w_5 need yet to be ranked. Is q to be given priority over s? Is there a possible middle way between the worlds?

Formally, dropping the IIA condition results in *too many* possible aggregation mechanisms which yield different results. The result of aggregation now depends not on the input (reasons) alone but also on the mechanism chosen to aggregate them. The aggregation mechanism thus becomes 'creative' rather than passive (MacKay 1980: 87). The choice between different aggregation mechanisms may again be based on reasons (e.g. reasons why q is more relevant than s) and can in this sense be rationalised. Reason-giving, however, will eventually end in a regress as long as there exist no 'final reasons' which do not require further justification.

Creativity implies that most sets of reasons will not be *sufficient* to determine a specific preference order over alternative worlds. Rather, the preference order ultimately depends on the mechanism chosen for their aggregation. Nonetheless, reasons are *necessary* to motivate the choice of an option, and changes in reasons should lead to changes in preferences. With the selection of an aggregation function, the decision gains an element of decisionism. Decisionism is not to be equated with arbitrary choice. The fact that a decision is not sufficiently determined by reasons does not mean that it cannot be rationalised and justified. Justification of actions (thus differing from justification of claims and beliefs) is not regressive: it is not necessary to name sufficient reasons, it suffices to name necessary and good ones. It is only the observer who is left with the well known problem (described by von Wright 1974, chapter four) of being unable to name sufficient conditions for actor choices and social events.

To sum up: although the decision what to want is not among the topics of classical decision-theory, it can to some extent be rationalised. This means that the selection of goals and other reasons for action (values, needs, conventions etc.) is itself based on reasons and that these reasons are, to some extent, accessible to the observer. The observer can name reasons why a particular goal was adopted by an actor and can thereby offer an explanation for the goal-choice and for resulting actions. The same applies to the selection of a mechanism for the aggregation of these into a preference order over alternative worlds. Preferences over options for action, such as policy options, however, are conditional not only on the volitive premises but also on opinions about the properties and effects of options for action. These opinions are cognitive attitudes making up the second important aspect in the formation of preferences: the cognitive one that complements the volitional one and will be dealt with in the following section.

4. DECIDING WHAT TO ACCEPT

The idea that actors can freely decide what to believe is equally, if not more, contested as that they can freely adopt and give up their goals or desires. It seems highly plausible that the primary and evolutionary function of beliefs was to enable us to achieve our goals: '... our original interest in truth was instrumentally based. Truths served us better than falsehoods and better than no beliefs at all in coping with the world's dangers and opportunities' (Nozick 1993: 68). In order to be instrumentally valuable, or, as Nozick terms it, 'serviceable', beliefs must be determined by something other than, and external to, the mind itself. Beliefs, so goes the classical interpretation, may not be influenced by anything other than evidence and, most importantly, may not be driven by desires.

The traditional conception of belief in decision-theory is one of subjective probability. Following Bayes, theorists in the classical framework have maintained that belief should not be conceived of as a binary yes/no attitude towards propositions but that one should rather conceptualise belief as a matter of degree.

The Bayesian concept of belief can be applied either to future events or to present states of the world that cannot be observed and to which probabilities are assigned.

Probability assignments are assumed to be 'updated' whenever actors are confronted with new evidence, according to the following formula:

$$p\textsc{ø}/x = [(px/\textsc{ø})(p\textsc{ø})] / [(px/\textsc{ø})(p\textsc{ø}) + (px/\neg\textsc{ø})(p\neg\textsc{ø})]$$

$p_\textsc{ø}$ is the 'prior probability' an actor assigns to a proposition ø being true before being confronted with confirming or contradictory evidence. $p_{x/\textsc{ø}}$ is the 'conditional probability' of an event x occurring, given that ø is true, and $p_{\textsc{ø}/x}$ is the 'updated probability' (cf. Goodin 2003: 113).

The Bayesian concept surely does justice to one central property of beliefs, that of transformability. The sole purpose of beliefs, as Nozick aptly points out, lies in the fact that they are not 'hard-wired' into the human genes but transformable in the light of new evidence (1993: 68). The transformation of beliefs enables adaptation to new circumstances and unexpected events. However, there are also some problems with the Bayesian approach. It seems that in order to take decisions and to act, certain assumptions must be treated as certain, they are required as premises for choice and action. For example, when making a choice, actors will take it for granted that they are actually facing the choice situation and not being deceived by an evil demon (see Nozick 1993: 95). Without any basis of certainty, probability assignments seem difficult.

What seems to be required are some premises – both for action and decision and for further reasoning. Isaac Levi, a critic of Bayesianism, therefore maintains that while something is believed, it is believed with certainty, and when the belief is dropped, this happens with similar certainty (1991). Nozick criticises this view as inadequate: we can obviously lose certainty in a belief without dropping the belief altogether. He instead proposes a concept of belief as context-dependent. If beliefs are instrumental for the pursuit of goals, their status may depend on the salience and possible consequences of the decision faced. Nozick uses the following example:

> I believe my new junior colleague is not a child molester. (Asked to list the people in the philosophy department who are not child molesters, I unhesitatingly place his name on the list.) Now the context changes; I need someone to watch for my young child for two weeks. A mistake here would be serious – the stakes have escalated. Now I think more carefully. It is not that I did not believe in my colleague's innocence before. In that context, for those purposes, I did believe it; I did not consider, or assign a probability to, the possibility of his being a child molester. In this context, with higher stakes, I consider what probability that might have (1993: 96).

Although the example, at a glance, seems compelling, problems remain. Is it really the belief that is context-dependent or rather the consequences drawn from one and the same belief? I believe that for cognition as for volition, it makes sense to draw a distinction between first and second-order mental states, in this case between belief and acceptance. Lehrer and Cohen regard beliefs as first-order states arising within us as a result of a process more or less beyond our control.[20] Beliefs are, in this understanding, determined by evidence, whether we want it or not. Acceptance, by contrast, is a conscious mental act, it is the decision to adopt a proposition as a premise for action and for further reasoning (Cohen 1989: 368). Being an action, it is not a matter of degree but the result of a binary yes/no decision: either I accept a proposition as a premise for action or I don't, there is nothing in between (Cohen 1989: 374).

Acceptance, Cohen points out, is similar to what used to be termed 'judgment': it is based on reasons rather than determined by evidence (Cohen 1989: 374.). Evidence can, of course, constitute a strong reason for accepting a proposition. When I am asked to state my 'belief' or justify my decision with 'beliefs', what I am really asked for is an expression of acceptance:

> … anyone's saying that he believes that p certainly does normally commit him to accepting any logical consequences of the proposition that p. But that commitment stems just from a fact about the speech-act of saying 'I believe that p'. By making this affirmative first-person confession one commonly expresses acquiescence in one's belief and thereby affirms one's acceptance that p, or at least one's opinion that the proposition p deserves acceptance (Cohen 1989: 371).

Like desires, beliefs are in Lehrer and Cohen's understanding nothing one could be reproached for, they are essentially private. As soon as they are expressed in speech acts, however, they will be treated as acceptances and require justification. Even if beliefs were objectively driven by nothing but reasons and evidence and frequently true, they would still require the metamental assent of acceptance in order to be justified and to serve as justification. Once they are made explicit as premises for further reasoning and action, they can and will be rationally criticised and defended.

The introduction of the second-order mental state of acceptance into the discussion of cognition and volition implies the assumption that cognitive processes are, to some extent, subject to voluntary control and guided by reasons and can be made rationally comprehensible. This means that actors can not only choose what to accept but can also wilfully adopt principles and methods of rational acceptance. Such principles may be epistemic, concerning the question of how much evidence is sufficient for acceptance of a proposition, or simply demand that one should draw logical conclusions and avoid accepting contradictory propositions. They may, however, also be ethical and prudential ones, defining the stakes for accepting a given proposition. The stakes for accepting that somebody is guilty of a crime should, for instance, be higher than the ones for accepting that somebody is intelligent, stingy or hospitable. In addition to this, acceptances about states of the world differ from acceptances about causal relationships between states of the world. While the former may be based on evidence alone, the latter require a different type of justification.

Like the adoption of goals and other reasons for action, acceptances constitute indispensable premises for action. If an actor is faced with a number of options for action but has no opinion whatsoever on what outcome would result from the choice of each, she lacks the basis for rational decision-making and can choose at best arbitrarily. Given that she accepts that the decision is relevant for her future well-being or the advancement of her goals and that time available for decision-making is scarce, the actor should make an effort to arrive at serviceable premises. In situations of incomplete or imperfect information, however, even the basis for assignment of probabilities may be lacking. In such situations, preliminary acceptances need to be found and intra- (as well as commonly inter-) personally justified.

Justifications for acceptances are reasons, which can be compared and weighed against one another (contrary to the Bayesian model, where evidence is weighed but not compared). Reason-giving is of course eventually regressive. However, if the acceptance of a proposition as true is regarded as an action, necessary reasons will again suffice instead of sufficient ones. The epistemic optimist would maintain that, in spite of the element of decisionism or creativity involved here, acceptances based on well assessed reasons should, in general, be more serviceable than arbitrarily or intuitively adopted ones. Lehrer argues that belief-acceptance, which amounts to intuitive acceptance, is available as a 'default mode' for cognition (1997: 92).[21] One method suggesting itself as producing more serviceable acceptances is reason-giving and reason-seeking in direct or indirect (mediated) communication. Few reasons can be obtained from experience and direct observation alone, which is why actors will seek communicative interaction in order to assess the quality of their acceptances and gain new ones. Formation and transformation of acceptances is a result of argumentative assessment of reasons. If such assessment yields acceptances which are instrumentally serviceable for the achievement of goals, their reasoned transformation should be a welcome result of interaction.[22]

Up to here, acceptances have only been discussed as acceptances of propositions referring to empirical states and events. However, assertions claiming moral validity can equally be assessed and accepted. These are to a particular extent dependent upon argumentative justification by reasons, on properly drawn conclusions and coherence. They are of special interest in that they constitute an interface between cognition and volition. Accepting a moral claim usually, although not necessarily, entails the adoption of respective volitive attitudes. If a moral acceptance is dropped, e.g. because it was shown to be inconsistent with a higher-order one, this will motivate the actor to rule out respective goals as reasons for action as well. Acceptance can, hence, immediately affect volition. With regard to their transformation, however, moral acceptances may in some respects differ from empirical ones. Because dropping or adopting a moral acceptance implies changing not only the cognitive but also the volitional premises of action, there are likely to be certain obstacles that do not exist for empirical acceptances. Moreover, it seems likely that, if people are insecure about the validity of moral claims and unsure which to accept, they choose the 'default mode', which, in this case, means not only belief-acceptance but also desire-satisfaction. Nonetheless, acceptances of both types, empirical and moral, entail the important function of being transformable, which they should also be empirically, most of the time.

Having established that the premises for the decision what to prefer are themselves to a considerable extent based upon voluntary decision, the following section will return to the topic of preference, dealing with how actors relate between goals and acceptances on the one hand and the empirical world on the other. Sticking to the concept of political preference, where objects are political programmes and strategies rather than states of the world, I maintain that the formation and transformation of preferences can and should be accounted for by reference to both volitive premises (goals and reasons) and cognitive premises (acceptances).

5. DECIDING WHAT TO DO

Having dealt with the cognitive and volitive aspects of motivation separately, it is now possible to join them again in the concept of preference. Preference, as pointed out in the second section of this chapter, is understood to relate between the individual mind and concrete options for action in the real world. Volitive attitudes are what motivates this process of relating but they cannot be translated into action and decision without cognitive premises. Political preferences, motivating the choice between available options (strategies, programmes), hence, evolve as conclusions from volitive and cognitive premises. Reconsidering the traditional model of rational choice, it becomes apparent that motivation for action as it is understood here considerably deviates from it.

The traditional model of rational choice regards action as jointly *determined* by beliefs and desires. Beliefs are driven by evidence alone: Bayesianism constitutes a frequent component of conventional models. Desires are regarded as given, stable and more or less universal, and their origin is rarely considered. Thin concepts of rationality entirely refuse to be concerned with the question of how beliefs and desires arise: they are simply assumed to exist and to determine action. But then, if a rationalist theory is not capable of recommending some actions and rejecting others, it must be regarded as one of (objectively) rational behaviour rather than one of rational *choice*.

The assumptions implied in the classical model of rational choice are, as noted before, of analytical rather than empirical nature. There may be cases in which they are, for their simplicity, of considerable heuristic value. Where the empirical and theoretical goal is to arrive at a better understanding of how preferences are formed and transformed, though, it is inadequate. A model of rational preference-formation and -transformation requires that the formation and transformation of the volitive and cognitive premises, which are both entailed in an adequate concept of political preference, be rationalised. This is enabled by following the Lehrer/Cohen-distinction between desires and beliefs as first-order mental states on the one hand and goals and acceptances as second-order mental states on the other hand.

In contrast to classical rational choice and decision-theory, where the *explanandum* is the actor's actual behaviour and preferences the *explanans* for it, the aim here is to account for the evolution and transformation of preferences. Preferences may be said to be derived as conclusions from their volitive and cognitive premises. Volitive premises arise from the aggregation of practical reasons, including goals. To be accepted as reasons to want something, goals and practical reasons themselves require reasons, they need to be justified. Acceptances, as cognitive premises, are equally based on reasons.

Reasons motivating volitive premises normally differ from those motivating acceptance, as Brandom's distinction into 'practical' and 'doxastic' reasons indicates (Brandom 1994). The case of moral reasons, however, shows that some reasons may play a role in both volition and cognition. The first-order mental states of desire and belief respectively constitute only one among many possible reasons that motivate premises of preferences. Desire-satisfaction and belief-acceptance operate as default modes of decision-making, most likely in situations of extreme uncertainty (where rational decision-making seems impossible) or ones in which stakes are low (and costly deliberation dispensable). Neither case, as I argue, is typical for the decision-making of collective and political actors, however.

The preferences evolving as conclusions from volitive and cognitive premises motivate actions. This does not mean, however, that they are preferences for actions as such. Rather, they are motivated by the outcomes which are expected to result from the choice of options for action. Outcomes have been defined as the sets of features of states of the world that are, in some sense, determined by an actor's choice. However, outcomes, or their prospects, are again not valued as such but for their properties. Philip Pettit (1991) has persuasively pointed this out:

> To desire a prospect is to prefer it to the prospects that you think of as alternatives. To desire a property is to be disposed to prefer a prospect that has it, assuming that there is only one, among a set of prospects that otherwise leave you indifferent. More intuitively, to desire a prospect is to opt for it, or to form the intention of opting for it, among the set of available alternatives; to desire a property is to value it, being disposed, if other things are equal, to desire any prospect that displays the property (1991: 153).

Among the consequences of an action, i.e. its outcome, are some that are more relevant than others. Those that are held to be most relevant are the ones that motivate the choice of an option, they are *reasons* for opting in this way and no other. Pettit goes on to contrast values with ends (or goals):

> ... the agent's ultimate points of reference, his ultimate motivational bearings,

must be given by abstract properties rather than by concrete outcomes. In more everyday language they must be given by the agent's values rather than by his ends. Certainly he may take his guidance in decision-making from the ends to which different choices are likely to lead, but how desirable he finds those ends will depend on his values (1991: 161).

I think that what Pettit refers to as 'values' are more appropriately described as 'reasons'. Pettit himself seems to regard the two as closely related when he describes the practice of seeking and giving reasons for choice: when asked for a reason for choosing an option, we explain which of the numerous expected properties of its outcome motivated the choice (Pettit 1991: 157–8). Reconsidering the twofold role of preferences as motivators for action and measures of individual welfare (Sen 1982), reasons seem to be on the 'motivating' side whereas values are on the 'measuring' (evaluating) side.

Being able to name reasons (motivators) for a decision surely affects the evaluation of its effects but is not sufficient as a measure of welfare or utility. As for descriptive and explanatory purposes (in contrast to normative ones), the motivating aspect of preference is of more central relevance than the evaluating one, the latter may be neglected but for these terminological concessions.[24] As soon as values are (on the motivational side) understood as reasons, the role of ends or goals becomes clearer, too. As argued in section 3 above, goals both require and constitute reasons. A goal without reasons for it lacks what Pettit calls 'ultimate motivational bearings', it is in this respect empty. Nonetheless, once adopted for reasons, goals can constitute powerful reasons for action themselves, although not the only possible ones, as classical rational-choice theory would have it.

Pettit's argument about the distinct roles of prospects and their properties is also helpful for the current project of joining the cognitive and volitive aspects of decision-making in the concept of preference. When confronted with a set of alternatives, actors need to carry out two separate parts of the same decision: they need to decide both 'what to want' and 'what to accept'.

The first part of this task consists in assessing reasons for preferring an outcome and aggregating accepted ones into a complete preference order over possible outcomes which constitutes a guideline for action. Reasons provide *criteria* with regard to which possible outcomes can be evaluated and *dimensions* within which they can be ordered. In contrast to doxastic reasons, which must not be contradictory, practical reasons are typically to some extent incommensurable (which is why aggregation is so difficult). The question here is: given my reasons, which outcome do I prefer?

The second step consists in assessing the available alternatives for their instrumentality to bring about the outcomes. The number of available alternatives is not always clearly restricted but may be more or less indeterminate. The same is even more true for reasons and outcomes. Outcomes may have properties other than those considered relevant for a chosen reason ('side-effects') which may come to be accepted and render new reasons effective. Acceptances about whether or not

a particular alternative causes a particular outcome are based upon other acceptances, all of which are necessarily transformable. Taken together, the constitution
of preference seems to be a process of complex interaction between cognition and
volition, both of which may nonetheless be regarded as rational(isable).

To illustrate: a political decision between three childcare programmes is
impending. One proposed alternative is to create tax abatements for parents who
employ professional carers to look after their children (a). A second proposal (b)
is to increase the number of all-day schools. The third option (c) is to leave things
as they are, with a status quo of half-day schools and without tax abatements.
Forming preferences over these options, voters will consider the likely outcomes
of each. Proposal (a) will enable young professional couples to stay in work and
pay for childcare. Proposal (b), too, will allow more women with children to stay
in work. The status quo (c) prevents female employment. Given that I prefer an
outcome with better job opportunities for women, I will assess the instrumental
quality of options (a) and (b) to achieve this outcome. Personally, I arrive at the
conclusion that option (b) is more likely to be successful and hence prefer it over
both (a) and (c).

The interrelatedness of cognition and volition in motivating choice becomes
even more apparent on considering that goals and values, which represent powerful reasons for action, can often be pursued only through the adoption of secondary goals, which are themselves based upon acceptances. Such secondary goals
are instrumental in the pursuit of superordinate goals and hence presuppose a
number of cognitive acceptances. The reasons motivating a preference on the volitive side are, at least in the case of secondary, or derived goals, based on cognitive
acceptances themselves. Since they join cognitive and volitive premises, derived
goals already constitute preferences.

Returning to the example, assume a (federal) decision over a policy option of
creating financial incentives for states to increase the number of all-day schools.
The reason driving the preference for this option is the goal to increase the number of all-day schools, while the cognitive premise of this preference consists in
the acceptance that financial incentives will be an instrumentally appropriate
means to achieve this. The goal of increasing the number of all-day schools is not
pursued on its own behalf, though. It is derived from a more abstract, superordinate goal with regard to which it is instrumental: the goal of improving female
employment rates and increasing job opportunities for women. This superordinate
goal could itself be motivated by an even more abstract goal of ensuring equal life
chances for men and women, or for the poor and the rich and so on.

Each derivational step from a superordinate to a subordinate, instrumental goal
is based on certain acceptances, in this case, that all-day schools improve female
employment and that life-chances depend on job opportunities. The relationship
between superordinate and derivative goals is thus based both on a reason-giving,
argumentative logic ('*because* female employment must be improved, all-day
should be introduced') and on an instrumental logic ('all-day schools should be
introduced *in order* to improve female employment'; 'they are the right instrument

to improve it'). The necessary specification and contextualisation of goals and values is both part of the decision what to want and part of the decision what to accept as instrumentally appropriate. If either the volitive or the cognitive premises for a preference (or derived goal) break down, so does the preference or goal itself.

Figure 1.4: The derivational structure of goals and goal-based preferences

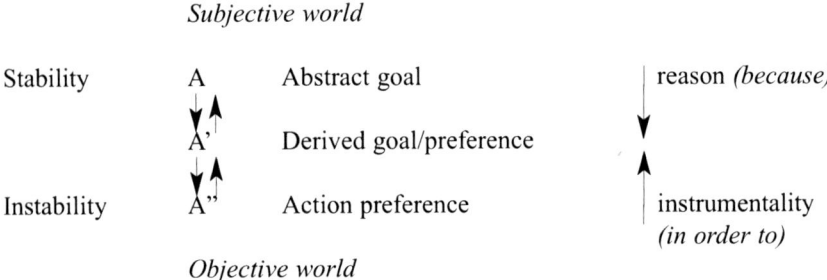

Figure 1.4 illustrates the derivational structure of goals and goal-based preferences. The top-down link between abstract goals and preferences over alternative options for action in the objective world is a reason-giving one: each primary, superordinate goal serves as a reason for adopting the secondary, derived goal. The bottom-up link between options for action and abstract goals is one of instrumentality: action preferences as well as all derived preferences are adopted because they are accepted as instrumentally useful for the achievement of abstract goals. If a goal is abandoned either temporarily or completely, all other goals and preferences that are derived from it lose motivation and should be given up as well. If acceptances about the instrumental qualities of a derived goal or preference change, all preferences further down in the derivational chain, i.e. derived from derived goals, should similarly lose effect: if I give up the acceptance that all-day schools improve job opportunities for women, I will no longer support the motion to create financial incentives to increase the number of such schools.

The resulting conclusion is that the relationship between subjective, abstract goals and options for action in the objective world is always a precarious one that can hardly be treated as determinate: political preferences over programmes, strategies and options are necessarily and rationally transformable.

6. THE NECESSITY OF PREFERENCE-FORMATION AND -TRANSFORMATION

It has already been noted that there exists a certain analytical value in the assumption of stable preferences, given prior to the interaction that is to be analysed. It seems problematic, however, to treat either stability or specific contents of preferences (e.g. 'selfish' goals) as components of the concept of preference itself or to translate the analytical into an empirical assumption. The formation and transformation of preferences is essentially important to how actors relate to the world and make decisions in it. My aim here is to point out that the adoption and changing of preferences over political programmes and goals can itself be rationalised, i.e. that it can be accounted for as rational, reason-based choice.

Obviously, it does not make sense to assume that all preference-formations and -transformations are due to reasoned deliberation rather than spontaneously arising mental or physical states. Nevertheless, I maintain that the preferences and goals that drive the political actions and decisions of political actors are usually rationally adopted and can be rationally transformed. Political preferences, it has been argued, are sensitive to changes in acceptances (which are themselves sensitive to changes in epistemic reasons) on the cognitive and practical reasons and their aggregation on the volitive side. Accordingly, they can empirically not generally be stable over a longer period of time. If political preferences are empirically transformable, and if their formation and transformation can be rationalised, then the development of an analytical framework to account for it is surely desirable.

Before I go on to discuss the implications of an assumption of rationally transformable preferences for the analysis of political decisions in the following chapters, the question of why the concept of preference should entail the notion of transformability will be discussed in some detail. For the cognitive aspect of preference, the case seems straightforward. Cognitive attitudes, whether conceptualised as beliefs or as acceptances, would lose their purpose if they were not responsive to changes in an actor's environment, i.e. to new reasons (consisting in arguments or evidence) for accepting propositions as true or false. The instrumental link between goals, preferences and actions is based on acceptances that each of the derived items is instrumentally appropriate for the pursuit of the respective goal. An actor who does not revise her decisions, although she comes to accept that other programmes or strategies are instrumentally superior to the ones she originally favoured, is not maximising utility. Hence, in assuming responsiveness to the environment, utility-maximisation entails transformability of political preferences. Actors with fixed preferences over programmes and strategies would lack the flexibility and adaptability that is required to pursue higher-order goals and to derive utility from their achievement. Accepting this is still in keeping with the traditional concept of instrumental rationality applied by rational-choice and classical decision theorists, even if the concept of preference is different.

Preference-transformations due to changes of acceptances would mean that the links drawn between alternatives and outcomes are revised – preferences over alternatives change while preferences over outcomes remain stable. What the new acceptances change, in other words, are assumptions about the respective outcomes that alternative strategies would produce. As the discussion above has indicated, however, changes in acceptances do not only concern the cognitive premises of preferences over given options but can affect the volitive ones as well – if these are derived from higher-order goals. There may thus be cases in which changes in acceptances, due to newly available information, change both preferences over outcomes and preferences over alternatives. In the example, changes in acceptances about all-day schools improving female employment render the *volitive* premises of the preference for the respective policy option (here: financial incentives) void. The outcome of an increased number of all-day schools will no longer appear desirable if the reasons for pursuing it as a goal are no longer accepted as valid.

As the volitive premises of preference must be regarded as prior to and motivating the cognitive ones, their transformation has more far-reaching effects for the decision at hand. If new acceptances concern only the instrumental use of a given option (e.g. the premise that financial incentives will be sufficient motivation for states to create more all-day schools), only the instruments would need to be reconsidered, not the reasons for action themselves. Comparing the acceptances upon which derived goals (such as increasing the number of all-day schools) are based with those upon which preferences over concrete options for action (for policy x rather than policy y) are based, though, it seems that the latter are usually held with less confidence and hence less stable.

As acceptances about the justification and rationality of higher-order preferences and goals commonly motivate a large number of derived preferences and choices, they are likely to be more fundamental and more deeply implicated in the system of acceptances than ones about concrete states of the world and decisions. Changing such fundamental acceptances might unsettle the entire motivational structure with which an actor relates to the world. Moreover, on taking a closer look at the fundamental acceptances upon which higher-order goals in the all-day school example are based, it becomes apparent that many of those acceptances are of a moral rather than purely empirical nature. The acceptance that increasing female employment is important in order to realise equal opportunities for men and women, for instance, is normative in that it implicitly views employment opportunities as particularly important to equality.

Such moral acceptances, as pointed out above, hold a dual status as both cognitive and volitive premises of preference and decision. The transformation of moral acceptances is therefore a point at which it becomes difficult to decide whether a change of preference is due to changes in its cognitive or in its volitive premises, i.e. whether the reasons for wanting something or the preferred instruments for achieving it have changed. Changes in practical reasons and their aggregation are the second possible cause, besides revision of acceptances, for a transformation of preferences. By taking into consideration the rationalisation and rational transformation of these volitive premises for action and decision, the present treatment leaves the common ground with classical decision-theory and moves beyond the purely instrumental concept of rationality. Although I maintain that a rationalisation of reasons for adopting preferences is possible, the case is clearly more difficult than the one for cognitive premises.

Different reasons matter to different actors, and it seems difficult to declare some of them to be more rational than others, partly owing to fears like Nozick's about the despotism in a substantial theory of practical reason. Some considerations are nonetheless due and possible. To begin with, goals are surely the most effective reasons for preferences, particularly where far-reaching decisions are concerned. Goals enable actors to make plans and pursue them over a longer period of time. To acknowledge the almost necessarily arising conflicts between the number of different goals one pursues and to deliberatively adopt a suitable mechanism for their aggregation may be regarded as one aspect of substantial rationality. As actors will hardly always be aware of the totality of reasons that might be relevant for a given decision, due consideration of and exchange about reasons constitutes a further requirement for rational decision-making, at least for far-reaching and political decisions. Finally, and surely more contestably, one might argue that, where ethical reasons and selfish goals conflict, making the former effective is the rational choice. This is more or less the essence of Broome's Kantian concept of categorically rational preferences (Broome 1991).

What the approach I take here seeks to enable is a rationalisation of empirical preference-formation and -transformation rather than a classification of reasons for action as rational or irrational. The number of reasons considered by the observer may be restricted for reasons of parsimonious analysis, as it is done in public-choice approaches, where specific goals are stipulated as the only reasons motivating actor choices. It also makes sense to assume that actors themselves try to restrict the number of reasons considered, a process that may be enhanced but also inhibited by communication with others. Where actors 'understand' the reasons others give for their preferences, they must at least consider these reasons themselves. Only if they come to the conclusion that another's reason is 'no reason at all', they reject the notion that this reason could in principle be made effective for their own decision. If other actors contribute new reasons to the domain of reasons considered, communication thus increases the number and heterogeneity of reasons but, if actors come to agree on a specific set of reasons to be relevant, reasons can converge as a result of interaction.

A degree of stability in practical reasons, and goals in particular, is an important aspect of actors' motivation and identity, however. Unless goals were held stable and made effective in a considerable number of decisions, there would be little point in adopting them at all. Their adoption is an important expression of autonomy and hence identity, a point that is of particular importance for collective actors. For collective political actors in particular, it makes sense to rationalise decisions on the basis of known goals, for instance by illustrating how one of numerous conflicting goals becomes effective in a given decision. Moral goals and reasons are of particular interest in this context.[25] Their categorical nature allows them to decide matters when decision-makers are trapped between conflicting goals that do not enable meaningful or rationalisable trade-offs.

Even if we assume stability and coherence with regard to the totality of reasons that are somehow relevant to an actor's action and decision, an actor who made the same reason or goal effective in every single decision would appear not only dogmatic but even irrational. His internal aggregation mechanism would be violating Arrow's non-dictatorship criterion, as one reason is obviously turned into an internal dictator (see section 3). As much as instrumental rationality (i.e.

utility maximisation) rules out stability of preferences on the cognitive side, demands for flexibility, adaptability and autonomy seem to rule out stability of preference on the volitive side. What counts as a reason in one context must be regarded as 'no reason at all' in another context. Each choice from a set of alternatives requires a new assessment and aggregation of practical reasons – preference orders cannot be assumed to be given independently of a specific context.

Taken together, these arguments suggest that transformability of political preferences over strategies, programmes and policy options is a requirement of rationality. Preferences must be responsive both to changes in acceptances and to the pertinence of reasons in a given choice situation. Simply sticking to one's preferences without proper assessment of their appropriateness appears to be a suboptimal, if not irrational, choice. In fact, I think that the latter constitutes the 'default mode' for preference-formation, which parallels the default modes of desire-satisfaction and belief-acceptance where the volitive and cognitive premises for preferences are concerned. To some extent, new situations always confront actors with the necessity of forming preferences over previously unknown options, which seems to rule out application of preference-adherence as a default mode. Choosing an option because it superficially resembles previously preferred options may be an appealing strategy in situations of high uncertainty, and is likely to serve the actor's goals better than random choice.[26] Wherever scarcity of time permits this, however, reducing uncertainty by means of information, communication and deliberation is obviously the superior strategy with regard to autonomy and rationality.[27]

7. SUMMARY

This chapter has advocated a concept of preference that entails the aspects of consequentialism and comparison, plays a twofold role in motivating actions and evaluating outcomes and relates the mind to the objective world outside the mind. Section 1 looked at different concepts of rationality and addressed the debate about whether rationality is a descriptive or prescriptive concept. I argued for an understanding of rationality as reason-based choice that extends beyond instrumental rationality, i.e. the choice of means, to the choice of ends of action. What matters in this context is not so much whether an action or decision is objectively rational but whether it can be accounted for by the observer by reference to the actor's reasons for it.

Section 2 discussed different possible concepts of preference and argued that a concept of political preference, where preference orders are defined over programmes and strategies rather than states of the world, should reflect both volitive and cognitive mental attitudes. The proper way to conceptualise and analyse the formation and transformation of preferences is, I maintain, via the rationalisation of these mental attitudes. Only if the adoption of cognitive premises (acceptances rather than 'beliefs') of preferences on the one hand and volitive premises (aggregated practical reasons rather than 'desires') on the other hand can be described as a voluntary and rational decisions can preferences themselves be dealt with within a rationalistic framework.

Section 3 addressed the formation and transformation of volitive premises of preferences. It was shown that any actor must consider a number of different practical reasons, including goals, interests, values and commitments, in forming preferences over possible states of the world. The intra-personal weighting and aggregation of practical reasons is, to some extent, contingent and is required anew wherever a decision between alternative options for action and their respective consequences is to be taken.

Section 4 looked at the formation of acceptances as cognitive premises for decisions. Following an argument made by Cohen and Lehrer, acceptances were distinguished from beliefs. While beliefs to some extent determine what one accepts as a premise for action and decision, it makes a difference whether a proposition is consciously adopted as a basis for practical inferences. The requirements for acceptances from which actions and decisions are inferred differ in several respects from the requirements for believing something. Acceptances as well as practical reasons (including goals) and their aggregation were argued to be products of metamental evaluation and assent. Section 5 pointed out how preferences over concrete options evolve as conclusions from these cognitive and volitive premises.

Section 6 contended that both the cognitive and the volitive premises of preferences over political programmes and policy options are necessarily subject to revision. For many purposes of analysis, it thus makes sense not only to assume the transformability of preferences empirically but also to make transformability part of the analytical concept of political preference.

Central questions pertaining to the empirical contents and properties of preferences and to how information about them can be obtained nonetheless remain open. In fact, I believe that a rationalisation of the cognitive and volitive premises upon which preferences are based contributes comparatively little to an analysis of consumer preferences or of everyday decisions of minor significance. The revealed-preference approach, which dominates economic research, may well provide more insights in these cases than an enquiry into the 'deep structure' of preferences.

The value I see in an analysis and rationalisation of the cognitive and volitive premises of preferences pertains explicitly to *political* preferences. Their formation and transformation is of central relevance to many political processes and therefore deserves particular attention. It is also of central relevance to normative theories of politics, most markedly of course, to the theory of deliberative democracy. Moreover, empirical aspects both of political decisions and of political actors not only enable but strongly recommend investigations into the acceptances and reasons preferences for policy options are based upon.

To begin with, stakes are higher for political decisions than for everyday consumer choices. Political decisions have considerable and long-term effects for large numbers of people. Even if they cannot be assumed to have the same salience for all voters in an election, politicians and representatives of interest groups may be expected to assign due relevance to political decisions. Moreover, political decisions are commonly decisions under high uncertainty. This uncertainty pertains both to questions about the outcomes given options will produce and to questions about the appropriate criteria to evaluate the expected outcomes. Whereas both of these aspects may appear trivial in consumer choices, they are (and should be) subjects of contentious public and non-public debates in democratic societies.

The fact that relevant reasons and acceptances are often publicly expressed is also one of the reasons why an analysis of preferences and their premises is not only desirable but also possible for political actors and decisions. The following chapter will look at the processes of communication and justification, which have been pointed out to be essential for the rational formation and transformation of preferences – for both individual and collective actors.

NOTES

1   See e.g. Tsebelis 1990: 35–36: '... when decisions are made and rewards or penalties are distributed, the less successful individuals will be eliminated'. However, this externalist account of rationality ends in the same circularity: rationality is defined as survival while survival is defined as rationality. De Sousa therefore argues that human rationality must be defined as an alternative to irrationality: 'Natural processes can maximize this or that property, but they cannot exhibit irrationality. ... The special rationality of persons ... consists essentially in the capacity to be irrational.' (1998: 123–4).

2   Beliefs are contradictory if someone holds that both p and ¬p are true (that it is the case that p and that it is not the case that p). Preferences are contradictory if one strictly prefers x over y and y over x. Somebody's preferences are intransitive if she prefers a over b and b over c but c over a.

3   Simon 1983: 7–8, quoted in Nozick 1993: 64. Note that this quote is Simon's definition of reason in general, not of instrumental reason: his understanding of reason and rationality is of the narrow, purely instrumental kind. This view was shared by, among many others, Bertrand Russell: '"Reason" has a perfectly clear and precise meaning. It signifies the choice of the right means to an end that you wish to achieve. It has nothing whatever to do with the choice of ends.' (Russell 1954: viii, quoted in Nozick 1993: 64).

4   In his defence of practical reason, Searle concedes that '[t]here is no x such that intention is to x as truth is to belief.' (2001: 137).

5   The recent works of Brandom (1994) and Searle (2001) can be seen as addressing practical reason from this empirical side without implying normativity. Habermas, although he does make normative appeals, similarly bases his *Theory of Communicative Action* (1984) on empirical assumptions about the nature and function of language and rationality.

6   Tsebelis, who shares the narrow concept of rationality, at least admits that '[a]s actors' goals become fuzzy ... rational-choice applications become less applicable.' (1990: 32–3). The 'fuzziness' of goals need not be due to the observer's incomplete perspective but can also

(and is more likely to) be a problem actors themselves face.

7   Minimisation is an alternative, although in situations of certainty 'minimise cost' may easily be read as 'maximise property'. 'MinMax' and 'MaxMin' constitute alternative choice rules only in situations of risk, where 'MinMax' is the term used for a strategy by which the chooser selects from all options the ones that minimise possible losses and then among these the one that maximises possible benefits, while 'MaxMin' signifies the reverse strategy.

8   Cf. Green & Shapiro 1994: 20: 'It is evident that ... neither the optimality requirement nor the consistency conditions ... can be relaxed without abandoning the entire rational choice venture.'

9   Preference relations may be either 'strict preference' (xPy, x is preferred to y), 'weak preference' (xRy, x is at least as good as y) or indifference ($xIy \leftrightarrow xRy$ & yRx).

10 The question concerned here is related to that of 'consequentialism', which can be given either a strict or a weak reading (see Levi 1991). A weak reading would regard the resulting fact 'that act A was carried out' as one of the intended consequences of this act A (Broome 1991: 124) and might hence allow for a consequentialist account of habitual or symbolic action. A strong consequentialism, by contrast, would require preferences to be based solely on considerations that are independent of the description of the act itself. That is, a given state of the world should be valued equally if it occurs as the result of an action as if it occurs as the result of other causes.

11 This is of course a simplification of the idea of expected utility. Given that there are n mutually exclusive possible outcomes of choosing option A, its expected utility would be defined as: $EU(A) = p(O1) \times u(O1) + p(O2) \times u(O2) + ... + p(On) \times u (On)$ (cf. Nozick 1993: 43). Moreover, the utility derived from an outcome may be conditional on whether it occurred as the result of act A or has different causes, which may be calculated into the utility function.

12 Scharpf (1997) addresses the problem of inseparable preferences with his concept of different possible 'action orientations'. The question arising in both cases is whether the utilities or disutilities inferred from feelings such as hostility, love or regret can simply be added to or subtracted from the overall utility of an action.

13 In epistemic accounts of democracy (e.g. Estlund 1990, 1997), the motivation for political decisions is regarded as a purely cognitive matter. In these approaches, preferences are either ruled out as input to collective decisions and replaced by beliefs or they are defined in a way that is in stark opposition to the standard economic concept.

14 Altruism and malevolence (or hostility) require the substantial, hedonistic ends of others to be satisfied or thwarted. Altruism is a desire to fulfil the hedonistic desires of others; malevolence a desire to prevent these from being fulfilled. In the absence of hedonistic desires, neither altruists nor malevolent people could be satisfied.

15 Lehrer 1981: 79–80; 1990; 1997; 2000: 25ff.; Cohen, L. J. 1989, 1992. Both draw an analogy between belief and acceptance on the one hand and desire and preference/goal-adoption on the other. I will deal with the latter in this section and address the former in the following section. While Lehrer is concerned with autonomy and freedom of choice in general, Cohen focuses on the cognitive and epistemic aspect.

16 This is one way of 'dissonance reduction' (see Elster 1990: 34–5). Another would be to devalue the object one has yearnings for ('the grapes are sour anyway', see Elster 1983).

17 Pursuit of goals, it seems, is necessarily consequential: what count are 'objective outcomes',

not decisions themselves. It has often been noted, however, that actors are commonly sensitive not only to outcomes but also to agency, i.e. to the question of who brought the outcome about (see Sen 2002: 237–8).

18 Arrow's 'Impossibility Theorem' (Arrow 1963) proves that there exists no function that aggregates indexical individual preferences into a transitive and complete social preference order and satisfies the conditions of non-dictatorship, citizen sovereignty, unrestricted domain, Pareto consistency and independence of irrelevant alternatives. Proponents of liberal theories of democracy, in particular William Riker, have used Arrow's results to defend a minimalist view of democracy, which reduces its function to 'permit[ting] people to get rid of rulers' (1982: .244).

19 The unrestricted domain condition requires that for any reason, every ordering of options is possible. If reasons were excluded because they suggest a particular ordering, the domain of reasons would effectively be restricted, resulting in inflexibility.

20 Lehrer (1981: 79–80) was the first to draw the distinction between belief and acceptance but Cohen (1989, 1992) is far more explicit on this topic.

21 Lehrer draws an analogy between desire-satisfaction (for volition) and belief-acceptance (for cognition), both of which constitute a kind of loss of control for the conscious self.

22 Differences in the transformability of acceptances may be accounted for by the degree to which they are implicated in a coherent system of other acceptances and with a likelihood of error that is assigned to them (cf. Gaus 1996: 41). The latter differs from the Bayesian concept of belief as a matter of degree in that the probability assignment is not part of the acceptance itself, which as a premise is not a matter of degree.

23 Pettit uses the terminology of belief and desire which has been abandoned here for all cases in which second-order states of mind are concerned. Throughout this quote, it would be in keeping with the concept of preference advocated here to replace 'desire' with 'prefer'.

24 'Values' are also discussed as moral reasons for action. To neglect the evaluative aspect of preference for descriptive and explanatory purposes does not mean to rule out moral reasons for action as motivators. On the contrary, they will be assigned important roles. The issue here is a purely terminological one.

25 The difference between moral goals and moral reasons may be explicated as follows: moral goals are like other goals in that they are wilfully adopted and systematically pursued over a longer period of time. They differ from material goals in that the reasons for which they are adopted are in the end cognitive rather than volitive – although moral goals themselves form part of an actor's volition. Moral reasons can be made effective in a decision without being pursued as goals: one can reject an option as unfair without pursuing the goal or realising maximal fairness.

26 Irrational adherence to preference might be interpreted as an instance of actors employing what Tversky and Kahnemann have called the 'representativeness heuristic': choosing something because it resembles a previously successful option (Tversky & Kahnemann 1974).

27 These considerations also seem to be at the heart of arguments about 'enlightening' or 'laundering' preferences (Goodin 1986). Public deliberation and exchange of arguments is supposed to help actors to determine how options relate to their goals or interests and adopt the respective preferences.

chapter two | communicative interaction and preference-formation

The goal of this second chapter is to move from the challenges of individual political preference-formation and decision to those of collective decision-making, and to point out relationships between the two levels. The link between them is the requirement for justification: individuals enter discourses in order to assess and improve the justification of their preferences. And justificatory discursive interaction forms and transforms individual political preferences, so that the result of the aggregation of individual preferences (i.e. the collective political decision) may be a different one post-interaction than it would have been pre-interaction.

The chapter draws on speech-act theory in the tradition of Austin, Grice and Searle in order to demonstrate the preconditions for effective linguistic interaction (section 1). Habermas and Brandom's theories of discursive commitment further illustrate why successful communication is unlikely to be without effects on practical reasons and acceptances (section 2). Political decision-making is described as a process of the discursive co-ordination of both (section 3). Two types of discourses are distinguished. The first type aims at the co-ordination of acceptances (section 4), the second at the co-ordination of practical reasons and their aggregation (section 5). Each type, it is argued, is an essential component of political decision-making processes. Just as on individual level, actors have to establish both cognitive and volitive premises for their political preferences, collectives have to resolve both cognitive and volitive conflicts in order to produce political decisions. Even if such conflicts can never be resolved entirely and once and for all, co-ordination remains central to the process of decision-making and is an important function of communication.

1. LANGUAGE AND ACTION

The first chapter has explicated political preferences as the result of rational choice rather than the input to it. If rationality is understood as the capacity systematically to respond to reasons, justification and linguistic interaction must play a central role in preference-formation. Reasons provide justification, and justification is essentially a linguistic activity (Brandom 1994: 204–6). Both Jürgen

Habermas and Robert Brandom have addressed the fundamental philosophical question of whether instrumentally rational action has priority over linguistic interaction or vice versa (see Brandom 1994: 229–33 and Habermas 1984, chapter I.1). Hardly surprisingly, both have argued for the priority of language over action and this is also the approach to be pursued here. It is in keeping with the conception of preference adopted before: if political preference is understood to evolve as the product of rational acceptance and rational assessment of reasons for action, then the ends for which action could be instrumental are only determined in the process of preference-formation. If preference-formation and -transformation is regarded as rational decision, they are systematic responses to reasons, which are available from linguistic interaction. Then, linguistic interaction and the contexts and circumstances in which it takes place can serve to explain the formation and transformation of political preferences.

Language being, as Searle (1995) forcefully argued, the fundamental social institution, giving priority to linguistic action over instrumental action seems to constitute a step away from the actor-centred perspective pursued here, towards an institutionalist perspective. I argue that this is not the case, at least not with regard to the theoretical approaches currently labelled 'institutionalist'. Institutionalism in the tradition of, for example, March and Olson (1989), has something in common with evolutionist rational-choice models, in that it regards preferences as determined by factors outside the individual actor's reach – in the former case, culture, in the latter case, nature. Where actors are instead regarded as choosing their ends freely and rationally, the concept of rationality is in fact a more far-reaching one, with the focus on individuals and their rational choices being maintained more thoroughly. The downside of this approach is that the aspiration to predict the precise content of preferences will have to be more or less renounced. The idea is rather to gain hypotheses on the probability of preference-transformation, on the likely structure of preferences and on the types of reasons that will dominate decisions, depending on the properties of institutions in which preferences are shaped and decisions taken. Language constituting the most basic of these institutions, presupposed by all other social and political institutions, it becomes necessary to start off with an analysis of the properties of language as the fundamental social institution.

Language is, first of all, a fascinating and powerful means to put ideas into other peoples' heads. It is, secondly, a means to co-ordinate action plans and thus necessary to achieve collectively ends that one cannot achieve individually. I believe that the former role is reflected in a norm of generality and the second in a norm of reciprocity; together, these set the normative framework for linguistic interaction. To be transferable from one mind to the other, what is being said must have meta-subjective qualities, it must be connected with a general claim to validity. Even when I relate a personal experience without relevance to my interlocutor's ends and beliefs, it is only accessible by virtue of being to some degree generalisable: the other understands what I felt in a certain situation because she would have had similar feelings in that situation.

The norm of reciprocity was elaborated by H.P. Grice (1979), who pointed out conversational maxims that regulate interaction and together amount to a principle of reciprocal co-operation. According to Grice, the co-operation principle is constitutive to any linguistic interaction: without co-operation, no meaningful exchange can take place. To abide by the co-operation principle is to regard the interlocutor as a rational being who is, in general, able to understand what I say and whose utterances I expect to be intelligible to me. Simply by not talking all at once, by listening to one another, by refraining from the use of physical violence, speakers co-operate to a degree that is, in some respects, remarkable. Conversational maxims further shape linguistic interaction and express that one is abiding by the co-operation principle.

The *maxim of quantity* demands that one say neither more nor less than necessary at a given stage. For instance, one does not normally repeat information that has been given before in the same interaction. Neither does one withhold information that is essential to others' understanding of a message. When first mentioning a person's name, for instance, one normally explains who they are and why they are relevant in the present context. The *maxim of quality* simply demands that an assertion is based on justified acceptances and that a promise is based on intention: 'Say nothing which you know is false and say nothing for which you lack adequate reasons/intentions.' The *maxim of relevance* demands that a contribution must be relevant to a conversation's topic and at the given stage of the conversation. The *maxim of manner*, finally, requires that the style in which an utterance is framed is not unnecessarily opaque, vague or ambiguous. Although maxims may occasionally be 'flouted', failure to respect them altogether amounts to a violation of the co-operation principle and hence to a breakdown of conversation.

Grice's theory of the norms guiding linguistic behaviour draws on speech-act theory in the tradition of John Austin and his student John Searle. Austin (2002 [1962]) was the first to direct attention to the fact that utterances constitute actions that change the world. The notion of 'performative verbs' indicates the impact of linguistic action on social reality. Performative verbs are verbs of saying in the first person singular present tense and may be combined with <hereby>:

<I hereby promise to pay you 20 € tomorrow.>
<I hereby declare the exhibition open.>
<I hereby assert that the present king of France is bald.>

The word <hereby> indicates the change effected in social reality. Once I have promised to give you the 20 € tomorrow, the promise is *there* and cannot be cancelled without violating conversational maxims. I cannot say:

<I hereby promise to give you 20 € tomorrow, but I will not give you 20 € tomorrow.>

Although I can of course indicate that I no longer intend to fulfil my promise, the fact that I have made it remains and has an impact on my future opportunities and actions. What is *done* by making an utterance, Austin termed the 'illocutionary act'. The illocutionary act is one of the three parts a speech act consists in:

> *Locution*: the act of saying, the realisation of a propositional content;
> *Illocution*: the action carried out in saying something, e.g. ASKING;[1]
> *Perlocution*: the effect a speech act has on the addressee (see. Austin 2002: 112–25).

As Karl Bühler (1999[1934]) pointed out, the linguistic sign constituting a speech act has three aspects. It is *symbol* in that it refers to objects and facts in the objective world, it is a *symptom* in that it depends on and originates in the sender (speaker), and it is a *signal* in that it appeals to the hearer (cf. Habermas 1984: 273–9). Bühler's so-called 'organon model' combines well with the typology of illocutionary acts John Searle has developed (Searle 1979). Although according to Bühler, the three aspects are present in any speech act, one aspect is clearly dominant in each of Searle's types of speech acts. Searle distinguishes:

> *Assertives* (e.g. ASSERTING, STATING, CLAIMING, DENYING), in which the symbolic aspect is clearly dominant;
> *Directives* (e.g. ORDERING, BEGGING, as well as interrogatives, e.g. ASKING), in which the signalling aspect is dominant;
> *Commissives* (e.g. PROMISING, OFFERING, THREATENING), in which the signalling aspect is equally dominant;
> *Expressives* (e.g. APOLOGISING, THANKING, REGRETTING), in which the symptomatic aspect is dominant (although they may function as signals);
> *Declarations* (e.g. DECLARING, BAPTISING, BLESSING), in which symbol and signal become one.

Both Habermas and Brandom stress the central role of assertives in linguistic interaction. They not only regard the act of asserting as prior to all other types of speech acts but also as the essential move in human action and interaction altogether. The reason behind this is, again, a priority assigned to cognition over intention, or language over rational action.

Searle (1979) draws a distinction between constative and directive speech acts which is taken up by Habermas (1984, 1: 323 ff.) and, less explicitly, by Brandom (1994: 229–38). Assertives are constatives and characterised by a 'word-to-world' direction of fit: if I assert that *p*, I assert that there exists a fit between my claim, that *p*, and the world, in which *p* is a fact. Both directives and commissives may be characterised as directives in that they are characterised by a 'world-to-word' direction of fit: they are satisfied when *p* has *become* a fact (which it is not at the time the speech act takes place).[2] In order to determine whether a directive has been satisfied, however, we require the capacity to establish a word-to-world direction of fit by asserting that *p* or not-*p*.

In his theory of intentionality, Searle makes a compelling analogy between speech acts and intentional states (beliefs, desires, intentions), which is based on the notion of direction of fit (Searle 1983). Like assertions, beliefs are characterised by a downward, 'mind-to-world' direction of fit, while desires and intentions have an upward 'world-to-mind' direction of fit (Searle 1983: 8). This idea is part of the concept of preference that was developed in the first chapter. The cognitive aspect of preference, acceptance, aims at a mind-to-world direction of fit, while its volitive aspect, the practical reasons motivating it, is concerned with the world-to-mind direction of fit. What follows is that the selection of reasons for action, i.e. of the volitive premises of preference, presupposes a background of acceptances with mind-to-world direction of fit. For discursive interaction, this implies that constative practices, as exemplified in arguing, should normatively and empirically precede directive practices, as exemplified in bargaining. In more simple terms: find out what the situation is first, bargain about who is to get what afterwards.

Typical arguing speech acts include, besides ASSERTING, ASKING, INFERRING, CONCLUDING, CONTRADICTING or CONCEDING. Typical bargaining speech acts include DEMANDING, OFFERING, PROMISING or THREATENING (see Holzinger 2004). The former all belong to the class of assertives, with word-to-world direction of fit, and stress the cognitive and symbolic function of linguistic interaction. The latter belong to the classes of directives and commissives, with world-to-word direction of fit, and stress the social and signalling function of linguistic interaction. This does not mean, though, that the volitive premises of preference evade argumentative contestation: '[b]eing rational is just being in the space of giving and asking for reasons, and being a rational *agent* is being in the space of giving and asking for reasons for what one *does*.' (Brandom 1994: 253).

The adequacy of both cognitive and volitive premises of preferences can be discursively assessed, and their assessment constitutes one motive to enter discourses. If discursive interaction results in transformation of preferences, this amounts to a perlocutionary effect of illocutionary acts such as ASSERTING, INFERRING or CONTRADICTING. As will be argued in the following section, perlocutionary effects may be caused not only by others' speech acts but also by one's own speech acts (such as ADMITTING or CONCEDING under the force of better arguments). Contrary to Habermas, hence, I regard perlocutionary acts and effects as an important feature of *all* communicative interactions, not merely of strategic ones (cf. Habermas 1984, 1: 292–5). Perlocutionary effects have central explanatory importance to the present project, regardless of whether communication is free and equal, as in Habermas' ideal, or systematically distorted and manipulated, as in many empirical cases.

One difference between cognitive and volitive reasons should be kept in mind, however: while one can have reasons or no reasons, good reasons and poor reasons for both acceptances and volitions, the Good is not in the same way One as Truth is One (Brandom 1994: 240). If I have good reasons to accept that p, you will also have good reasons to accept that p, you should in fact accept that p. If I have good reasons to do A, by contrast, this does not imply that you have good reasons to do A – you might have no reason whatsoever. Accordingly, my being justified in doing A does not imply that you are equally justified in doing A (Brandom 1994: 240). Which of the many possible reasons for action are reasons for both of us, or even reasons for all rational actors, remains to be discursively established.

2. DISCURSIVE ACCEPTANCE AND COMMITMENT

Habermas was the first to make linguistic pragmatics fruitful to social theory. In his *Theory of Communicative Action* (1984), he famously distinguished communicative from strategic action, assigning priority to the former. The utopian element of his linguistic idealism is represented in the idea that communicative action, which he regards the fundamental, original mode of human interaction, is not based on consequentialist logic but aims at '*Verständigung*'.[4] Habermas' central claim is that 'reaching understanding is the inherent telos of human speech' (1984: 287). If, in addition to this, language use (as symbolic interaction) is regarded as the distinctive feature of human beings, prospects for peaceful cooperation seem bright. These are the philosophical background assumptions on which one of deliberative democracy's promises is based: that linguistic interaction will yield consensus. But why should the product of processes of '*Verständigung*' be in any respect 'good', 'right' or true?

The answer to this question must be sought in the norms guiding communication which, being constitutive of it, are equally inherent in human speech. As constative speech acts are regarded as fundamental, the deontic consequences (rights and duties) deriving from assertions must be the focus of analysis. Although Habermas assigns central relevance to them, his discussion of the ways in which validity claims (to rightness, authenticity and truth) are raised and discharged is somewhat brief and vague (1984, 1: 305–19). Searle pointed out that 'the point or purpose of the members of the assertive class is to *commit* the speaker (in varying degrees) to something's being the case, to the truth of the expressed proposition' (1979: 12, my emphasis). Grice's maxim of quality similarly refers to a *duty* to prove that one is abiding by it by being able to name reasons for a claim one has raised.

The most comprehensive theory addressing the significance of assertions, however, is Robert Brandom's, which is essentially a theory of deontic statuses. According to Brandom, in making an assertion, a speaker displays and incurs a *commitment*. Whether *entitlement* to this commitment is attributed depends on the speaker's being able to justify it by naming reasons for it.[5] If a hearer attributes entitlement to a commitment, she can inherit entitlement and use the respective assertion as a premise for further reasoning.

Epistemic progress, hence, is warranted by two things. First, if justification is regarded as an indicator of truth, assertions to which entitlement is attributed on the basis of justification will be likely to be true and serve as adequate premises for the subsequent discourse. Secondly, entitlement inheritance enables a division of epistemic labour. If every speaker had to justify every single one of her assertions and acceptances (which are potential assertions), communicative reasoning would never get very far. Interlocutors must be able to draw on a background of accepted premises in order to arrive at new insights.

In communicative action, interlocutors assume the roles of speakers (first person), hearers (second person) and listeners (third person).[6] The speaker is in the position to express commitments (i.e. acceptances) and to incur further commitments that may be inferred from what she says. For instance, if a speaker asserts that she owns a dog and thereby expresses a commitment to this claim, she will incur a commitment to the claim that she owns a mammal, even if she has not explicitly asserted this. The hearer's role is to attribute or withhold entitlement to commitments. Brandom assumes that for many assertions, particularly observation reports, entitlement is attributed 'by default' (1994: 176–8, 189). If the hearer refuses to grant entitlement by default, she may demand reasons to justify a claim. Alternative moves consist in querying a commitment in order to find out whether the speaker actually acknowledges it (in the above case, asking whether she means to assert that she owns a mammal) or challenging it by making an incompatible assertion (1994: 192–3).

A typical challenge would consist in asserting that not-p when another speaker has asserted that p. Obviously, any challenge entails acknowledging one's own commitments, which are consequently, open to challenge themselves. Unless the hearer explicitly challenges a claim, he implicitly attributes entitlement to it and accepts it as a premise for further interaction. A possible reaction to a query or challenge is to disavow a claim by acknowledging that one is no longer committed to it. As will be argued below, however, this move is connected with severe problems with which Brandom himself is not concerned. The role of the listener differs from that of the hearer, in that the listener is not in a position to ask for reasons or to query and challenge assertions and, hence, has no chance of becoming a speaker and asserter himself. One consequence of this lack of opportunity is that listeners cannot be assumed to embrace an assertion when they fail to challenge it: listening has an impact only on other speakers' scores but leaves one's own score unchanged.

Following Brandom, all three (speaker, hearer and listener) engage in a process of 'scorekeeping': for every single participant (including themselves), they keep a mental record of the assertions that have been made, the commitments that have been acknowledged and the entitlements that have been attributed. What commitments a speaker is regarded as entitled to, therefore, depends on the score of the discourse. A claim that has been vindicated once need not be vindicated again and may be employed as a premise for inferences – 'assertions are fundamentally fodder for inferences' (Brandom 1994: 168, emphasis omitted). In the conflict over importing embryonic stem-cell lines (which will be discussed in chapters four and five), for example, the claim that such cells could not develop into embryos was successfully vindicated at an early stage. Consequently, entitlement to this claim was granted and speakers' commitments to it no longer required justification.

However, if she has formerly acknowledged an incompatible commitment, a speaker may lack entitlement to a claim that her interlocutors embrace. In this case, hearers and listeners will expect her publicly to disavow her earlier claim before they attribute entitlement to the new commitment. If I insisted on the claim that stem cells can develop into full embryos although my interlocutors deny my entitlement to it, I would be excluded from the inferences they draw from this premise. In this case it was inferred, for instance, that if stem-cell lines were not embryos, they were a commodity, and that EU law on free trade would not allow a ban on importing them. If I wanted to commit myself to the claim that the ban is incompatible with EU law, my interlocutors would be likely to demand that I disavow my earlier commitment first.

This process accounts for what Habermas calls the 'force of the better argument'. As Brandom argues, 'the practical significance of lack of entitlement consists in liability to *punishment* of some kind' (Brandom 1994: 179). In the case of the speaker committed to a claim incompatible with one that is collectively embraced by her interlocutors, the punishment may simply consist in a kind of tacit exclusion from further reasoning for which the claim is required as a premise. However, if the justificatory case for a claim p is so strong that it is impossible to warrant entitlement to the claim that not-p, anyone unable to embrace p will appear irrational because no acceptable reasons can be named for this stance. Being regarded as irrational is certainly a severe punishment, even if it is not inflicted intentionally by interlocutors.

The concept of preference as the result of rational decision implies that rationalisation is not only an interpersonal, discursive requirement but also an intrapersonal one. Actors are expected (by other actors and by observers) to decide rationally; they believe that they should decide rationally and, most of the time, they want to decide rationally. Acceptance and assertion are therefore clearly interdependent. Assertions can have perlocutionary effects on acceptances, and they are made with the perlocutionary aim of affecting other actors' acceptances. The same holds for goals and other reasons constituting volitive premises for preferences. Even though some reasons for action (such as desires) may have their origin in actors themselves, equally they require justification to be rationally adopted and depend on discursive assessment.

Both Habermas and Brandom stress the fact that not only cognitive attitudes but also actions require justification and are open to discursive contestation.[7] Brandom distinguishes doxastic (cognitive) from practical discursive commitments: '[e]ach is essentially something that reasons can be given for and for which reasons can be asked, and one cannot give reasons unless one can acknowledge doxastic commitments by making claims' (Brandom 1994: 233). In justifying actions or intentions to act, that is, one raises further claims and incurs new commitments that require further reasons, which are new claims, and so on. Where the reasons named for an action are cognitive commitments, they can be dealt with in exactly the same way as ordinary assertions.

The justificatory chain for assertions typically ends in observation reports or axioms that do not demand further vindication themselves (see Brandom 1994: 222). The justificatory chain for intentions, or volitive premises of preference, similarly, often ends in a statement functioning as an unjustified justifier: 'because I want it'. Discourses generally enable actors to assess and refine rationalisations and provide alternative ones. Insofar as the degree and quality of rationalisation improve a decision (in that rationalisation produces the desired effects and increases overall happiness or satisfaction), the decision to enter a discourse is clearly a rational one. If actors need yet to decide what to accept (because information is incomplete) and what to want (because they hold more than a single practical reason), communicative interaction is indispensable.[8]

The ways in which assertions are challenged and justified differ for different types of discourses and different types of topics. As Brandom points out, default attribution of entitlement is common in everyday conversations. It is in some senses analogous to the default modes of belief-acceptance and desire-satisfaction that were discussed in the previous chapter: where very little is at stake, one can resort to less costly modes of decision-making, both for collective decisions (in communicative interaction) and for individual ones (in preference-formation). As attributing entitlement by default also signals willingness to co-operate and acknowledgement of the other's co-operation, it may be necessary to enable communication and to keep it going. Harald Müller describes how, in a tough negotiation between representatives of the former Soviet Union and the United States, the presence of a child and the shift to less controversial topics which this inspired enabled the negotiation to move on at moments where it seemed to be stuck (Müller 1994: 34). Assessment of claims, however, requires challenge and justification and, hence, a break with the default mode. If we want to achieve epistemic progress or co-ordination of action plans, we have to move to less easy modes of discursive interaction that are more than self-sufficient.

The ways in which assertions can be challenged and justified depend on the kind of claim they make. Habermas distinguishes descriptive, normative, evaluative, expressive and explicative validity claims. Descriptive claims are discharged by demonstrating the existence of empirical facts. Normative claims are discharged by demonstrating the acceptability of actions and decisions with regard to accepted norms.[9] Evaluative claims are discharged by demonstrating the preferability of some values over other values. Expressive claims are discharged by demonstrating the authenticity and transparency of self-ascriptions. Explicative claims, finally, are discharged by demonstrating that symbolic terms have been produced according to axiomatic rules (Habermas 1984, 1: 39–40). Brandom is less concerned with universal validity claims and their eventual discharge than with their local justification. He points out that claims normally do not need to be justified 'all the way down' but that they can be defended as inferences from existing, accepted premises. Entitlement to a commitment, whether doxastic or practical, is demonstrated by naming the premises from which it was derived as a conclusion. These premises need no further justification unless they are explicitly challenged, too.

In everyday discourses, all types of claims distinguished by Habermas typically play a role, although some are dominant in specific types of discourses, of which Habermas develops ideal types (Habermas 1984, 1: 23). In *Between Facts and Norms*, he applies his ideas to political discourses, distinguishing pragmatic, moral and ethical-political discourses (1994 [1992]: 195–9). Pragmatic discourses are described as appropriate where the conflict between actors (or rather, between their validity claims) is one of fact. The conflict over the use of nuclear energy, for example, is a predominantly factual one: actors disagree over the risks and the consequences of nuclear power for the environment compared to other energy sources. Moral discourses are seen as appropriate where the question at hand is one of principle. The conflict over abortion is an example of such a primarily moral disagreement.

What Habermas describes as ethical-political discourse is probably closest to most real-life political discourses: the issue here is what 'we' shall do in a given situation at a given moment in time, what is right for 'us' with regard to our local tradition, values and way of life (1994: 199). The question of whether to increase or reduce immigration, for instance, can hardly be resolved without reference to the specific community and its present condition. As Habermas acknowledges in a postscript, no empirical discourse is ever pure in this sense but rather a mix of the three types of which one is typically dominant (1994: 667). The type of discourse one is confronted with may be inferred from the type of claims that are raised and defended: descriptive claims in pragmatic discourses; normative and evaluative claims in moral discourses; and all three in ethical-political discourses.

The role of expressive and explicative claims is somewhat unclear. Expressive claims may indicate that a speaker is not employing assertions strategically but with the goal of reaching understanding. Explicative claims I regard as more relevant than Habermas does. The interpretation of fundamental values is often a matter of correct specification. Is justice to be understood as equality of opportunity or as distributive justice? Can there be degrees of a right to live, depending on developmental stage? Even if the problem behind this is still how to rank competing values, the concrete conflicts may well be about the correct explication of a concept like 'justice' (cf. Richardson 2002: 104).

In what follows, I will use my own distinction between two types of discourses, which will be presented in sections 4 and 5 of this chapter. My distinction draws on both Habermas and Brandom and is more or less analogous to Habermas' original one between 'theoretical' and 'practical' discourses (Habermas 1984, 1: 23). In contrast to Habermas, and following the concept of political preference presented in the previous chapter, my ideal-types are based on the intentions with which people enter a discourse rather than on the types of claims they raise there. They either seek to assess and co-ordinate the cognitive premises of their preferences, their acceptances, or to assess and co-ordinate the volitive premises of their preferences, i.e. the reasons for preferring outcomes and their aggregation. Before I go on to discuss these types of communicative interaction in more detail, however, I want to point out why preference co-ordination is a necessary precondition for political decisions and how this requirement of co-ordination affects individual preference-formation and decision-making.

3. POLITICAL DECISION-MAKING AS DISCURSIVE PREFERENCE-CO-ORDINATION

There are many goals that actors cannot possibly achieve on their own; and there are many conflicts that can only be accommodated, and demands that can only be met, through collective decisions. Political decisions result in explicit, collectively binding general rules that, in the ideal case, should receive the consent of all those affected by them – through either their acknowledgment of the 'rightness' of the norm itself or of the fairness of the procedure by which it was produced. Individual preferences in non-political choice situations, such as consumer choice, differ from political preferences first of all in that they are indexical (cf. Estlund 1990). If A wants x for A and B wants y for B, there will be no conflict if x and y are ordinary goods. If I buy chocolate ice cream for myself, I should be indifferent with regard to other consumers' choice of ice cream. Customers' demands jointly determine the price and availability of goods without any requirements for co-operation and co-ordination.

Political preferences, by contrast, need to refer to *general* rules. If A wants to implement x as a general rule, this will have consequences for B, if B is a member of the same collective. If A wants x to become a general, binding rule, and B wants y to become such a rule, the situation is one of conflict, where, assuming non-dictatorship, neither actor can achieve her goal without the co-operation of the other. Unless actors somehow co-ordinate their preferences over options for political action, no political decision, whether consensual or majoritarian, would ever be possible. By co-ordination, I mean the process of reaching any kind of agreement on a joint course of action. The result can range from agreement over available options and decision rules or a shared set of acceptances to consensus on a particular policy option or even a political programme.

By means of comparative evaluation, actors form political preferences for options for collective action (resulting in general, collectively binding rules) *over* other options for collective action. Such collective action not only interferes with individuals' freedom (which decisions of a major corporation could also do) but imposes new rights and duties on citizens: the duty not to smack one's children, the right to vote at 16, 18 or 21 years of age, or, for a soldier, the obligation to take part in a war the government has declared (cf. Pettit 1997, Richardson 2002: 28–36). An actor intending to render an individual political preference subject to collective action will first of all need to indicate what other choices the option she has in mind is to be preferred, that is, what the alternatives to it are. Choice, as was pointed out in the last chapter, requires at least two options that are comparable and, in principle, substitutable.

For legislative decisions, one option necessarily features as an item in the set of alternative options: the status quo of legislation (which may be no legislation). For executive decisions the present practice, which again may be inaction, will similarly constitute a status quo. The first challenge for actors seeking to bring about a new political status quo will consist in persuading fellow citizens that the option they have in mind is, in principle, substitutable for the status quo and can seriously be compared with it. This activity aims to define a new political choice set and to point out that choice from this set is a necessity other actors should be concerned with. One way to describe it is as the 'politicisation' of a topic that was previously not on the agenda. Many proposals fail at this early stage of preference co-ordination because they simply are not being taken seriously and are not regarded as viable alternatives to the status quo. However, even if the initial proposal fails to be vindicated as a serious option, it may still serve as a challenge to the status quo and change the political agenda. One effect of this may be that other actors develop their own more successful proposals to supplant present legislation.

Once a set of options has been established, the likely consequences of implementing each of these options will be discussed. Options in the set may be understood as practical commitments that need to be justified by those preferring them. The justification of an option consists in assertions about its consequences and the desirability of the state of the world it will produce. Predictive assertions draw on acceptances about the world and accepted expectations with regard to the future. Estimating the likely consequences of an option newly on the agenda confronts actors with the need to form new acceptances on a new topic. The next step, of preference co-ordination, hence, consists in co-ordination of the cognitive premises of actor-preferences, that is, of the acceptances they make relevant to the decision at hand.

Assuming that the states of the world the alternative action plans seek to bring about are identical, the challenge of co-ordination will consist solely in arriving at a joint set of acceptances. The 'policy entrepreneur' initiating a new decision will, at this stage, appeal to goals that she knows are widely shared and try to persuade fellow citizens of the instrumental adequacy of her proposal. Even if she knows that some other actors oppose the goals she pursues with her proposal, a necessary condition for its success will be to have convinced those who *do* share her goals as practical reasons that the policy she proposes is an adequate means to the shared end. Obviously, actors assess and transform their acceptances all the time in everyday discourses. It makes a difference, however, whether they are sought as serviceable premises for a specific collective decision. In this case, the need for co-ordination is much more evident and the pressure to reach a consensus increases.

In academic debates, where the point is not to co-ordinate action plans but (at least officially) to track truth, dissent and contestation are understood to promote epistemic progress and are sought on their own behalf. In political debates, by contrast, the need for (a certain degree of) consensus reduces the extent of contestation, so that only claims that are clearly controversial need to be challenged. Faced with the need to determine what 'we shall do', with the need to take a decision, we cannot engage in endless deliberation about what 'we should do'.[10] Certain types of scepticism – is there anything like an 'empirical world?', 'is our perception entirely determined by cultural frames?' etc. – that are common in academic debates lack justification in political ones. Here, the need to decide simply appears to be too urgent to bother with such questions.

Political debates in this sense assume a kind of middle position between everyday conversations, where entitlement is frequently attributed by default, and academic discourses, where it is frequently denied by default. Because the eventual decision will affect everybody, the consequences of both default entitlement and default challenge will have to be considered by speakers. The specific 'default and challenge structure of entitlement' (Brandom 1994: 176) that a political discourse displays determines the qualities of its results. More challenge does not always amount to better quality or less challenge to poorer quality, though this may often be the case. Unwarranted challenges may be a means to prevent decision-making altogether and to preserve the status quo; while predominance of the default mode may lead to undeliberated, myopic decisions and favour manipulative strategies. The correct balance between default and challenge may be different for every single decision-problem.

Co-ordinating preferences to establish a set of collective options to choose from and to arrive at a set of shared acceptances (on the issue at hand) amounts to a co-operative definition of the situation and conditions under which the collective decision takes place. The final step of co-ordination, once the situation has been sufficiently defined, consists in a co-ordination of the various reasons motivating preferences over options. Assuming that a joint set of acceptances has been established, the number of individual reasons, combinations of reasons and compromises between reasons should determine the number of items on the set of alternatives. Preference co-ordination can thus be understood as a circular process:

Figure 2.1: Definition of choice set and co-ordination

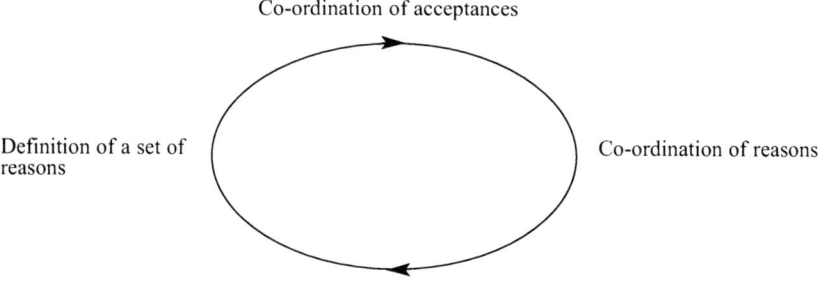

Co-ordination of acceptances

Definition of a set of reasons

Co-ordination of reasons

The set of options determines the kind of information that is sought and the conflicting acceptances that need to be co-ordinated. Successful co-ordination of acceptances thus presupposes a set of options with regard to which acceptances are relevant. In the stem-cell example, the apparently obvious alternatives of either maintaining the status quo (which amounted to a permission) or enacting a ban turned the previously only academic discussion over the potency of stem cells into a politically relevant question. The subsequent co-ordination of practical reasons presupposed a background consensus of shared acceptances. In the stem-cell conflict, the agreement that stem-cell lines are not embryos allowed the debate to move on to addressing the moral reasons behind the preferences for each of the options. The discursive assessment and co-ordination of practical reasons, however, also informs the definition of the choice set and is likely to challenge the existing one. In the stem-cell case, a third option was brought up, namely to allow the importation of existing lines but not of lines produced after the decision. This new option lead to new factual controversies about its likely consequences. The processes of preference co-ordination and the political discourse are therefore never complete but accompany decision-making and continuously yield new decision-tasks.

In preference-co-ordination, the co-ordination of acceptances thus precedes that of practical reasons, although in individual preference-formation, the decision what to want has a certain priority over the decision what to accept. There are two reasons for this. The first derives from the precedence of the cognitive over the volitive that is implied in the theory of communicative action embraced here. Only because they can draw on a discursively acquired fund of acceptances can individuals set priorities before they assess the quality of alternative options. In interactive processes, however, a joint definition of the situation has frequently yet to be established. The second reason is that the volitive premises of preference are more fundamental to actors' identities, implying that their challenge and transformation requires a higher degree of co-operation, which may only be possible once a background consensus has been established on the cognitive side. Because acceptances refer to external, empirical reality rather than personal motives and identity, it is simply easier to co-ordinate them than it is to co-ordinate goals and moral reasons.

Unless we assume that a perfect consensus – not only with regard to acceptances, but also with regard to collective goals – can be achieved, though, the circle of preference-co-ordination needs to be interrupted at some stage, in order to arrive at a decision. Two ways of interruption are conceivable. Actors might decide to accept a compromise in which they consensually embrace a solution that is suboptimal with respect to what they ideally wish to accomplish but superior to no decision at all. For a compromise, it does not matter whether an option is preferred on the basis of different acceptances or for different volitive reasons. Compromise is thus possible at any stage after a choice-set or choice dimension (i.e., decision-problem) has been defined. The second mode of interruption is majority voting. It equally presupposes a set of options on which voters are to be asked their preferences. For aggregation to be meaningful, however, co-ordination of both acceptances and practical reasons may be required. For instance, preferences for which the same normative dimension is deemed relevant are likely to be 'single-peaked', which prevents aggregation problems of the type described by Arrow from occurring (see Dryzek & List 2003, List 2002). Preferences based on incompletely informed acceptances are undesirable from a normative point of view and may be regretted at a later stage.

A further particularity of political decisions has to do with the fact that actors are often composite rather than individual actors. For the observer, this has certain advantages in that decision-making here constitutes a social rather than intra-subjective process and is therefore more easily accessible (Zintl 1994). The co-ordination of preferences and their cognitive and volitive premises, however, will differ from that of individual citizens in several respects. First of all, while individual actors necessarily pursue more than a single goal, collective actors typically derive their legitimacy and existence from the pursuit of a single goal or the defence of a single value. Although goals and values are open to different specifications, and although the preferences derived from such superordinate goals may well be competing, the range of possible practical reasons will be more restricted for collective than for individual actors.

In addition to this, collective actors face principal-agent problems that affect the way in which they transform their acceptances, practical reasons and preferences. If they engage in discursive preference co-ordination, the representatives, or agents, of collective actors (for example, union leaders) are faced with a dilemma. On the one hand, they must be sufficiently flexible to adopt their positions to new information and priorities; on the other hand, they must remain faithful to the will of their members, or the principal, of their organisation. If the members do not take part or even follow the discourse themselves (and even if they do), they are likely to stick to positions that their representatives may want to give up in the course of the decision-making process. Thus, principals will demand that their agents be maximally responsive to their preferences. Without a sufficient degree of independence and discretion, however, agents cannot be sufficiently co-operative to enable preference-co-ordination and compromising.

A last problem, which has been hinted at in the last section, concerns the practice of 'scorekeeping'. While Brandom assumes that interlocutors can, at any stage of the 'game', disavow claims and commitments, I think that the very point that motivates the assessment of preferences and assertions – the inherently deontic character of language use – also constrains it. If a speaker is discursively forced to give up a commitment, this will not only be an unpleasant experience but might even amount to a loss of face. Assuming that people want to *be* rational, that they want to have true acceptances and valid practical reasons, the experience of the failure to achieve one's aspiration may be useful (in that it renders acceptances and practical reasons more rational than before) but must also be painful. Assuming that people want to *be regarded* as rational by others, being unable vindicate one's assertions will result in a loss of esteem, an effect that increases with the size of the audience (Brennan & Pettit 2004: 142–5). As professional politicians and representatives typically enjoy a high degree of publicity, they will be less willing to disavow commitments than ordinary citizens. It further follows that commitments are generally more likely to be disavowed in intimate circles than in public. The probability of preference-transformation and -co-ordination thus depends, among other things, on the size of the forum.

4. CO-ORDINATION AND TRANSFORMATION OF ACCEPTANCES: LEARNING AND EPISTEMIC PROGRESS

The topic of the present section is the discursive formation and transformation of acceptances. As noted above, empirically, this story cannot be told separately from the processes of choice-set definition and the co-ordination and transformation of goals and practical reasons. Nevertheless, there are specific properties and specific problems pertaining to processes of acceptance-co-ordination, which will be discussed in this section. To begin with, one should keep in mind the differences between everyday conversations, academic discourses and political discourses, although several points concern all three of them. Anyway, the distinction is of an analytical rather than empirical nature. As soon as the practical commitments made in everyday conversations affect more actors than the speaker herself, the interaction gains a political aspect. Reasons will now be asked for and more rigorously challenged. Communication ceases to serve as an end in itself and becomes a means to co-ordinate action plans. Academic discourses are rarely completely separate from political intentions and ideologies. Political discourses, finally, are informed by both everyday conversations and academic discourses and permanently refer back to these.

It is the *political* aspect of discourses that determines the role the co-ordination of acceptances has in them. While all sorts of factual discourses can be expected to have an effect on actors' acceptances, the *co-ordination* of these does not become relevant unless discourses are to result in practical commitments that affect other actors apart from the one who holds them. If factual reasons are eventually meant to justify political action, they are assessed from a different point of view than if they result in actions that have consequences only for the actor herself , or in no relevant action at all. I may well be indifferent whether or not a friend regards star signs as a sound basis for the choice of a wife. However, if the two of us are to co-operate on some action plan we will need to establish what game theorists term a 'common prior': we will need to decide what we are jointly to accept as premises for further decisions. If my interlocutor's decisions are to affect my own prospects, it would normally be in my own interest to make sure that they are not based on astrological considerations. In discourses with a political aspect, the establishment of a common prior of shared acceptances, which is a precondition for co-ordinated action, is therefore a particular goal of communicative interaction. This goal will be a background condition for the assessment and transformation of acceptances in political discourses and is likely to enhance their convergence and coherence.

The motive for actors to enter into discursive interaction has already been established: actors depend on a fit between their mind, their acceptances and the world. The idea of truth entails the idea that there is but one correct representation of the world as it is and that it is our cognitive goal to attain this. Discourses provide both new evidence (observation reports of other speakers) and assessment of assertions. If an acceptance can be discursively vindicated, it may be assigned positive justificatory status, which is regarded as an indicator of truth. Both evidence and justification (evidence may be understood as special kind of justification) improve the rationale for a decision, which must be the goal of any rational actor.

However, even if it is rational for actors to seek benefit from discursive interaction, the question remains why exactly they should contribute to the discourse themselves. Why give up strategic advantages by betraying information that is more valuable when it is exclusive? The answer lies partly in the logic of communicative action and must partly be sought in the type of discourse (everyday, political, academic) and its institutional contexts. The most extreme example of strategic language use is lying. If we assume information to be strategically relevant, lying or deliberately withholding information may even be regarded as constituting the dominant strategy for all players.

Economists therefore typically maintain that talk, where it does not serve as strategic signalling, is 'cheap'. This means that it is no more costly to claim that p when one knows that p is false than to claim p when one knows that p is true. If any advantage can be gained from dishonestly asserting p as true, lying constitutes a rational move for actors to make. Making a claim is regarded as having no effect on the state of the world defined by a distribution of goods. If the conditions of cheap talk obtain, all actors will be aware of this. Cheap talk therefore rules out discursive transformation of acceptances, as other speakers' assertions will not be considered for their assessment. It is highly plausible to assume, though, that in many cases, all players would be better off if everybody told the truth than under conditions of cheap talk. Players are then stuck in a collective (n-player) prisoner's dilemma, where the equilibrium is suboptimal compared to the outcome that could be achieved by mutual co-operation. Can actors possibly escape this dilemma?

The deontic structures guiding language use that have been identified by Brandom and Habermas point in a different direction from that indicated by economic theories of linguistic interaction. In making an assertion, a speaker claims commitment to it. Commitment is universal: if speaker A is committed to the claim that p in forum one, he should also be committed to it in forum two. Unless he disavows his claim, the commitment will continue to be assigned to him, it is part of his score. The deontic score defines a state of the world and distribution of goods: someone else's promise is a good to me.[11] The liar must hence take pains not to betray the dishonesty of his commitment by making contradictory claims in different forums, at least if the membership of the forums overlaps to some extent. This already reduces strategic opportunities because different commitments might be serviceable in different forums. Once a speaker is found guilty of faking commitment, he is faced with further trouble. In a community where assertions 'are treated as having the significance of promises', failure to keep such a promise will warrant subsequent distrust: actors disqualify themselves from 'counting in the future as eligible to undertake commitments' (Brandom 1994: 180). In more simple terms: once exposed, the liar will not be believed again (see also Mackie 1998).

Depending on the context, moreover, honesty may even be entirely irrelevant. For entitlement to be attributed, dishonest commitments require just as much justification as honest ones. Assertions can be assessed regardless of a speaker's intentions. As long as justification is an indicator of truth, false claims, whether they originate in ignorance or strategy, should be more difficult to defend and less likely to be successful. If a claim does not reflect rational acceptances as it should do, the one raising it will probably lack adequate reasons and hence will not be attributed entitlement. If reasons are nonetheless named, these will equally have to pass the test of discursive assessment.

If a lie is indeed successfully vindicated, it may be rational to accept it as true, even if the dishonesty has already been exposed. In academic debates, raising provocative claims to which one is not actually committed, in order to see whether they can withstand assessment, is a common strategy in the pursuit of epistemic progress. Things are different, though, wherever entitlement is attributed by default. Observation reports are not normally challenged and thus easier to fake (although the risk of disclosure may be higher). As evidence is the central argument in factual discourses, this constitutes a first backlash against the idea that justificatory discourses necessarily promote truth. Moreover, where entitlement is attributed on the basis of social status and power rather than justification, manipulation can be easily accomplished.[12] The resulting question is thus: in what kinds of contexts is co-ordination of acceptances most likely to be successful?

As mentioned before, political discourses differ from academic ones in that they result in practical commitments (commitments to act) and thus have practical relevance for all those involved. While the ultimate goal of academic discourses is 'knowing-that', the goal of political discourses rather is 'knowing-how' (see Brandom 1994: 23). The quest for know-how presupposes a well defined goal. If know-how is attained, the goal can reliably be achieved. There may, however, be different ways to realise the same goal. Only if these are equally costly (none having significant advantages over others), should it not matter which one is chosen. Knowledge *that* is relevant in so far as it is instrumental to, and required for, knowledge *how*. It then assumes the role of evidence or information. Information differs from knowledge in that it is not without purpose: it is always for and about something. Evidence is similarly purpose-bound: it concerns the (empirical) truth of a proposition.[13]

In political discourses, the propositions in question will typically appertain to the viability and instrumental quality of options for action. Where acceptances are co-ordinated, (empirical) evidence will thus constitute the most important argument, or doxastic reason. As noted before, evidence and information can have great strategic relevance. If an actor possesses information about how to attain a certain goal, sharing this information might reduce access to the goal. Moreover, even without lying, actors can employ evidence and information selectively, withholding whatever contravenes their interests.

Rather than claiming either the economic or the discourse-theoretic interpretation of linguistic interaction to be the correct one, it makes sense to acknowledge the force of both arguments and to distinguish situations in which talk is cheap from those where it need not be cheap. Actors may be assumed to be aware of whether they and their interlocutors are in a position to act strategically in a discourse. They may be assumed, that is, to know the degree to which talk is meaningful or cheap.

Apart from many situations in which strategic incentives impede the exchange of information, at least three are conceivable where the assessment and co-ordination of acceptances is likely to be successful. First, there are situations in which actors share the same goal but hold different opinions on how it is best to be reached. Second, there are situations in which actors have no individual goals or interests involved in the question at stake. Third, there are situations of high uncertainty and over-complexity, in which actors are insecure about how best to pursue their goals (and maybe even about what their goals should be; but that question has to wait for the next section).

Situations in which actors have a joint goal or shared volitive premises for their preferences, and differ only on the instrumental quality of options, are the easiest case. It is the case typically assumed by epistemic democrats: the goal all citizens pursue is supposed to be the common good; the conflict is a factual one about how this is best to be realised. Although the assumptions of epistemic democracy are somewhat unrealistic (and in my opinion, not even normatively appealing), decision-problems of this type do play a role in politics. In democracies, these are not typically the ones that yield legislative decisions but rather they precede and accompany such decisions. One place where co-ordination of this type may be observed is the social interactions and decision-making processes taking place within collective actors such as political parties, trade unions or other associations. A joint set of practical reasons being constitutive for such organisations and competing interests ruled out, the task of assessing and co-ordinating acceptances should be an easy one to accomplish.

Under conditions of mutual trust, where each actor believes that every other actor not only shares the relevant goal but also renounces the pursuit of conflicting goals, actors have no incentives to employ their information strategically. On the contrary, there are likely to be rewards (such as esteem) for valuable contributions. However, although co-ordination may be assumed to be easy, assessment is unlikely to be very thorough or very successful. The problems associated with discursive interaction in groups with joint goals or interests have been forcefully described by Cass Sunstein, who diagnoses a 'law of group polarization' affecting those groups (Sunstein 2003). People sharing the same goals, especially if they form organisations, are likely also to have similar lifestyles (to read the same books and newspapers, for instance) and to be exposed to similar evidence.

The pool of arguments and information the group can draw on is thus limited by the very fact of their association (Sunstein 2003: 84). Critics of deliberative democracy have pointed out that participants in deliberative forums, even where access is formally unrestricted, are far more likely to be upper- or middle-class whites than economically disadvantaged or members of ethnic minorities. The rules of deliberative discourse, requiring generalisation and abstraction from everyday problems, tend to be such that people lacking the respective discursive skills and culture are unlikely to be noticed and respected. The heterogeneity of such forums is therefore limited and the inputs to it systematically biased (Sanders 1997, Young 2003). For assessment of reasons to be conscientious and exhaustive, though, the pool should be maximally diverse and comprehensive: challenge requires dissent.

An equally serious problem arises from tendencies towards wishful thinking. Individually, most people are aware of this danger. Escaping it is one motive for exposing one's acceptances to critical review in discourses. People are probably less aware, however, of biases existing in the groups in which they co-ordinate their acceptances. On the contrary, they will be grateful for any arguments favouring their wishful thinking. Acceptances in biased groups are therefore easily transformed by discursive interaction: but typically towards more extreme positions.

> Members of a group will have thought of some, but not all, of the arguments that favour their initial inclination; ... In discussion, arguments of a large number of individuals are stated and heard, but the total argument pool will be tilted in one or another direction, depending on the predispositions of the people who compose the group (Sunstein 2003: 84).

In addition to this, Sunstein remarks a 'rhetorical asymmetry' which, where quantitative issues (for example, the sum of funding or compensation, years in prison) are concerned, favours persons urging higher awards. The trick here seems to be to present a question that is (quantitatively) evaluative as a categorical, all-or-nothing one. Categorical axioms ('every capitalist is a fascist', 'never compromise on the right to life') provide a strong and easy rationalisation that compromises cannot withstand. Group-members opposed to this kind of categorical thinking have little choice but to leave the group in which it prevails, thus reducing the argument pool further. Biased groups, therefore, not only tend to become more extreme but are also highly obstinate to correction. If their strategic capabilities depend on the adequacy of acceptances, however, polarised groups are unlikely to be very successful. Moreover, inability to compromise makes it difficult to exert influence on executive and legislative decisions. Where associations are politically successful, we should therefore expect practices countervailing the tendencies of group polarisation.[14]

The second type of situation in which actors may exchange information and assess their acceptances without acting strategically are situations in which neither of the actors has any interests or goals involved in the decision that is to be made. Just like situations of the first type, they play a frequent role in real-world politics. Experts are typically assumed to be the kind of persons who are at once disinterested and well informed. But why should anybody, lacking individual interests, have acquired a rich fund of information on any specific topic? The question is a serious one: in several branches, such as pharmaceutical research, it is difficult to find persons both equipped with a certain type of knowledge and without economic interests at stake in decisions to which this knowledge is of relevance. The incentives for experts, if they are to be serviceable in political decisions, must be such as to reward honesty and conscientiousness and to punish strategic use of arguments.

One group of actors informing political decision processes consists of the staff of administrative bodies in which people are employed as experts on specific topics and gain further expertise through their everyday work. Further expert information is increasingly being sought in various types of commissions and advisory committees. Their members are typically recruited from the academic world. Here, knowledge and expertise, as well as the ability to present them persuasively, yield actors social esteem and status, which is often increased by being appointed as a member of a prestigious committee. Discourses in expert committees differ from academic discourses within disciplines and professions in that they are purpose-bound: they are meant to inform practical decisions on specific topics, not to pursue truth on its own behalf.

The problems that occur when academics are employed as experts in political decision processes arise mostly from a role conflict that has been aptly described by Kenneth Arrow. Arrow draws attention to the adverse effects scientific ethos has in decision contexts, leading to 'excessive caution, manifested by delay and by conclusions which preserve scientific value by being ambiguous' (Arrow 1995: 271). For example, experts may be unwilling to embrace either of the options in a set of alternatives and instead provide additional ones without declaring a clear preference for one of these either. He further notes that, while specialisation increases the efficiency of research, it also increases the costs of communication (Arrow 1995: 271). Expert committees frequently fail to present the results of their proceedings in a manner that is easily accessible to non-expert political actors. What they produce is often more useful and interesting to their own disciplines than as a basis for political decisions.

An even more serious obstacle arises from the incentive structures prevailing in academic discourses. In these, hyperbolic scepticism and fierce challenge of commitments are not predominantly part of a scientific ethos but rather a source of esteem and success. If expert bodies are composed of members of competing disciplines, traditions and schools of thought – which is reasonable to avoid the negative consequences of group homogeneity discussed above – consensus will be most unlikely to occur. Dissent, which is a necessary requirement for epistemic progress, will prevail over co-ordination. 'Bargaining over beliefs' (Goodin & Brennan 2004) is not what academics tend to engage in because the truth is but one and cannot be compromised on.

However, the scientific ethos and culture, although it has disadvantages for decision purposes, seems to favour the transformation of acceptances. Yielding to the force of the better argument and accepting evidence produced according to certain standards is part of the background consensus of academic discourses. It would be wrong to assume, though, that anybody, including experts, could be without practical preferences and commitments. In particular in the social sciences, some schools of thought, such as Keynesianism or neo-classical economics, are intertwined with political ideologies. Fundamental assumptions about causal relationships that lie at the heart of these political ideologies are likely to give rise to differing interpretations of the same evidence and events.

Even if, on the surface, the discourse is a purely factual one, value dimensions cannot be entirely kept out of it. As the necessity to question and co-ordinate values, which are practical reasons, is not understood as part of the task, value conflicts are not solved but constitute a further obstacle to agreement. Although transformation of acceptances is possible in expert discourses, there are mechanisms inherent in them ever producing new disagreements and preventing consensus. While the problem with shared-goal groups is polarisation, the problem with expert groups is indecision.

The third type of situation where communicative interaction is unlikely to be 'cheap' are situations of high uncertainty and over-complexity.

> First, in the face of uncertainty, and more so in the wake of a shock or crisis, many of the conditions facilitating a focus on power are absent. It is difficult for leaders to identify their potential allies and to be sure of what strategies are most likely to help them retain power. And, second, poorly understood conditions may create enough turbulence that established operating procedures may break down, making institutions unworkable. Neither power nor institutional cues to behaviour will be available and new patterns of action may ensue (Haas 1992: 14)

What Haas observes for political leaders is equally or even more true for other actors involved in and affected by policy-making processes. Turning to expert groups or 'epistemic communities' (Haas 1992) is one way of dealing with uncertainty. The point here, however, is rather that actors themselves will have more incentives to share information in order to arrive at a suitable definition of the situation and problem (see Keck 1995).

Each actor may hold certain pieces of relevant information exclusively but, taken by themselves, these cannot be made instrumentally useful. All actors' pieces taken together, though, might, like the pieces of a jigsaw, reveal a useful representation of the world on which strategic action can be based. Moreover, not all pieces of information that are instrumentally relevant are also strategically relevant. As noted above, there are cases in which the sharing of information reduces access to one's goals, but not all cases are like this. Only in competitive zero-sum games does any gain of the other constitute a loss to ego, wherefore any actions providing the other with new opportunities would be avoided (Scharpf 1997: 84–9). In 'individualistic' variable-sum games, by contrast, the payoff the other receives is of no effect to ego: all that counts are ego's gains and losses (Scharpf 1997: 85/86). Individualistic action orientations in fact constitute the standard assumption of neo-classical economics and rational-choice theory, which is reflected in the criterion of separable preferences (see chapter one, section 2). Scharpf further notes the possibility of 'solidaristic' games, in which the gains of the other positively affect ego, who would hence prefer a payoff structure from which both benefit over one in which only ego benefits (1997: 85–6). Solidaristic action orientations may be expected to occur wherever actors share a set of political goals or reasons.

In the case of individualistic action orientations, uncertainty and iteration of the game may turn the dilemma of actors strategically withholding information into a co-ordination problem. Here, defecting has no advantages over co-operating, if the other player co-operates. Only if the other keeps defecting in repeated games, is co-operation likely to be abandoned. In case of solidaristic action orientations, payoffs will be symmetric and the game one of pure harmony, where the co-operative solution constitutes a stable equilibrium.[15] These game-theoretic considerations match well with the constitutive principles of language use pointed out by Grice. In both cases, co-operation represents the equilibrium solution and failure to co-operate yields the lowest collective payoff. Grice's contribution to the matter is that he points out why unilateral defect must and will be sanctioned: it follows from the basic principle of reciprocity that co-operation in linguistic interaction always takes two and cannot be adhered to as a strategy if the other defects.

Games of co-operative exchange and fitting of pieces of information in the face of uncertainty are well described by the term 'information pooling' (cf. Grofman & Owen 1986). An empirical example of it might be the 'open method of co-ordination' (OMC) introduced as a new instrument of governance in the European Union. The OMC has been employed as a forum for exchange and co-ordination in several policy areas, among them employment and health policy. Both policy areas are highly complex, so that actors perceive a lack of information that would be required as a premise for a rational choice of policies. Information-pooling must be expected to have a marked effect on actors' acceptances and hence on the probability of preference-transformation.

Uncertainty means that actors cannot decide what to accept and lack the premises they need to form preferences about what to do. Information and arguments offered by other speakers provide rationalisations for acceptances that will be highly welcome and quickly translated into own acceptances. A likely danger for actors in situations of insecurity and instability of premises therefore is that of 'jumping to conclusions'. That is, they are at risk from undeliberated, hasty decisions that are made for the purposes of stability and certainty rather than being based on thorough assessment. A factor contributing to this is that assertions provided as information or evidence in information pooling settings are unlikely to be queried or challenged.

Challenges always constitute a riskier step in communicative interaction than default attribution of entitlement, as they signal mistrust and suspicion. Actors unused to co-operation and unfamiliar with cultures of rigorous challenge are therefore likely to avoid moves that seem unco-operative and/or risky. They will tend to assume that they can judge and decide for themselves whether or not to accept challenges as premises. Accordingly, even if acceptances are transformed by information pooling processes, co-ordination is a side-effect rather than an explicit goal of interaction. A certain piece of information may be accepted by a majority of actors because it is persuasively presented or matches their inclinations but persistent refusal to accept something as a premise in the face of better arguments is not sanctioned.

Contradictory and incompatible arguments may well co-exist in the information pool, therefore, without contradictions being argumentatively eradicated. Consequently, actors might benefit from information-pooling by becoming better able to achieve their individual goals without arriving at anything like a joint definition of the given problem and situation or even joint goals of action. As uncertainty is reduced, actors are also likely to recognise the type of game or dilemma they are involved in and the dominant strategies in this game. The information that decreases uncertainty brings with it a learning potential that might increase conflict. Like expert groups, information-pooling settings are therefore ill suited for decision-making purposes.

Neither of the three types of situations identified as enhancing meaningful (non-cheap) linguistic interaction is representative of the public political discourse that is understood as essential to democratic decision-making. On the contrary, all three seem to be parasitic on democratic deliberation. They represent the 'easy cases' of co-ordination, which have little to do with conflict-accommodation. I maintain, however, that all three types of situations form part of the larger-scale public debate and decision-making process.

To begin with, even in modern heterogeneous societies, a set of joint goals or practical reasons may at least be appealed to. In particular situations of crisis, caused by wars, terrorism or profound economic turmoil, people are likely to interpret the decision-problem as one of finding the right way to achieve a joint goal. Accordingly, situations of crisis increase the danger of a polarisation of public opinion. While, on the one hand, a focus on joint goals entails certain dangers, it is, on the other hand, a prerequisite of trust in politics and politicians. Without a certain degree of trust (but also without a certain degree of scepticism), democratic institutions could not survive (see Zintl 2002).

Experts, too, are involved in all public discourses. Not only as members of advisory bodies, but also in television talk-shows, newspaper forums and public events, they frequently inform discourses with allegedly disinterested intelligence. In fact, it is only in *public* discourses that the potential of expert advice can be fully exploited. The adversary procedures that characterize competitive politics are 'specifically designed to bring out unstated assumptions, differing interpretations of the facts, and gaps in logic or in evidence' (Majone 1989: 40; see also Arrow 1995). Competition should force politicians and political parties who seek to win majorities for their proposals to take any effort to produce the most convincing evidence and compelling arguments and challenge those of their opponents.

Uncertainty, finally, is a basic condition of all human decision-making and thus of political preference-formation. It may well be assumed that most people most of time and on most topics neither know what to accept nor what to want (Offe 1992: 128). Citizens are frequently confronted with new political questions and new options for action, while being unable to tell how these are going to affect their goals and interests. Political discourses between 'ordinary' citizens, although they are significant for political preference-formation and action, can therefore hardly be led by strategic considerations. As people are frequently insecure, not only about what to accept but also about what their political goals and practical reasons should be, discourses are likely to affect the volitive premises of preferences as much as the cognitive ones. I maintain that the exchange and co-ordination of practical reasons is, in fact, the crucial point in the debates preceding a political decision. After all, the decision is not about what to accept as true but about what to do – and why. This is the topic of the next section.

5. DISCURSIVE CO-ORDINATION AND TRANSFORMATION OF REASONS: *VERSTÄNDIGUNG* AND CONSENSUS

If actors have differing and competing acceptances about the effects of political programmes, strategies and policies, information may resolve the conflict and decision-problem. The more difficult case, however, is the one where actors pursue different goals and make different practical reasons effective for their preferences. In this case, discursive co-ordination of action plans becomes truly remarkable. And it is also the point where the present project leaves the common ground with economic theories and sides with theories of communicative action and deliberative democracy.

In particular, insecurity plays a different role where the volitive premises of preference are concerned. If actors are insecure about what states of the world they prefer or should prefer, information may, far from solving it, rather increase the problem. Where only acceptances are at stake, insecurity and incompleteness of preference-orders represents merely a superficial conflict, which may or may not be resolved in the processes of discursive co-ordination. Where practical reasons are at stake, conflict and incompleteness are more fundamental. Here, actors are confronted with severe internal dilemmas – with the problems of deciding what to want (see chapter 1, section 3). As argued before, actors must be expected to have and accept a set of practical reasons. Given this set, it was further argued, there exists no one aggregation-rule that yields a meaningful complete ordering of preferences over outcomes of alternative actions for any given choice situation. For every new choice situation, such as the decision between options for political action, the volitive premises of preferences have to be determined anew. Arrow's challenge to collective decisions occurs here as a challenge to individual decisions (cf. Steedman & Krause 1986). How are actors to decide how to weigh their various practical reasons against one another, without employing an arbitrarily chosen decision-rule?

I argue that the discursive exchange, contestation and co-ordination of reasons can produce aggregation rules for practical reasons that yield complete prefer-ence-orders and escape the unattractive prospect of blank decisionism. Pure deci-sionism removes the link between action and individual goals and utility. Although it entails freedom of choice, this kind of freedom seems to be of little value to the actor. I assume that, besides the instrumental motive of acquiring information that was discussed in the last section, the need for an appropriate aggregation procedure to apply to one's own practical reasons is the fundamental motive for engaging in communicative interaction. Justifications of practical rea-sons, which are offered in 'practical' discourses, provide rationalisations of possi-ble actions.[16]

It would be wrong to assume, though, that, except in a few extraordinary cases, actors simply maximise rationalisation. For political decisions in particular, this would amount to a kind of higher-order decisionism and would eventually turn the discourse into an end in itself. If an actor's practical reasons as well as their respective weights in any given choice situation are entirely contingent, the actor could just as well 'let things happen' or decide by chance. If motives for action were completely transformable in discourses, entering a discourse would in an important sense constitute a risk of losing one's identity. A liberal perspective, however, demands that preferences be regarded as to some extent autonomous (cf. Goodin 2003, chapter two). So does any approach choosing the rational individ-ual (i.e. the actor acting for reasons) as the fundamental unit of analysis.

An exchange and co-ordination of practical reasons for collective action has several prerequisites. To begin with, it requires a shared set of acceptances, or joint definition of the choice situation (see above). Secondly and like the exchange and co-ordination of acceptances, it requires a sufficient degree of mutual trust that the intention of the other is not a malevolent manipulation for her own prac-tical reasons. It further requires reasons that are moral or ethical, in that they entail the wish to make them subject to a general political rule. Reasons that are not gen-eralisable may still require argumentative justification but they are not transfer-able, i.e., they cannot be made available as motives for other actors. Where rea-sons are not generalisable, their exchange is pointless but for strategic reasons. In this case, there can be no *Verständigung* about practical reasons and bargaining is the only possible way to co-ordinate action plans.[17]

Successful co-ordination of reasons normally also requires a set of shared prac-tical reasons that can be appealed to (cf. Richardson 2002: 183). Although it is con-ceivable that a moral reason – which, to begin with, is in Brandom's sense a dox-astic one – develops such persuasive powers that it is established as new practical reason, this case seems rather exceptional. A set of shared moral and ethical con-victions must rather be regarded as a precondition of trust and co-operation.[18] The problem actors face is not uncertainty about which practical reasons, of interest or moral, could be relevant for decisions, but insecurity about how to weigh conflict-ing and partly incommensurable reasons against one another and how to specify abstract reasons (such as fundamental values) for the given context.

Typical moves in the exchange and co-ordination of practical reasons will therefore consist in appeals to and justifications of existing reasons. In fact, any justification or petition for an action that appeals to a higher-ranking reason in a sense implies that this higher-ranking reason is shared. The pragmatic phenomenon of implicature that was described by H.P. Grice (1979) in the context of conversational maxims can serve to illustrate this. Consider the following sentence:

<We should not introduce tuition fees because that would deprive children from poorer backgrounds of the opportunity of higher education.>

The sentence makes a factual *presupposition*: that the introduction of tuition fees would deprive poor children of opportunities. This factual presupposition claims a shared set of acceptances on which the decision can be based. It can do so either justly (because agreement over the consequences of tuition fees has in fact been established) or manipulatively (in order to pretend that there can be no rational disagreement over this claim). At the same time, it *implicates*[19] something: namely, that the deprivation of poor children of the opportunity of higher education is a bad thing and that the hearer shares the value of safeguarding poor children's opportunities to higher education.

As a pragmatic phenomenon, implicature is best understood on the basis of a theory of speech acts and linguistic interaction. Reconsider Grice's conversational maxim of relevance. By employing the proposition 'that it would deprive children ...' as a reason, the speaker implicitly claims that it is a relevant reason (rather than no reason at all). If the speaker named reasons which he knew were not relevant to the hearer(s), he would be violating the maxim of relevance and behaving in a non-co-operative manner that risks the breakdown of communication. By justifying our practical commitments with adequate and generalisable reasons, we acknowledge others' rationality, which is an important requirement for a democratic discourse to work. At the same time, the recourse to implicatures can also serve as a powerful means of manipulation. Implicatures produce a supposition of commonality and alliance that can prevent questions and challenges and cause decisions to be taken on the basis of vague feelings rather than rational assessment of reasons.[20] Whether the consent is real or illegitimately suggested, presuppositions and implicatures are a valuable source of information for the observer, as they reveal a lot about shared assumptions and shared practical reasons.

For the co-ordination of reasons, it makes a considerable difference whether the discourse is a political one or merely an instance of everyday conversation. As noted above, where the reasons that justify practical commitments are entirely idiosyncratic and non-generalisable, even non-political conversation is hardly possible and bargaining is the only way to co-ordinate action plans. In an extreme case of everyday conversation, reasons are sufficiently general, i.e. accessible to the other, but do not need to be co-ordinated. For instance, if I discuss my choice of career with a friend who will not be affected by my choice, the reasons I name for my commitment will be general in that my friend would probably consider the same reasons if she were in my position: that my job should be interesting and challenging; that I expect an adequate salary; that I still wish to have enough spare time to spend with my family and so on. However, I may well decide that, for me, having enough spare time to spend with my family is the most relevant reason for my choice of career; while for my friend, a high salary might be more important.

Things are different where one actor's actions affect another actor's prospects. Here, general rules and norms of conduct begin to play a role and the justification of practical commitments gains a political aspect. When confronted with a new political decision-problem, actors yet need to establish relationships between their own practical reasons and the possible outcomes of available options for action. In this context, I may try to justify my practical commitment of, for example, voting for option A by reference to non-general practical reasons ('I vote for A because A is in my very own economic interest'). If I seek to convince others that they should vote A because there are good reasons for it, however, the reasons I name must be general.

Reasons that can be successful in persuading other actors are:

- reasons of sub-group interest, which might motivate actors belonging to the same sub-group to prefer a specific outcome and thus option;
- reasons of collective (all-group) interest, which might motivate all members of the collective that is taking the decision to prefer a specific outcome and option;
- moral reasons, which might motivate all actors who share the fundamental values they are based on to prefer a specific outcome and option.[21]

These different types of reasons have differing prospects of being successful. Reasons of sub-group interest may be very successful where actors are members of a formal organisation, such as a political party or trade union. They will be less successful where group membership is not clearly defined and where it is less constitutive of the identity of the person, who may be a member of several groups with conflicting group interests: the groups of women, Catholics, the self-employed, parents, etc. In this case, whoever is seeking to convince me that option A is in my interest because I am a woman would additionally need to convince me that my membership of the group of women is the relevant membership in this context. Moreover, the fact that, with regard to long-term political decisions, citizens are placed behind what John Rawls called a 'veil of ignorance' (1971: 12) makes it myopic to base decisions on contingent group membership: I may be in the group of the self-employed today but I may well be in the group of welfare recipients in the future.

However, appeals to the collective interest are similarly confronted with problems. As Arrow's impossibility theorem indicates, deriving a group interest from individual interests is a serious challenge. Although actors may generally be expected to believe that this is a task that can, in principle, be accomplished, very different interpretations of the common interest may co-exist (Offe 2001). A further requirement for such appeals to be successful is that actors actually perceive themselves as members of the collective and accept that what is in the collective interest is equally in their own interest. Finally, but probably most importantly, the persuasive power of reasons of interest is restricted by the fact that 'being in one's interest' is a matter of degree rather than a categorical property. Options or outcomes will always be in some respects and to some extent in our interest, otherwise they would not be debated as alternatives of policy choice. There simply exists a too wide range for interpretation and disagreement over the collective interest to expect a broad consensus on it (see Greven 2003).

Moral reasons escape some of these problems. They display a categorical and imperative logic that enables them to be decisive where decisions on the basis of interest are difficult to rationalise. The claim that it is morally wrong to kill somebody for reasons other than self-defence asserts universal validity in all possible worlds. Accepting this claim commits one not to consent to a decision that takes or risks someone's life, regardless of what other positive or negative consequences that decision may have. Decisions based on moral reasons also defy strong consequentialism, which considers only the resulting distribution of goods, and instead focus on the way in which a situation was brought about. Decisions based on reasons of interest follow a different logic. If it is in my interest that petrol taxes remain low, it is only so all other things (such as whether or not I own a car) being equal.

While in the case of moral reasons, a comprehensive understanding of the outcomes of a decision is not required, reasons of interest depend on a thorough description of an action's consequences to be persuasive. The common good or collective interest is a consequentialist notion referring to a specific group and time. The morally right is a transcendent notion that is independent of time and context. As the political norms in which the decision is to result must be general and universal (at least for the particular community), the implicit universality of moral reasons recommends these as a basis of choice, which will contribute to their discursive success (cf. Greven 2000: 61).

As moral reasons can only be appealed to if they are already shared, typical strategies will include moralising, insisting, repeating and emphasising duty and guilt.[22] Appeals to reasons which the interlocutor already shares obviously cannot be reduced to illocutionary acts in the way Habermas does it (Habermas 1984, 1: 292–5). Rather, they are always made with the perlocutionary goal of changing the other's effective practical reasons and intentions. Speech acts are in this sense strategic or instrumental. The instrumental character of interaction is constrained, however, by the fact that, if they engage in an exchange of practical reasons, actors allow for the appeals of other speakers to have perlocutionary effects on their own motivation. If I subject my own motives to contestation and revision, I cannot be acting entirely instrumentally.

Few actors, however, can be expected to assign precedence to a single moral reason over all other practical reasons, including personal goals and interests. An actor who does this would qualify as a 'fanatic' whose internal aggregation mechanism violates Arrow's condition of non-dictatorship: the single moral reason dictates all her decisions (cf. Steedman & Krause 1986: 208). Moreover, where (as in most cases) more than one moral reason is acknowledged to be relevant, the question how to weigh reasons against one another is not easily solved by categorical logic. Being forced by discursive principles to employ generalisable reasons, people may, from several possible moral argumentations, choose the one that best serves their interests and advocate it. This reduces the probability that a single reason will dominate the collective decision.

Generalising the justification of one's practical commitments nonetheless always entails a risk of being convinced by the better argument. Elster (1995) has described this phenomenon as the 'civilizing force of hypocrisy'. Practical commitments based on 'selfish' reasons evade certain argumentative challenges. Their justification eventually boils down to the indexical statement 'because I want it', which can hardly be further contested (although it is a perfectly acceptable reason for many everyday decisions). Once I have agreed to follow the norm of generalisation, my reasons become contestable and I might, at least discursively, be forced to give up my stance. Generalisation also helps to break with default modes of entitlement attribution: general and moral reasons are more likely to be challenged because, in accepting them even implicitly, actors can incur a commitment to specific actions and decisions.

Whether reasons of sub-group or collective interest or moral reasons dominate a discourse and eventually motivate a collective decision will depend on the decision-problem and the course of the discourse and is hardly predictable. In any case, the discourse provides opportunities for individuals to arrive at rules for the aggregation of practical reasons into complete preference-orders over options and their outcomes. In other words, political discourses can enable the formation of a political will that is free in the Kantian sense of not being arbitrary. This is not to say that it is impossible for actors to find aggregation rules by themselves; in fact, this is what they have to do whenever they take private decisions. However, political decision-problems tend to be more complex: they involve interests other than one's own which one may feel morally inclined to respect; they concern issues that are beyond everyday experience; and they have far-reaching consequences that are difficult to predict. Decisions between options for political action, for instance in directly-democratic polls, therefore seem to be particularly prone to be taken by way of unreflected decisionism.[23]

Communication helps actors decide how to weigh various reasons against one another and to determine which aggregation rule to use in a given situation. In an ideal case, an act of collective creativity might arise from such interaction, in which exercise of individual and collective autonomy coincide. The individual derives a preference over options from her practical reasons not by way of decisionism but by rational deliberation and decision. Individual preferences deriving from deliberation will be less idiosyncratic and more similarly structured. As a result of this, meaningful aggregation of individual preferences into a collective preference order may also be accomplished (cf. Miller 1991, Dryzek & List 2003, List 2002). Contrary to the suggestion of Arrow's impossibility theorem, it would then make some sense to speak of a 'collective will', for which individual wills are nonetheless constitutive. Richardson concludes that '[w]ith the truth about what we ought to do depending both on external standards and on how actual democratic deliberation turns out, democratic processes are normatively fruitful ones' (2002: 141).

Various courses that a process of co-ordination of practical reasons might take and various resulting aggregation-rules are conceivable. One possibility is that a single reason of moral or collective interest dictates all, or at least an overwhelming majority, of individual decisions over the given alternatives. This might be an ideal of *Verständigung* but is unlikely to occur very often except in situations of crisis and high emotions. Greven points out that, in the face of the 'acid bath of modernization and secularization', joint normative reference systems have ceased to exist (2000: 57). Politics alone can set norms with collectively binding force. Where, under these conditions, a joint reason is nonetheless established, it is not unlikely to represent a result of manipulation by a particularly persuasive interlocutor or of collective polarisation, both of which are undesirable in modern democracies.

Another possibility is that actors arrive at an explicit or implicit consensus that neither moral reasons nor reasons of collective interest are tenable in the case of the present decision and allow non-general, indexical reasons to guide it. This is probably the least likely case, as it implies that a political decision is neither required nor desirable. A similar but more probable case is one in which actors end up being guided by considerations of sub-group interest. In this case, sub-groups are successful at establishing one reason as having priority over all others, albeit only for members of the respective group. This might be the result of group polarisation as described by Sunstein (2003, see above). One example of it is the groups of pro-lifers and pro-choicers on the issue of abortion that have formed in the United States: one group considers only the moral reason that human life must be preserved at any cost while the other considers only the moral reason that freedom of choice and self-determination must be guaranteed for everyone, including pregnant women. Although this case is objectionable with regard to social peace and collective identity, it may at least enable meaningful aggregation of individual preferences if the decision is a binary, yes/no one or if all sub-group preferences are single-peaked on the decision at hand.

Finally, communication might produce a 'deep compromise' (Richardson 2002: 144–9) or 'principled compromise' (Gutmann & Thompson 1996: 88–93) between conflicting and seemingly incommensurable practical reasons.[24] This compromise would be at once an intra-personal and an inter-personal one. If citizens, when confronted with a new set of alternatives for political action, have conflicting preferences within different dimensions and thus difficulties in forming a complete preference-order over the available alternatives, deliberation can help them to arrive at a non-arbitrarily chosen formation rule. A formation (or aggregation) rule would essentially provide actors with a mechanism for weighing their various practical reasons or domains of choice.

Assigning weight to two or more dimensions constitutes a compromise between them. If the reasons concerned are reasons of interest, compromising should be comparatively easy. Interest is a matter of degree and the goods concerned are likely to be partitionable and available in differing amounts. As empirical research shows, however, the intra-personal calculation of anything like indifference curves is more of a problem for actors than economic theories tend to assume (cf. Slovic 2000, Shafir *et al*. 2000). Moreover, even if indifference curves could be obtained, that would not relieve actors from the need to choose a specific point on the curve if more than one is available.

Because their categorical logic enables easier rationalisation both internally and socially, moral reasons tend to be more persuasive. Making compromises where moral reasons are concerned seems to be ruled out by these very reasons themselves. In the debate about abortion, the decision-problem seemed to consist in choosing one moral reason – preserving life or granting freedom of choice – to guide the decision. Any compromise option that would have restricted freedom of choice or the protection of unborn life is hard to defend without violating the categorical logic of the norms involved.

Co-ordination of practical reasons, however, can, if successful, enable compromises and trade-offs even between moral reasons that are difficult or impossible intra-personally. It makes a difference whether a reason that is incommensurable with the one I hold to be most relevant for the present decision is represented internally or by another person or group of persons. In the latter case, the moral reason represented by the other also constitutes an interest, in so far as it is one of the interests of a group that their moral convictions be respected. Between conflicting interests, it is far easier to establish a compromise solution, that does some justice to each. In addition to this, interests favour consequentialist action-orientations. If moral reasons conflict, the consequences of preferring either one over the other in a given choice situation should be very seriously considered.

In Germany, a solution to the abortion problem was found that sacrifices both freedom of choice and protection of unborn life to a certain degree on behalf of the other: women must see a counsellor before deciding to end a pregnancy and abortions are restricted to the first three months of pregnancy. This compromise does not seem argumentatively defensible in a coherent, deductive way on the basis of either of the fundamental values involved. Nonetheless, it has found wide acceptance and prevented either pro-life or pro-choice campaigners from resorting to violence.

It seems that most people in Germany today prefer the compromise over either of the extremes, as it does some justice to two fundamental values of which neither can be entirely sacrificed to the other. Interaction and social compromise have, hence, both provided individuals with an aggregation-rule for their individual practical reasons and enabled meaningful aggregation of individual preferences, which are now based on an identical dimension and (most likely to be) single-peaked. The fact that the aggregation rule was democratically arrived at is another argument for it – not only normatively, from an observer's perspective, but also empirically, for the very actors trying to form preferences over alternatives. In this sense, democratic discourses and decisions cannot be reduced to the interpretation of moral principles and common values. Instead, the choice of an aggregation rule for practical reasons and its justification amount to the moral and political construction of norms (Forst 2007b: 252, 268).

Exchange of reasons can lead to co-ordination and convergence in several ways. It can help identify more clearly the relevant alternatives and produce new ones (Dryzek & List 2003: 22). In this sense, it produces new input to the circle of preference co-ordination. It can further help to identify the relevant reasons or dimensions of choice. Moreover, it may help to establish a ranking between these dimensions and to assign weights among them and thus provide individuals with an aggregation-rule for their conflicting reasons. Such would be instances of meta-co-ordination leading to meta-agreements, which seem far more realistic than substantial ones (List 2004). Even if neither of these steps of co-ordination leads to consensus, they increase the structuration of individual preferences and therefore enable a collective aggregation mechanism that escapes the problems of Arrow's theorem (Dryzek & List 2003, List 2002).

Convergence of practical reasons, and thus of preferences, is most likely to occur if the following conditions obtain.

To begin with, things are far easier if a set of shared highest-ranking values already exists and if the individual orderings of these are similar. In this case, the task consists primarily in finding an adequate specification of values for specific contexts and aggregating values with interests. Group homogeneity and a clearly defined decision-problem are likely to be positively correlated with the existence of such a shared set of values, while heterogeneity and competing 'frames' for a decision-problem can be expected to be negatively correlated.

Secondly, things may be easier where the overall number of actors with different goals and moral reasons involved is lower. In a large forum, there will simply be more speakers offering alternative views, aspects and options. Individual preferences are therefore more likely to be unsettled in large forums, which will result in shifting majorities. In so far as co-ordination of practical reasons always involves compromises between reasons and between groups or persons, the increase in transaction costs with the number of speakers will also have to be considered. However, if the interlocutors are unwilling to compromise, a smaller group-size may also make co-ordination more difficult, as the implicit or explicit recourse to majority decisions is problematic.[25]

The setting must, thirdly, be sufficiently dialogical: every potential speaker must get a chance to speak and commitments must be challengeable. Unequal opportunities to participate are likely to result in reservations: feeling excluded keeps the focus on one's own interests and values and countervails respect for and interest in other positions. It also makes a big difference whether one simply listens to questioning of one's own practical reasons or whether one has to defend these reasons explicitly and in public.[26]

It is further helpful if there exists a sufficient degree of trust that others' appeals to moral reasons are authentic and not driven by intentions to manipulate. Trust is promoted by the expression of respect, by taking other speakers'

contributions seriously and by pointing out joint interests and consensual acceptances. Mistrust of an interlocutor can be expressed and is increased by challenging presuppositions and implicatures. While suspicions can prevent co-ordination
and decision altogether, too much trust may also lead an inadequate assessment of
reasons and open doors to manipulation.

Finally, there should be no adversary, competitive logic of action intervening
if practical reasons are to be successfully co-ordinated. This would be the case
where participants compete for best reasons and best arguments in the pursuit of
esteem or status rather than seeking to achieve 'good' or 'rational' collective decisions. To some extent, adversary logics of interaction obviously promote the
assessment of practical reasons (although they are more important in the assessment of acceptances). However, where argumentative challenge and success lacks
a political goal and instead becomes an end in itself, co-ordination is rendered
impossible.

6. SUMMARY

The first two sections of this chapter have pointed out justification (or generality)
and reciprocity as norms implicit in linguistic action and constitutive rules of communicative interaction. They fill Habermas' assertion that 'reaching understanding is the inherent telos of human speech' (1984, 1: 287) with meaning. Assigning
priority to communicative action over instrumental action in the way Habermas
and Brandom do, talk can rarely be regarded as 'cheap' in the economic sense. In
undertaking speech acts, actors incur commitments that change the state of the
world in which they find themselves. Engaging in linguistic interaction, actors
implicitly express respect of others' rationality and autonomy, which is a precondition of democratic politics.[27]

Given that actors are always involved in communicative *and* instrumental
action, motives for entering a discourse have to be established. Section 2 pointed
out two possible motives that connect with the concept of preference as motivation for action and decision which was developed in the first chapter. The first of
these motives is that of achieving a fit between mind and world, which is required
for instrumental action. The second motive is that of finding out for what purpose
action is eventually is to be instrumental, i.e. what one actually wants. The problem here is, as pointed out in section 3 of chapter one, that of arriving at an aggregation rule for individual practical reasons.

Section 3 represented political decision-making as a process of discursive preference-co-ordination. Ideal-typically, this process is a circular one, consisting in the
definition of a set of alternatives, exchange of information and the co-ordination of
goals and practical reasons. Two types of discourses were distinguished with regard
to the motives of actors entering them, with regard to the kind of justification
required in them and with regard to the kind of co-ordination and conflict-accommodation achieved in them. In 'theoretical' discourses, where acceptances are

exchanged and co-ordinated, doxastic commitments are undertaken and justified by reference to evidence and causality. In 'practical' discourses, where practical reasons are co-ordinated, practical commitments are justified by reference to interests and/or moral rules. Communicative interaction in theoretical and practical discourses helps actors break with the default modes of belief-acceptance and desire-satisfaction in the formation of political preferences. To arrive at superior justifications, however, assertions need to be challenged and contested rather than uncritically accepted.

Section 4 dealt with the exchange and co-ordination of acceptances in political contexts. It was argued that strategic incentives for dishonesty or withholding information may be overcome if either of three conditions obtain: if actors share a joint goal, if they are disinterested in relation to the issue that is to be decided, or if they find themselves in a situation of high uncertainty and over-complexity. Each of these conditions, however, also entails a specific risk for the interaction to take a problematic course. A joint goal increases the risk of polarisation and biased or wishful acceptance. Disinterested actors, typically experts, may be unwilling to decide (and, from the point of view of normative democratic theory, they should not do so). Uncertainty, finally, is not necessarily a suitable basis for thorough assessment and may give way to strategic logic as soon as it is sufficiently reduced.

Section 5 addressed the question of how practical reasons are exchanged and co-ordinated in political discourses. Although the pragmatic question of how best to achieve a given goal is clearly an important aspect of preference-formation and interaction in politics, the issue of what individual and collective goals should be seems to me to be the more crucial and truly political one. In economic theories, this issue is usually entirely neglected, while in deliberative approaches, it is too often dominated by an epistemic conception of democracy. Epistemic democrats hold that there is an independently existing truth about the common good that democratic procedures are supposed to 'track' or 'discover'. Contrary to this position, it was argued that democratic deliberation can be normatively fruitful in that it creatively establishes new priorities, alternatives and solutions.

If the co-ordination of practical reasons is successful, it can help to solve an individual and a collective aggregation problem at once. Individuals will be enabled to arrive at a non-arbitrary and rational decision on how to aggregate their diverse and conflicting practical reasons into a complete preference-order over alternative actions. If the reasons or dimensions on which individual preferences are based are similar, and if dimensions are similarly weighted, meaningful aggregation, on which Arrow's theorem casts doubt, is a possibility. If individuals are willing to prefer a decision at least partly on the grounds that it was discursively prepared and democratically decided on, individual preference-formation is, to some extent, driven by collective preference-formation – but nonetheless rational and autonomous. And one goal of democracy is, as Sunstein points out, 'to ensure autonomy not merely in the satisfaction of preferences, but also and more fundamentally, in the processes of preference formation' (1990: 12). This view of individual and collective decision-making might, following Greven, be seen as a 'democratic decisionism' (Greven 2000: 51–62).

Empirically, political discourses obviously do not take the form of a single conversation (Chambers 1995: 249). Rather, a political discourse takes place in a number of different institutions and forums, with only partially overlapping membership. Different institutions and forums, if they are deliberately established, are typically devoted to specific tasks: the definition of alternatives, pooling of information, establishing priorities, developing mediating proposals, finding compromises or evaluating the success of a previous decision. This also means that discussions have no definite end or beginning but are taken up again and again with different focuses. The co-ordination and transformation of preferences need not be the result of a singular instance of communicative interaction either. It is more likely to be a gradual process stretched over a longer period of time. In particular, where interaction is public, changing one's position may, as was pointed out, also represent a loss of face and thus be avoided at least in the immediate situation.

While this chapter focused on the constitutive rules of communicative interaction and on *motives* why actors enter discourses in which their acceptances and practical reasons are assessed and challenged, the following chapter will turn to institutional *constraints* on interaction. Different modes of communicative interaction can be realised in different types of political forums. Constraining and enabling interaction, institutional properties will have effects on the formation and transformation of preferences. The following chapter develops ideal-type modes of interaction and describes their possible institutionalisations. The identification of such ideal-types and of relevant characteristics of political forums will enable the formulation of more specific hypotheses about where, why and how preferences are likely to be transformed.

NOTES

1   It is common practice in linguistics to indicate illocutionary acts by small capitals.

2   For directives, word-to-world and world-to-word direction of fit collapse into one: when a speaker declares that p, p becomes a fact simply by virtue of this declaration. The case with expressives is somewhat more difficult and controversial in linguistic theory. The understanding I find most convincing is that which conceives of expressives as a special case of assertives, in which the subjective world plays the role the objective world plays in assertives (cf. Tugendhat 1979, discussed in Habermas 1984, 1: 313–5). Searle himself insists that the category of direction of fit cannot be applied to expressives (1979: 15–16).

3   Only if volition is regarded as beyond actors' control and evaluation and perfect information is assumed can the role of linguistic interaction be reduced to signaling. Austen-Smith (1992), however, who adopts this view, illustrates its inadequacy himself: he claims that 'persuasion' is the central point in political discourses but fails to see that a signal, if it is perceived as such, cannot possibly persuade.

4   There exists no adequate translation for this term. It is characterised by a process-product

ambiguity, in that it can refer either to a process of 'reaching understanding' (the term his translator Thomas McCarthy employs) or to its product, agreement. Habermas obviously exploits this ambiguity: it distracts attention from the fact that the process may not always yield the product.

5 Commitment and entitlement correspond to the traditional deontic concepts of obligation and permission (cf. Brandom 1994: 160). Rainer Forst speaks of the speaker's moral duty to justify his assertions and intentions and the hearer's corresponding right to receive a justification (2007a: 61).

6 On the differing roles of hearer and listener, see a debate between Habermas and Brandom (Habermas 2000, Brandom 2000). Habermas criticises Brandom for assigning priority to the listener role where it is due to the hearer role.

7 See Habermas 1984, vol. I, chapter 1 and Brandom 1994: chapter four. Judgment and action are, according to both Habermas and Brandom 'precisely the sorts of things reasons can be given for and for which reasons can be asked' (Brandom 1994: 230). Note that Brandom uses 'judgment', which is equivalent to my 'acceptance', not 'belief'. Following the distinction between beliefs and acceptances that was embraced above, beliefs defy the application of deontic concepts such as commitment and entitlement precisely because they are not actions. In this sense it is actions in general that allow and demand justification.

8 Discursive assessment may in some cases be a purely intra-personal process (see Goodin 2000, 'Democratic Deliberation Within'). In this case, the deliberator assumes the roles of both speaker and hearer in turns, querying and challenging her own assertions. However, the intra-personal form of assessment is clearly derivative from the inter-personal one.

9 Habermas argues that the 'rightness of norms of action' is assessed when assessing normative validity claims. However, the rightness of norms can only be assessed by referring to other, superordinate norms. Following a theory assigning priority to linguistic interaction over rational action, the highest-ranking norms should be those guiding language-use: reciprocity and generality (see also Forst 2007b: 249).

10 According to Richardson (2002: 76, 136), democratic deliberation is addressed solely to the question of what we should do. This position has been criticised by authors highlighting the necessity of decision, e.g. Greven 1991, Shapiro 1999.

11 Of course, I cannot know for sure whether the promise will be kept. However, neither can I be sure what the worth of shares I bought today will be tomorrow, although they definitely constitute a good.

12 For an overview of strategies used by politicians to ensure default attribution of entitlement where it is not warranted, see Gastil 1992. Among these strategies are the use of presuppositions and implicatures, generic language, nominalisation, euphemisms, loaded metaphors and many more. Among deliberative democrats, it is controversial how much rhetoric should be permitted in political discourses. Habermas' position is to rule out all kinds of perlocutionary intentions, which rhetoric implies, from communicative interaction (1984, 1: 286–95). Simone Chambers has recently argued for a less 'socratic' understanding of public reason, which allows for rhetorical means and emotional appeals (2004).

13 On the different functions of data, information, evidence, argument and conclusion in the policy-making process, see Majone 1989, chapter 4, particularly pp. 66–8.

14 The existence of practices countervailing polarisation may indeed be one explanatory variable

to account for the success or failure of social movements and political parties. The success of the German Green Party, which developed from a social movement into a well established governmental party within 20 years, might thus be explained by the fact that movement and party have always been highly heterogeneous. The failure of several other parties on the left of the political spectrum might correspondingly be due to too much homogeneity and resulting polarisation.

15 On types of games and mechanisms for the solution of collective action problems, see Holzinger 2003.

16 See Habermas 1984: 19: 'The medium in which we can hypothetically test whether a norm of action, be it actually recognized or not, can be impartially justified is *practical discourse*; this is the form of argumentation in which claims to normative rightness are made thematic.'

17 It is interesting to note, in this context, that economic models of bargaining have nothing to do with communicative interaction at all. In these ideal-type models, perfectly informed players simply calculate the possible compromise and signal consent in it.

18 In game-theoretic terms, co-operation is an option only in mixed-motive games.

19 Grice distinguishes 'implicate/implicature' from 'imply/implication'. He uses the latter for expressions in which something is logically implied and the former for utterances where something is contextually presupposed (somehow 'between the lines').

20 See Gastil 1992: 180–2 on the manipulative use of implicatures. For example, the German politician calling a rival 'the biggest instigator since Goebbels' thereby implicated a comparison of this rival with Goebbels. This comparison could not have been defended as an explicit claim, but the implicature could be used to propose the idea to listeners.

21 The last two stand in a kind of analogy to Habermas' distinction between moral and practical-political discourses, in that moral reasons would dominate moral discourses and reasons of interest practical-political discourses (cf. Habermas 1994: 187–207).

22 Schumpeter claimed that, for the average citizen, 'mere assertion, often repeated, counts more than rational argument' (quoted in Sanders 1997: 354). What is obviously irrational where empirical questions are concerned may help individuals to consult their feelings on how to weight conflicting practical reasons. See also Chambers 2004 for a defence of emotional speech and rhetoric means in political discourses.

23 Which is a reason for many deliberative democrats to reject direct democracy (see Offe 1992, 1998 and Goodin 1986, 2003).

24 On commensurability of practical reasons as a precondition of rational choice, see Richardson 2002: 106 and Richardson 1994, sec.17.

25 Implicit majority decision can occur when an overwhelming majority of interlocutors embraces a certain assumption as a premise for further arguing and decisions, leaving disagreeing members with the alternatives either to quit the discourse or to adopt the premise even if they do not think it correct. Unwilling to renounce all influence on the eventual decision, they may choose to yield to the implicit majority verdict and remain in the discourse.

26 Steiner *et al.* have developed a set of indicators of discourse quality that take the dialogical quality of an interaction into consideration in order to measure discourse quality in a somewhat objective fashion. Indicators are the level of justification (from 'no justification' to 'sophisticated justification'), the content of the justification (egalitarian or non-egalitarian), the mutual respect expressed by participants (are counterarguments and mediating proposals

valued?) and the amount of 'constructive politics', i.e. the degree to which compromises are sought and justified (see Steiner *et al.* 2005, Spörndli 2004).

27 Respect may, of course, be expressed dishonestly. To the extent that this is the fact, the discourse is non-democratic.

chapter three | institutional context and modes of interaction

The last chapter pointed out that the discursive co-ordination of acceptances and practical reasons can induce rational preference-transformation, and that political decisions and the formation of political preferences require such co-ordination. The goal of this chapter is to identify modes of political interaction that promote or impede co-ordination and preference-transformation. To begin with, I discuss the relationship between actors and institutions and point out why institutions should be considered as important constraints on interaction, rendering some modes of interaction more likely than others (section 1). Moreover, I will address the idea that deliberation can be employed as an instrument in institutional design in order to increase the quality and efficacy of decisions (section 2). Based on the assumption that, for communicative interaction to have effects on actor preferences, justificatory and co-ordinative incentives must be given, I identify four ideal-typical modes of interaction and discuss their possible institutionalisation (section 3). To the extent that a mode of interaction is successfully institutionalised, hypotheses on whether and how action plans will be co-ordinated and preferences transformed can be derived (section 4). The theoretical framework for the analysis of interaction and the effects of institutional properties on actor preferences and their transformation is thus being completed.

1. ACTORS AND INSTITUTIONS

The relationship between actors and institutions is central to all social sciences. The term 'actor' simply denotes any entity capable of intentional behaviour, usually a human individual. The term 'institution', by contrast, is more ambiguous. To many sociologists, anything that is, in the widest sense, a product of human interaction may be referred to as an 'institution'. As opposed to this, political scientists tend to restrict the use of the term to formal institutions. In the most narrow sense, these are organisations such as, for example, the Westminster parliament, the European Commission or the United Nations. In a wider sense, political institutions are said to include all legally binding and legally sanctioned norms, from traffic regulations to criminal law to the voting rules for the election of representatives.

The relationship between social norms and positive law can be seen as circular in character: laws represent and are built upon pre-existing norms and normative beliefs and are, at the same time, internalised by actors and used as norms and rules of conduct. Positive law might hence be regarded as a formalisation of social norms, or, in other words, as an institutionalisation of institutions. The sanctions for violation of social norms may be equally severe as those for breaking the law. The difference is that, in the latter case, sanctions are not only regarded as legitimate but are to be enforced upon everyone to whom the law is addressed (typically, people living in the territory of a given state) and to apply in every given situation.

The issue of sanctions is dominant in economic treatments of institutions. Here, institutions are seen as constraints on individual action. By demanding behaviour that follows certain rules, and by imposing sanctions on deviant behaviour, institutions increase the costs connected with particular courses of action or even rule them out altogether. At the same time, institutions provide a degree of certainty about the behaviour of other actors, which is crucial in situations of interdependence. By relieving actors of the burden of deciding under conditions of uncertainty, institutions play an enabling as well as a restricting role (Windhoff-Héritier 1991: 40–1). This will be equally true for formal and informal institutions. What matters are the probability and severity of sanctions, on the one hand, and the expectation that others will abide by the rules, on the other hand. Economic perspectives might therefore renounce the distinction between formal and informal institutions and focus instead on the consequences of institutions for individual choice sets and choices. Empirically, however, formal institutions are far easier to observe and can be claimed to exist 'objectively', which commonly leads to a certain bias towards formal institutions.

A too-wide 'sociological' concept of institutions, moreover, would lead to problems for actor-centred analysis as it entails a challenge to fundamental assumptions. As pointed out before, a general principle to guide action, namely that of rationality, may constitute an integral requirement for the perception of individual identity. The general rules embodied in formal and informal institutions can similarly be regarded as possible and likely components of the identity of those who abide by them. The idea that institutions both constrain and enable actions may therefore be taken even further, to the notion that action is determined by institutions. In this conception, institutions not only prevent actors from choosing particular courses of action but make it inconceivable for actors to do so: institutions, in this sense 'influence behaviour not simply by specifying what one should do but also by specifying what one can imagine oneself doing in a given context' (Hall & Taylor 1996: 948). Sanctioned options would not even occur to actors, or feature in deliberation. The result of such a wide understanding of institutions at the analytical level is a complete breakdown of the distinction between identity and institutions.

A far-reaching commitment to institutionalism would also imply an epistemically constructivist stance: the observer will have to regard the results of her own research as determined by the culture she lives in and the institutions she is part of. If one seeks to refuse this pessimist view, the free will of actors and their successful representation of an independent, 'objective' reality will need to play a role in theorising and, hence, lead the analyst to abandon the determinism between situation and decision. An actor-centred or action-theoretical approach must imply a certain amount of epistemic optimism, i.e. the assumption that there exists an objective reality that actors and observer have access to.

Moreover, a liberal-democratic view demands institutions to be so constructed as to serve and protect individual interests, not as to produce them. The institution of democracy, in particular, has the essential purpose of enabling individuals to exercise their autonomy as rational, goal-oriented actors. Without autonomy of preferences, the entire project of democracy becomes pointless. In this case, democracy becomes an end in itself, as institutions must be expected to simply produce the preferences that are necessary for their own reproduction. In the case of the fundamental institution of democracy itself, this effect may be desirable. But the measures for individual welfare cannot themselves be products of democratic decision-making. It is only as a means for individuals to pursue and protect their welfare that democracy is meaningful, not as an end in itself (cf. Elster 1997).

Epistemic optimism also seems to be a precondition for political optimism: if politics is about the creation of institutions in the form of collectively binding rules, it will be essential to policy planning and implementation to assume that the actions and decisions actually 'make a difference'. That is, the institutions political actors seek to create must not be regarded solely as a function of already existing institutions. A political science that regards politics as meaningful and seeks to be either critical or constructive cannot therefore assume a radically institutionalist and constructivist perspective. In addition to, and in a consequence of the epistemic optimism they imply, action-theoretical approaches also entail more potential for generalisation and for a systematic framework of hypotheses.

In the context of this book, institutions are particularly relevant with regard to their consequences for the probability of preference-transformation. In the last chapter, it was pointed out that rational transformation of preferences is enabled and promoted by the interactive exchange and co-ordination of acceptances and practical reasons. Accordingly, properties of institutions will be considered with a focus on their constraining or enabling effects on linguistic interaction. Given that different types of linguistic interaction advance the change of acceptances and practical reasons, an institutional setting in which a specific type of interaction is produced can be made instrumental for the transformation (or preservation) of preferences.

2. DELIBERATION AS INSTRUMENT

If one takes the promises of deliberative democracy – epistemic progress and consensus – seriously, it follows that deliberation can be used as an instrument in the pursuit of these goals. Hardin (1999) has argued that deliberation is best understood not as a normative theory of decision-making but as a method for evaluating options and preparing decisions. He points out that long before the 'deliberative turn in democratic theory' (Dryzek 2000: 1), deliberation was used instrumentally by officials and representatives, albeit in a hardly democratic fashion. Citizens were not normally involved in this sort of communication, their role was reduced to participation in elections. What is more, deliberation in committees and bureaucracies is most likely to be a feature also of any well-functioning authoritarian regime.

The previous chapter has indicated that although equality, openness and heterogeneity contribute to the epistemic success of discourses, democracy is neither a necessary nor a sufficient condition for it. The size of a forum is likely to impede on the probability of consensus: wide democratic participation is an obstacle to rather than an instrument for the co-ordination of preferences. Despite these shortcomings on the participatory, input-side of democracy, the idea of rational and consensual decision-making enjoys great popularity among opinion leaders, politicians, social scientists and ordinary citizens. While the democratic quality of deliberative institutions and decision-making is an issue that needs to be addressed from a normative perspective, my focus here is a different one.[1] Before considering the question of how deliberative institutions can be rendered more democratic, it is essential to show how institutional factors affect chances for epistemic progress and consensus. Regardless of whether or not existing deliberative institutions satisfy participatory expectations, their potential to transform preferences in such a way as to produce knowledge or consensus yet needs to be demonstrated analytically and empirically.

The institutional focus on deliberation can be justified from several perspectives. Zintl (2006) points out that the appropriate objective for rationalist theories of politics should not be to explain individual actions but rather to show how institutional logic and constraints affect the likelihood for certain patterns of behaviour to occur. Holzinger (2005) shows that the context within which communicative interaction takes place determines the choice of communication modes such as arguing or bargaining. From his work on group polarisation, Sunstein also draws the lesson that we should devote more attention to the question of how institutional factors influence the course discourses are likely to take (Sunstein 2003: 98). Moreover, given the ubiquity of communicative interaction in both private and political life, it is not only necessary to ask *how* deliberation is to be institutionalised but also *where* it is to be institutionalised. Is it more important in the preparation of decisions, as a tool for decision-making itself or in the evaluation of decisions? Is the instrument of deliberation more successful at tackling some types of conflicts than at tackling others? As Ian Shapiro aptly concludes: 'Asking the question whether deliberation is a good thing is a bit like asking the question of whether a saw is a good tool. If you are making shelving it is, but not if you are trying to repair a watch' (2003: 127).

Focusing on the institutional contexts within which deliberative interaction and preference-transformation are more or less likely to occur also addresses a point that deliberative democrats are often criticised for neglecting: the problem of institutionalisation. Habermas himself has been reluctant to offer specific proposals as to how his ideas are to be translated into institutional structures. Others have proposed different types of forums for citizen participation and deliberation but have been less clear on the exact role these institutions are to play in the political decision-making process.[2] The problem here seems to be that authors have a normative ideal of a power-free and inclusive discourse in mind. This ideal either cannot be institutionalised at all, or only outside established political institutions and without significant impact on these. In order to be useful not only as a normative ideal but also as an empirical theory of politics, however, deliberative democracy must detach itself from counterfactual ideals and come to embrace the fact that institutions can be more or less deliberative – and more or less democratic. Only if the more deliberative institutions do indeed increase the probability of epistemic (or rather: pragmatic) progress and consensus (or rather: successful coordination) can the appeal for more deliberation be justified empirically.[3]

It seems that the promises of deliberative democracy are in fact being taken quite seriously, with the theory constituting the dominant discourse in democratic theory (cf. Bohman 1998; Dryzek 2000). Linked to the success of deliberative theory is the call for institutional reform and the creation of new, deliberative institutions. The overall number of extra-parliamentary, or mandated, forums or commissions has increased largely in most Western countries over the last two decades (van Thiel 2004). Some of these are charged with preparation or evaluation of decisions, others with decision-making itself.[4] It is beyond doubt that politician's reasons for setting up such institutions are instrumental. Instrumental for what, though?

It would be somewhat cynical to assume that purely selfish motives such as blame-avoidance are the only ones, although they definitely play a substantial role. Rather, there exist a number of possible motives that are, in most instances, mixed and which motivate the concrete choice of composition, tasks and decision-rules for a new institution. Among these are the necessity to cope with complexity and uncertainty and find instrumentally appropriate policies for existing goals, the wish to increase participation and legitimacy and the need to win the consent of conflicting interest groups. The institutionalisation of a conflict will also be the result of a meta-conflict about how a problem is best to be dealt with, or, in other words, about the rules of the game. The default solution here is reliance on established parliamentary procedures. Parliamentary decision is always a natural option on the set of institutional alternatives, although the precise procedure can be challenged as well. The meta-conflict and the motives involved in it are reflected in institutional variables, the empirical impact of which can be assessed empirically: does the choice of strategy (i.e. institution) yield the intended result? Could the strategy be improved?

This chapter will, from the theory of preference developed in chapter one and the theory of communicative action presented in chapter II, deductively derive hypotheses on the likely effects of institutionalised modes of interaction on preference-transformation. Modes of interaction and the way in which they are translated into institutionalised forums thus come into play as the independent variable, while preference-transformation is the dependent variable. Four properties of interaction were selected to define ideal-type modes of interaction, which are developed in section 3 of this chapter: the ratio of speakers, hearers and listeners, the definition of the conflict, the definition of actors' roles, and the definition of the task or function of interaction. Each of the four properties can occur in four (nominally) different values. It is assumed that on the basis of the theoretical considerations in chapters one and two, the effect of each of the properties in a specific value on the probability and type (cognitive or volitive premises) of preference-transformation is to some extent predictable.

As pointed out in the last chapter, two aspects are particularly important as prerequisites for preference-transformation and hence deserve particular attention: the justificatory and the co-ordinative pressures and incentives exerted in a given situation of interactive decision-making. Only if both preconditions are fulfilled can changes in the premises of preferences be expected. Each of the properties of interaction will therefore be assessed for its impact on justification and co-ordination, from which hypotheses on preference-transformation will be inferred.

However, a problem with properties of interaction is that it is plainly impossible to create *ceteris-paribus* conditions that would allow us to analyse the effects of each of them separately: neither of the variables can be voluntarily controlled. By contrast, properties of interaction (i.e. variables in specific values) empirically tend to occur in clusters. This strong correlation between properties of interaction and types of institutionalised forums can also be accounted for conceptually: properties of interaction correspond to the differing motives for which forums are instrumentally constructed. The empirical and conceptual arguments for clusters of properties justify the application of ideal-types. Properties of interaction that are not employed for the definition of the ideal-types will be considered only as possible intervening variables, just like the large number of other contextual factors that can affect outcomes.

Such intervening variables have an influence on when and how precisely the independent variable (mode of interaction and its institutionalisation) affects the dependent variable (preference-transformation).[5] For example, the causal relationship between the institutionalised mode of interaction and actor preferences may be interrupted by external events with far-reaching consequences, such as a terrorist attack, which leads to changes in preferences even where the institutional context would normally rule them out. A mediating variable may further allow to account not only for the fact of preference-transformation but also for its course. The framework developed so far only aims to accomplish the former, while a more complex, multi-variable one might also be capable of explaining why precisely an actor ended up with a preference for A over B rather than vice versa. One important contextual factor to be considered is the system of primary (constitutional) institutions within which new forums are created and charged with tasks. A different system of government and political culture will set different constraints and create different opportunities for interaction in a newly established body. The assumption, then, is only that *ceteris paribus*, approximation to one of the ideal-types increases the probability of a specific outcome.

3. CONTEXTUAL DETERMINANTS OF INTERACTION

3.1 The ratio of speakers, hearers and listeners

The 'scale problem' has often been remarked as a challenge to theories of deliberative democracy (Parkinson 2003). Electorates are much larger in modern democracies than in ancient ones, in which participation was restricted by status. A debate in which every citizen was present to justify their position for even a single minute would last years and be an impossible thing to organise. But even forums of the size of ancient city states (or even modern parliaments) do not allow for a thorough exchange and assessment of arguments and positions. Hence, deliberative institutions, where they are proposed and implemented, entail forums that are smaller than the respective electorate. From the background of a theory of communicative interaction, interaction can be considered under two different aspects concerning the number of interlocutors. First, the number of hearers may be higher or lower. Secondly, the number of speakers may be higher or lower.

The first aspect is that of publicity and secrecy, which has been widely discussed by deliberative democrats.[6] If the number of hearers is high, interaction is public in nature. Modern communication technology (radio, TV, internet) can easily increase the number of hearers to millions or even billions. The number of speakers can, quite obviously, not be higher than the number of hearers. Speaking requires at least one interlocutor; and contributing to a discussion typically implies willingness to hear the contributions of other speakers. Where the number of speakers approximates the number of hearers, an interaction may be classified as dialogical.

The constitutive feature of a dialogue seems to be that every hearer has the chance to become a speaker and to query, challenge or simply comment on other speakers' assertions. A situation is monological if these constitutive features of a dialogue do not fully obtain and it is the more monological the less they obtain. In the traditional definition, a monologue is the speech of a single person, addressed to listeners rather than hearers. A listener, as noted before, is distinguished from a hearer by two things. Contrary to the hearer, the listener cannot react to commitments undertaken by the speaker. As a consequence, she can observe a speaker and engage in keeping score of their commitments without incurring her own commitments. More than that, the listener simply cannot undertake commitments even if she wants to. The discursive role of the listener reduces to silent evaluation without active participation. The hearer of a monologue thus necessarily becomes a listener.

The monological character of interaction is partly a function of the number of interlocutors. The more participants there are, the more of them will be turned into listeners without a chance to undertake or challenge commitments. Even where the floor is not occupied by a single speaker, contributors will begin to address the audience rather than one another. This is because the listener is far more convenient to address than the hearer: the possible gain, consisting in persuasion, is the same. The risk, consisting in challenging questions and counter-arguments, is far lower. The stronger the competition for floor-time is (depending on the number of potential speakers), the more difficult interventions and challenges will become.

Speakers will then react to one another without actually interacting with one another.

Combining the dimensions of publicity–secrecy and dialogue–monologue, four types of communicative situations can be distinguished:

Table 3. 1: Publicity, secrecy, dialogue and monologue

	Publicity	*Secrecy*
Dialogue	discussion, deliberation	bargaining, private conversation, counselling
Monologue	speeches and announcements, public debates	diary, soliloquy

A secret monologue seems to be a less likely and politically irrelevant case. Even the deliberative processes going on *within* our own minds are more appropriately and more commonly described as a dialogue. The only cases approximating a secret monologue would be a private diary or a soliloquy, although most people keeping a diary would probably admit that, when writing, they are at least imagining a reader other than themselves.

The number of situations constituting secret dialogues is larger. Private conversations take place in small circles and are not easily accessible to further speakers, hearers or listeners. For counselling situations between a lawyer or a psychotherapist and their clients, secrecy is even a matter of contract. Politically relevant examples of secret dialogues are contexts of bargaining and mediation. Bargaining is dialogical because each participant is a veto-player who must be given the chance to make threats and offers and to signal refusal or consent. It usually takes place behind closed doors, to enable trades in votes, logrolling, compensations and thus, compromise.

Public monologues are equally common in political life. Politicians frequently address the electorate in speeches and announcements that are directed at listeners, not hearers: there is no way to reply to them, they are entirely uni-directional. Maybe somewhat surprisingly, the typical 'debate' also qualifies as a monologue. A debate, as the term is traditionally used, is distinguished from a discussion or conversation by its competitive element. The point in a debate is not to track truth or to reach a consensus but to win a competition for support or votes. In debating clubs, where the debate is essentially an end in itself, participants try to display rhetorical skills and argumentatively defeat their opponent.

Where defeat rather than persuasion is the goal, the audience assumes the role of a referee. In debating competitions, the audience normally elects a winner. In consequence, speeches are directed at listeners, not hearers and potential speakers. The same holds true for parliamentary debates. Although parliaments are frequently idealised as deliberative forums, interaction in them is typically far away from the dialogical ideal of deliberation.[7] Speakers do not intend to convince other members of the house, but voters at the TV-screens, opinion leaders such as journalists, or, at most, members of their own party, none of whom normally gets a chance to become a speaker. Contributions to parliamentary debates therefore have more or less the same monological, uni-directional character as other public speeches and announcements.

Two types of interaction that qualify as public dialogue I respectively label 'discussion' and 'deliberation'.[8] The point in what I define below as a discussion is a definition of the given situation by means of information pooling and argumentative contestation rather than making a decision. This requires a larger number of contributors and is likely to be public as there appears to be no sound justification for keeping empirical information and generalisable arguments secret.[9] A second type of public dialogue takes place where deliberation is successfully institutionalised. In ancient times, deliberation among citizens reportedly happened in city democracies and, in modern times, different types of participatory procedures are seen as institutionalisations of it. The point in deliberation is less an exchange of information (which is in a sense presupposed), but an exchange and co-ordination of individual practical reasons for preferring or rejecting options. Such a process must obviously be a dialogical one that does not require secrecy: reasons that are named by speakers in justifying practical commitments are potentially shared and hence public ones. As will be further elaborated below, it is the private character of practical reasons that requires bargaining to be secret.

Nevertheless, there is a certain contradiction between dialogue and publicity, just as between monologue and secrecy. If the dialogue is fully public in the sense of being accessible to any potential hearer or speaker, competition for floor-time will increase and render interaction more monological. The mere presence of listeners (who do not compete for floor-time but engage in scorekeeping and can be convinced) will further contribute to this tendency. To secure the dialogical character of such forums, it will thus be necessary to restrict their overall size from the beginning. The restriction in size need not imply secrecy, however. Rather, the doors can be closed without being tightly closed. Where participants can still carry arguments and information in and out of the forum and where the proceedings of the forum are presented to a wider public, the publicity of reasons and justification can be preserved in spite of limited access.[10]

Whether interaction is secret or public, dialogical or monological is assumed to be an important determinant for the probability of preference transformation. Following the concept of preference developed in chapter one, preference change can have either of two origins: a change in cognitive premises (acceptances) or in volitive premises (practical reasons and their aggregation). Accordingly, the dimensions isolated here should be considered separately for their effects on each type of premises. The impact of publicity, secrecy, dialogue and monologue on the probability of preference-transformation is due to two factors, which must be understood as preconditions for preference change.

The first of these is the force to justify one's position and preferences in terms of generalisable, impartial and hence public reasons that can potentially be shared by other actors. Only non-private reasons (whether epistemic or practical) can induce changes in the cognitive or volitive premises of preference, because these are the only ones that are transferable and can assume inter-subjective validity. Elster notes that 'secrecy tends to induce bargaining, and publicity to induce argument', as 'the norm against expression of self-interest will be stronger in public settings than if the debates are conducted behind closed doors' (1995: 252, 249). It seems that, once an actor's self-interest is expressed or perceived in an interaction, all further arguments brought by the respective person will be treated as private and non-generalisable.[11] The reason why closed doors encourage bargaining is that, behind them, the point is less to convince one another of the benefits of a course of action than to settle on a course of action. Otherwise, the doors could as well be left open: it can do no harm to convince more people (although increasing the number of speakers might be an obstacle).

This leads to the second precondition for preference-transformation, which Elster finds to be in contradiction with the justification-condition. Publicity, and in particular the presence of listeners, promotes a competitive, adversary logic of interaction as well as precommitment-strategies and inflexibility (Elster 1995: 249–50). One cannot 'win' anything by publicly yielding to the force of the better argument. Defeating an opponent in an argumentative competition first of all requires that one demarcate oneself from them, which is likely to lead to actors assuming more extreme positions than they normally would.[12] Giving in to stronger reasons and admitting errors can in such a context generate opprobrium and is often perceived as a loss of face. The amount of opprobrium increases with the size of the audience and thus with the degree of publicity (see Brennan & Pettit 2004, chapter ten). The resulting inflexibility of positions raises the stakes for co-ordination. Elster concludes that we are, consequently, stuck with the second-best and third-best options of secret bargaining and public argument (or rather: debate), which are arguably the most frequent ones.

Distinguishing the dimensions of publicity–secrecy and dialogue–monologue, however, leaves a more favourable picture. Consider first the effects of each factor on justification and coordination:

Table 3.2: Publicity/Dialogue – effects on Justification and Coordination

	Justification	Coordination
Publicity	+	+
Secrecy	-	+
Dialogue	+	+
Monologue	-	-

It becomes clear that, while the effects of publicity and secrecy on the preconditions for preference change are contradictory, the effects of dialogical and monological interaction are unambiguous. Dialogue clearly promotes justification, as reasons can easily be queried and challenged. It also promotes co-ordination, in that interaction of a dialogical kind can only be sustained if actors succeed in establishing a set of joint acceptances and reasons. Acknowledging the validity of the other's points, admitting errors and misunderstandings, conceding and compromising are necessary elements of two-directional communicative action. This is in essence Habermas' 'telos of reaching understanding', discussed in the previous chapter, that is 'inherent in human speech'.

Justification, although it is often the purpose behind a monologue, is nonetheless hardly improved by it. What is being justified in a monologue is subject to the choice of the speaker, who is more or less free to raise claims without justifying them, to presuppose justification where none has been given and to ignore relevant counterarguments wherever she pleases. Although a listener may be convinced by an eloquent speaker's reasons, he will also be aware of the discursive limitations of the situation. In particular if the listener is critical of the speaker's position, a monological performance, however brilliant, is unlikely to transform his preferences. Justificatory monologues are hence more likely to reinforce existing preferences (offering new arguments for preferences actors already hold) than to transform them.

Interaction that ranks high in both the dimensions of publicity and dialogue and which therefore promotes the transformation of preferences will be labelled 'discursive'. Discursiveness of interaction is assumed to be the single most important causal factor for preference change.

Definition discursiveness: Interaction is discursive if it is both public and dialogical.

According to the matrix above, rational preference-transformation can only be expected where the institutional setting promotes discursive interaction, i.e. where both publicity and dialogue obtain:

Table 3.3: Definition Discursiveness

	Publicity	*Secrecy*
Dialogue	+	-
Monologue	-	-

3.2 Types of conflict

A second important factor that is likely to affect the probability of preference-transformation is the type of conflict with which actors are confronted. The origin of political conflict, to begin with, is actors' differing acceptances and incompatible goals. If no such differences did exist, co-ordination and thus meaningful communicative interaction would be unnecessary. Preference-transformation would then occur only spontaneously, not in consequence of interaction. This type of purely intra-personal, endogenous preference change is beyond the focus of this project and will therefore be neglected. The cases which are of interest here are those where a discursively identified conflict, or difference, affects either of the decisions involved in preference-formation.

Holzinger distinguishes three types of conflicts: conflicts over facts, conflicts over values and norms, and conflicts of interest (2004: 199–200). The type of conflict is supposed to motivate the choice of either of the communication modes of arguing or bargaining. The communication mode of arguing demands a dialogical structure of assertion, challenge and justification, which has been identified above as a prerequisite for preference change. The communication mode of bargaining aims at a consensual compromise but makes a defence of the own position by means of generalisable reasons dispensable. Following Holzinger's analysis, conflicts over facts and norms should increase the probability of preference change while conflicts of interest should decrease it.

For conflicts over facts, the case seems particularly clear. The truth is something actors normally conceive of as one and as existing prior to and independent of their contingent positions: 'Whatever the correct position is in each case, it does not depend on the agreement of the parties to the conflict' (Holzinger 2004: 199). Accordingly, the truth of a proposition is nothing that could be settled by compromise or majority vote.[13] Trying to establish the truth of a proposition, actors have no choice but to argue. Observation and trial-and-error experiments surely play a role in this process, too, but in order to be made serviceable in the pursuit of truth, they need to be translated into argumentative justification. Evidence is but one justifying reason that can be named for a given assertion.

If actors need to co-ordinate their divergent epistemic acceptances, they will have to argue until the 'force of the better argument' has left only a single position tenable. If the force of the better argument drives not only discursive (possibly hypocritical), but also intra-personal acceptance, we should expect the justificatory discourses by which factual conflicts are resolved to motivate changes in the cognitive premises of preference and hence expect the probability of preference-transformation to increase where conflicts concern facts. However, although reaching agreement may be present as a 'telos' in factual disputes, it can never be their explicit goal. The goal is to track truth and the adversary logic that promotes the pursuit of truth ensures that complete agreement can never be achieved.

The case with conflicts over norms and values seems similar. As pointed out in the previous chapter, the difference between factual and normative discourses is mainly that in the former, observation reports (i.e. evidence) typically function as unjustified justifiers while for the latter, ultimate, highest-ranking values assume this role. In so far as we assume a 'moral truth' existing prior to and independent of our conflict and respective positions, moral conflicts can be understood as a specific type of factual conflict which is to be resolved in the same manner. If another speaker can, by means of logic, thought experiments or empirical information, be convinced that a statement or action is not in keeping with fundamental values, their commitments will be revised. However, does a change in normative acceptances constitute a transformation in the cognitive or in the volitive premises of preference? Does a normative reason justify doxastic or practical commitments?

As argued above, the appeal to norms or values implicates that these are shared by the interlocutor. That a value is shared does not mean that it is simply acknowledged as a possible justification for a given commitment. Rather, it implies that the value generates practical reasons for action which are supposed to motivate the same choice of alternatives. A conflict over values is therefore not a conflict over the existence and validity of ultimate values – which are supposed to be shared – but over how these values are to be specified in context and over how they are to be weighed against one another. For a resolution, conflicts over values require that actors co-ordinate the aggregation procedures they apply to their own diverse and typically conflicting practical reasons.

As actors typically struggle to find a rationalisable stance in matters of fundamental values, there are strong incentives for justification and co-ordination in such conflicts. What is an acceptable compromise between shared, but conflicting values and a presumably right or good solution is presumed to be that which can reasonably be agreed upon. The discursive success or failure of justifications can then be expected to affect the volitive premises of preferences. Nonetheless, it also seems possible that values and the practical commitments that can be justified by reference to them are discussed in a more theoretical sense and without being relevant to the participants' immediate action-orientations. In this case, conflicts of value are in a sense redefined as conflicts of fact, as it sometimes happens in academic discourses concerning normative theories, for example in practical philosophy.

The case is different where the reasons that motivate practical commitments are not based on shared highest-ranking values. The lack of shared practical reasons is the primary characteristic of conflicts of interest. 'Selfish' reasons of interest are a typical case of non-transferable reasons: your interest in policy A is a reason for you to promote A, but it is no reason for me to want it. In competitive situations, it may on the contrary even be a reason for me not to want it. However, reasons can fail to be shared without being selfish. In a given situation, non-selfish moral reasons named for a practical commitment may turn out to be non-transferable. A justification in terms of a fundamental value that is not shared, though, is not relevant to the hearer and thus futile.[14]

If justification is lacking, so too is a prerequisite for preference change. Nonetheless, there may be strong incentives for co-ordination if non-co-operative strategies prevent all actors from achieving their individual goals. Such co-ordination in the absence of shared reasons (and even in the absence of shared acceptances) is achieved by bargaining. In this case, other speakers' preferences and the cognitive and volitive premises they are based on are not regarded as potential motives for their own decisions but as constraints on one's prospects. Incentives for co-ordination without pressures for justification are unlikely to have a positive effect on the probability of preference-transformation. The challenge in such situations lies solely in achieving the best possible deal with regard to one's existing preferences. The consensus emerging from successful bargaining then displays actor preferences over joint action under the constraints of each other's preferences.

In a political context, all conflicts are in the end conflicts about what to do, collectively. Factual conflicts are conflicts in a political context only in so far as different action strategies follow from differing acceptances about the world, moral conflicts are conflicts only in so far as different ultimate values demand differing policy choices. Conflicts of interest, where they are politicised rather than left to market mechanisms, indicate a need to establish new decision-systems to deal with them. The ability of a government to establish such implies a power to manipulate its institutional parameters and affect relative bargaining power (Scharpf 1997: 201). The political conflict about collective action is hence involved in all other types of conflicts and entails aspects of all of them. A decision about political action in the name of the collective is subject to particular justificatory pressures along the dimensions of fact, value and interest. Collectively binding decisions would be impossible, though, in the absence of majority rule – at least as long as we assume that unanimous consensus is an unrealistic goal in either dimension. Once a majority has been established in a conflict over action, further co-ordination is not necessary, so that incentives for it are likely to be reduced.

Empirically, it will hardly ever be possible to classify a conflict as pure with regard to its origin. Factual questions are often intertwined with questions of value, and conflicts of value sometimes conceal conflicts of interest. In particular, conflicts of interest are unlikely to remain unaffected by normative and factual disagreements. Holzinger (2004: 200) therefore argues that while in conflicts of fact and value, arguing should prevail, bargaining and arguing are likely to coexist in conflicts of interest. Where a mode of interaction is institutionalised to deal with a conflict, what matters is not what the actual mix of aspects involved in it is, but what the conflict to be dealt with is *defined* as by the actors involved in the decision.

The definition of a conflict is part of the meta-conflict surrounding the creation of a new institution and will affect actors' behaviour regardless of the actual nature of the conflict. If a conflict is defined as a factual one, actors will refuse to compromise and deny the legitimacy of different opinions. If a conflict is defined as a conflict of value, actors will seek to justify their positions in terms of shared ultimate values rather than instrumentally and try to co-ordinate their preferences. If a conflict is defined in terms of interest, this will undermine moral motivations: if I believe that everyone else is deciding selfishly, I will rank my own self-regarding reasons higher than my other-regarding reasons for the given decision (cf. Brennan & Pettit 2004: 260–3, 300–4). From the definition of the conflict that the institution is to tackle we can draw conclusions regarding the preconditions for justification and coordination.

Table 3.4: Type of conflict – effects on justification and co-ordination

	Justification	Co-ordination
Factual conflict	+	-
Conflict over values	+	+
Conflict over interest	-	+
Conflict over action	-	-

Table 3.5: Type of conflict – transformation of acceptances and practical reasons

	Transformation of acceptances	Transformation of practical reasons
Factual conflict	+	-
Conflict over values	+	+
Conflict over interest	-	-
Conflict over action	-	-

Factual conflicts offer good conditions for justification but poor ones for co-ordination (as compromises over facts are ruled out). Value conflicts offer good preconditions both for justification with regard to the highest-ranking principles and for co-ordination (assuming that these are shared, compromises on how to specify and combine them must be sought). Conflicts of interest are unfavourable for justification, which interests do not seem to require, but they may under conditions of interdependence motivate co-ordination. Conflicts over action do induce public defences rather than reciprocal justification and thus do not yield new reasons. They neither enhance co-ordination, as they can be resolved by majority voting.

Assuming that the probability of preference-transformation depends on the justificatory and co-ordinative pressures exerted in communicative interaction, the type of conflict that is at stake will affect the conditions for changes and acceptances and practical reasons as shown in Table 3.5.

In sum, both factual conflicts and conflicts over values promote preference change on the basis of communicative interaction, while conflicts that are defined in terms of interest tend to prevent preference-transformation and instead advance maximisation and efficiency considerations. All three types of conflicts are normally entailed in conflicts over political action. However, when a conflict has reached the stage at which the decision is solely about which option for action to choose, coalition-building and vote-seeking tend to replace justification and co-ordination of differing acceptances and practical reasons. Once a compromise between conflicting interests has been established or a majority decision been taken, actors may nonetheless begin to value the solution as such and turn it into a basis for further co-ordination.

3.3 Roles people play

The specific nature and parameters of an individual conflict may have a decisive impact on institutional processes and outcomes and so may the particular actors with their individual skills, knowledge and personality. However, what matters from the present perspective is how actors are defined and what roles are assigned to them rather than what their actual empirical properties are. The selection of members of newly established decision-making bodies and forums is driven by the goals and acceptances of those actors involved in the aforementioned meta-conflict surrounding the creation of a new institution. The selection process, or mandating, of members typically follows a selection-rule that requires candidates to be suitable with regard to a particular dimension. In other words, there is supposed to be a reason for which actors are selected as members, and this reason determines the role they are to play in the respective institution and process.

In political contexts, four types of actor roles may be expected to be of particular importance: the expert, the citizen, the interest-group deputy and the elected representative. The citizen role is commonly contrasted with that of the consumer, where the consumer role is typically evaluated negatively or as a misperception of the citizen role (e.g. Elster 1997: 10–11). The only context in which the consumer role is more or less explicitly appealed to is that of opinion polls. Otherwise, and regardless of whether or not economic models of democracy such as Anthony Downs' (1957) reflect an empirical reality, the consumer role is criticised rather than appealed to in political contexts. Where either of the other four roles is appealed to, the appeal is loaded with a specific set of expectations that will affect incentives for justification and co-ordination and, in consequence, the probabilities that cognitive or volitive premises of preference are transformed.

Experts. Where participants of interaction are defined as experts, the expectation is that of an informed but disinterested verdict on the given conflict or problem. Experts are selected for their superior knowledge and experience in the field concerned. Candidates for this role are principally researchers and academics. Persons selected as experts will, if they seek to fulfil these expectations, try to present their knowledge in an unemotional, conscientiously precise and accessible fashion (with a certain contradiction between the final two). Justification and openness to challenge are part of the academic ethos and the expert role model, so that one of the prerequisites for preference change is obviously promoted where the role of interlocutors is defined as that of experts. What is lacking in this case, however, are incentives for co-ordination. An expert is not a better expert if she agrees with her colleagues but, on the contrary, may be seen as falling short in dimensions such as innovativeness and originality. Adversary and competitive logics promote dissociation and the development of contending schools and counteract the co-ordinative forces of justificatory language-use. Compromises between contrary acceptances are ruled out by the paramount goal of truth.[15]

Citizens. The concept of the citizen is much discussed in philosophical and political-science literature. Again, what is of interest here are the role expectations evoked when actors are appealed to *as* citizens rather than historical and analytical specifications of the concept. The appeal to citizenship is commonly connected with a republican rather than liberal view of politics and society. The individual member of a society is viewed as taking an active role in shaping the conditions under which she lives rather than as a mere consumer of policy outputs. Active citizen-participation in policy-making is supposed to be driven by considerations about the common good, by moral values and the collective interest rather than selfish individual interests. In the normative ideal, the citizen is well-informed, takes into consideration positions and opinions other than her own, weighs reasons and evaluates alternatives and seeks deliberative interaction (Ackermann & Fishkin 2003: 21–4). Whereas the consumer obtains esteem and gratification for instrumentally rational choices, the citizen receives esteem for responsible, moral and informed choices. Where this role-model and normative ideal is appealed to, actors may be expected to adapt their behaviour correspondingly. The citizen role entails pressures for justification in terms of transferable and shared reasons but also urges co-ordination and compromise. Where citizens interact in a forum, the point is to arrive at a common verdict on 'what *we* ought to do', taking all things into consideration. An acknowledgment of the need for collective action and decision is implied when one assumes the citizen role.

Interest groups. Interest-group participation is sought essentially for two reasons. First, it appears to serve purposes of democratic representation and legitimation. Groups are, in this case, regarded as part of the civil society and as reflecting a plurality of experiences, values and preferences. A decision in which relevant interest groups had a say can be expected to enjoy higher public support and acceptance, even if their actual influence was minimal. A more important second motive for involving interest groups in decision-making is to surmount or circumvent the veto-points these groups occupy. Veto-points need not be understood in the strict sense of fully effective veto rights. It suffices here to regard them as obstacles to the implementation of an intended policy. Interest-group resources are, typically, the creation of publicity, promotion of public protest and voters' displeasure, as well as non-co-operation where they are involved in the implementation of policy programmes (such as doctors and nurses in health-care programmes). Originally, interest groups were typically defined in terms of interest and thus of private, non-transferable practical reasons. However, there are also organisations that claim to promote general and shared interests which are nonetheless regarded as interest groups (e.g. Greenpeace).

Although they represent positions that may, in principle, be justifiable in terms of shared ultimate values, justification tends to play less of a role where interest groups are involved in decision-making. The positions that interest groups represent are constitutive for their existence and identity, so that to challenge positions would imply to challenge existence. The waiver on justification need not, of course, hold for every concrete position on a given policy. However, involving interest groups *as* interest groups in decision-making entails an acknowledgment of their constitutive goals and values, which, consequently, escape the need for further justification. In addition to this, interest-group deputies face principal-agent conflicts: as agents, they cannot question or revise positions without the consent of their principal. If justification is nonetheless enforced, the reasons provided are likely to be of an indexical, non-transferable kind: 'because we want it'. While pressures for justification are low, incentives for co-ordination are high for interest groups. As it is obvious that its goals cannot be achieved without the collaboration of other actors, the interest group's charge is to maximise goal-achievement under the constraints of other actors' preferences.

Elected representatives. Arthur Benz points out that the relationship between elected decision-makers and their electorate can be viewed either in terms of suspicion, as a principal-agent contract, or in terms of trust, as a relationship of democratic representation (2002: 280–6). Iain McLean discusses different ways in which the parliament can be said to represent the people: as (statistically) accurately reflecting the plurality of its groups and interests or as temporarily and conditionally in charge of its well-being (McLean 1991). According to McLean, the former view is displayed in systems of proportional representation, while the latter is realised in purely majoritarian (first-past-the-post) systems. If elected representatives are to be conceived of as agents, the case is hardly as clear as for interest-group representatives, though. Do the parliamentary majority and minority have the same principal (the people) or different principals (the majority and minority of voters, specific social groups and economic interests)? Are there in either case specific or well-defined goals they are expected to maximise? Does the principal have the opportunity to sanction or replace the agent at will?

While the agent-status is obviously problematic for elected politicians, so is the status of trusted responsible representatives. These ambiguities in role-definition and perception contribute to the particular justificatory pressures connected with the appeal to actors as elected representatives. As such, they need to defend decisions, which cannot be trusted to be good or correct by default, in terms of a common good. However they choose to define the common good, the reasons they name to defend their decisions must be transferable and must ultimately appeal to shared values and goals. This kind of justification is not only a necessarily evil for elected representatives, but also a way of recommending re-election: although they can, as agents, not be sanctioned immediately, they must seek to secure and gain voter support. At the same time, the kind of justification employed by elected representatives often comes as a product rather than as a contribution to the process of communicative interaction.

With regard to co-ordination, incentives also point in a different direction. Although collaboration and compromising definitely play a role in parliamentary politics, such behaviour does not form part of the role expectation for elected representatives and is therefore typically informalised and kept secret. The representative must try to present herself as a knower, as a competent and moral decision-maker. Concessions and admissions of errors and opinion change are interpreted as indicating weakness and unreliability, and thus feared as a loss of face.[16] In sum, while the actor role of elected representative is to some extent favourable for one prerequisite of preference change, justification, it is highly unfavourable for the other, co-ordination. Table 3.6 summarises the expected effects of attributed actor roles on the preconditions for justification and co-ordination.

The actor roles of expert and citizen are assumed to enhance justification, while

Table 3.6: Actor roles – effects on justification and co-ordination

	Justification	Co-ordination
Expert	+	-
Citizen	+	+
Interest group	-	+
Elected representative	+ / -	-

the actor role of elected representative is ambiguous and that of interest group deputy negatively affects the conditions for justification. With regard to co-ordination, the actor roles of citizen and interest-group deputy affect preconditions positively, while the actor roles of expert and elected representative tend to preclude it. Given that justification and co-ordination respectively promote the transformation of acceptances and practical reasons, we expect the effects on preferences will be as shown in Table 3.7.

Table 3.7: Actor roles – effects on transformation of acceptances and practical reasons

	Transformation of acceptances	Transformation of practical reasons
Expert	+ / -	-
Citizen	+	+
Interest group	-	-
Elected representative	-	-

Only in the citizen role, both conditions for preference-transformation are evidently fulfilled. For all other roles, either justificatory or co-ordinative incentives are lacking. The expert role is somewhat ambiguous with regard to the transformation of acceptances. While yielding to the force of the better argument (particularly of evidence) is part of the role expectation, there are also incentives for obstinacy and insistence in opinions. This does not imply that the persons acting as experts, interest-group deputies or representatives do not rationally revise their preferences in many contexts. All that is claimed here is that preference-transformation is not part of their specific role expectation.

3.4 Tasks and functions

The process of policy formulation and selection may be subdivided into different stages. It starts with the definition of a problem, of relevant goals and alternatives, proceeds with a normative evaluation of alternatives and negotiations over the distribution of goods, and ends in a collectively binding decision. Mandated institutions, where they are involved in policy-formulation (not merely implementation), are typically charged with one of first three tasks, while legislative responsibility in the end remains with the parliament. At each of the stages, justification and co-ordination are more or less important for interaction, with the likelihood of preference-transformation varying correspondingly.

Definition. At the stage where a decision problem and situation are defined, the exchange and coordination of acceptances plays the central role. Definitions are obviously subject to strong justificatory pressures, with empirical evidence constituting the ultimate justifying reason (see above). There are also incentives for co-ordination, as a joint definition constitutes the common prior that is indispensable for evaluation, distribution and decision. However, definitions can often be arrived at in an additive manner. It is not yet necessary to decide whether A or B is a more relevant aspect, x or y the better alternative. Instead, it suffices to ascertain that A *and* B are relevant and that x *and* y are alternatives. Practical commitments and reasons for them need not yet be assessed at this stage either. Thus, where the function of interaction is definition, transformation of acceptances is likely to be enhanced while practical reasons are less likely to be affected.

Evaluation. Where alternatives are to be evaluated, with the goal of arriving at a consensus on one of them, practical reasons come into play. Actors need to justify their preferences over courses of collective action by recourse to values and interests. If evaluation is to be an interactive process, pressures for co-ordination are high. Only one alternative can be recommended, which needs to be justified in terms of transferable and shared reasons. Such reasons must be weighed against one another and compromised on in order to arrive at a majoritarian or even consensual decision. As definition logically precedes evaluation, a common prior may be presupposed at this stage, so that acceptances are less likely to be transformed. Instead, the focus will be on the aggregation of shared practical reasons, so that it is a transformation and convergence of the volitive premises of preference that should be expected.[17]

Distribution. The distribution of goods, or benefits and disadvantages from collectively binding decisions, is necessarily a competitive matter. If distribution is made subject to a co-operative decision-making procedure, this implies that each of the participating actors has a certain potential to block or sanction policies, while none can realise the expected benefits unilaterally. If distribution is not decided on in an hierarchical mode, but by co-ordination of actor preferences, justificatory pressures are low. The reasons for each actor to maximise benefits are indexical and do not point in the same direction. However, the impracticability of unilateral strategies constitutes a strong incentive for co-ordination, although the absence of justification and shared reasons leaves little room for preference-transformation.

Decision. The ultimate goal of politics is a collectively binding decision. Such a decision will in nearly all cases require a majoritarian procedure as a 'closing device' (Gaus 1996). In order to win a majority for a proposal or win support for a decision, they need to be justified and defended in comparison with competing proposals and alternative decisions. As far as decision rules provide the majority with the necessary discretion, however, the time for co-ordination has passed once a majority has been established. Preference-transformation is therefore unlikely to occur in the closing procedure of majoritarian decision-making itself.

Discursiveness, which is a function of the dialogical and public properties of a forum, was pointed out as the first defining variable for ideal-type modes of interaction that can be institutionalised to play different roles in the political decision-making process. The implications of the respective definitions of the type of conflict, actor roles and the task of an institution now allow us to state the second. As illustrated above, certain properties of interaction increase incentives for co-ordination and compromise and thus produce favourable conditions for preference-transformation: conflicts defined as being about values or interest, actors assuming the roles of citizens or interest groups and institutions charged with evaluation or distribution all promote co-ordinative actor strategies. *Definition of co-ordinativeness:* Interaction is co-ordinative where the setting provides incentives for the co-ordination of acceptances and practical reasons; and the more co-ordinative, the more incentives it provides.

Co-ordination is promoted where:
- the conflict is defined as being predominately one of interest or value;
- actors assume the role of citizens or interest-group deputies;
- the task a forum is charged with is one of evaluation or distribution rather than definition or decision;
- the necessity and desirability of a collectively binding decision is acknowledged.

The dimensions of discursiveness and co-ordinativeness now enable the definition of ideal-type modes of interaction in political decision-making. The institutionalisation of these modes of interaction, I argue, can be and is in fact attempted in the creation of new political forums.

4. MODES OF INTERACTION AND THEIR INSTITUTIONALISATION

Using the dimensions of discursiveness and co-ordinativeness as axes yields a two-dimensional space in which real instances of interaction can be positioned (see Figure 3.8). The x-axis indicates co-ordinativeness, the y-axis discursiveness. A linear function indicates the inferred probability of preference-transformation, given that actors' preferences differ in their premises: the higher the interaction scores on both co-ordinativeness and discursiveness, the higher is the probability that preferences will be rationally transformed. The zero-point and origin of this function denotes one extreme of interaction, where no incentives exist either for co-ordination or discursive interaction. Accordingly, preference-transformation is ruled out. Preference-transformation is equally ruled out if interaction is zero on either of the two axes, even if the value on the other one is very high. Cases in which discursiveness is maximal but co-ordinativeness zero or vice versa are the second and third extremes. Finally, if discursiveness and co-ordination are equally high, preference transformation becomes maximally probable – this is the fourth extreme case.

For any given real instance of interaction in the two-dimensional space, the probability of preference-transformation can be estimated by dropping a perpendicular through function f on the x or y axis. For the very different cases i (high on discursiveness but low on co-ordinativeness) and j (high on co-ordinativeness but low on discursiveness), the model yields the same probability of preference-change. Case k is as high on co-ordinativeness as j, but higher on discursiveness, and therefore has a higher probability of rational preference-transformation.

On both dimensions, a point exists at which interaction is, respectively, more discursive than non-discursive and more co-ordinative than non-co-ordinative.

Dropping a perpendicular from each of these points divides the two-dimensional space into four sections. It makes sense to assume that the point on the function where the two straight lines meet is also the point where actor preferences are as likely to be transformed as they are to remain stable, i.e. where the probability of preference transformation is 0.5.

Figure 3.8: Discursiveness, Co-ordinativeness and Probability of Preference Transformation

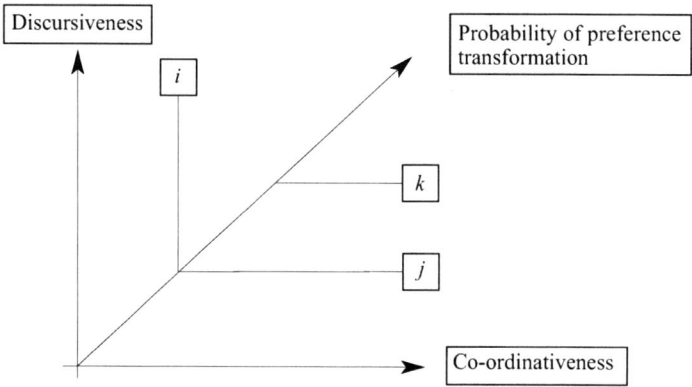

Figure 3.9: Sectors in the discursiveness/co-ordinativeness matrix

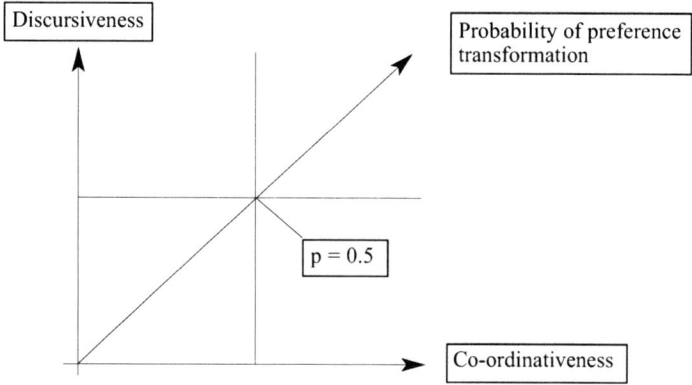

Only in the top-right sector is preference-transformation likely to occur; in the other three, it is more or less unlikely to happen. With each of the sectors, one ideal-type mode of interaction can be associated. Each of them, it will be argued below, has its place in the policy- and decision-making process. The table below translates the axes scheme into a four-field matrix:

Table 3.10: A matrix of ideal-type modes of interaction

	Non co-ordinative	Co-ordinative
Discursive	Discussion	Deliberation
Non-discursive	Debate	Bargaining

The properties of a setting that affect the way people interact in it can now be assigned to these ideal-type modes of interaction:

Table 3.11: Ideal-type modes of interaction and their properties

	Discussion	Deliberation	Bargaining	Debate
Communication	Dialogical publicity	Dialogical publicity	Dialogical secrecy	Monological publicity
Conflict	Factual	Value	Interest	Action
Actor roles	Expert	Citizen	Interest group	Representative
Task	Definition	Evaluation	Distribution	Decision

The construction of the ideal-types is, first of all, conceptually justified. Each mode of interaction can be institutionalised in different ways. For the analysis of the results of such institutionalisation – which amounts to the creation of new political forums – the respective ideal-types serve as useful points of reference. In addition to this, I believe that such ideal-types function as normative ideals in the constitution and composition of new forums. Institutional parameters require a justification in terms of instrumentality and justice. If 'definition' is the task assigned to a forum, the factual nature of the conflict it is to deal with is implicitly acknowledged, experts constitute an instrumental choice of members and dialogical publicity is a defensible style of approaching a decision. Similar arguments can be made for citizen-deliberation and interest-group bargaining. The task of decision itself, by contrast, cannot be mandated: negotiations in other forums take place within the 'shadow of hierarchy', which promotes, enables and sanctions agreements (Scharpf 1997: 197). Even where the government apparently gives up or delegates responsibilities, it still takes a decision to do so, for which it may be held responsible. The default mode of resolving a conflict over collective action is a decision by the actor who is charged with it in modern representative democracies: the parliamentary majority or the government. The mode of interaction ideal-typically connected with majority decisions is that of the parliamentary debate.

All four ideal-type modes of interaction in the form in which they are defined above represent logical and empirical possibilities. At each of the four interfaces between the sectors in the axes scheme, hybrid modes are conceivable. Deviations from ideal-types in one direction or the other may be used to account for deviations from hypotheses on preference transformation. It may be worth mentioning, however, that the ideal-types presented here are in no respect advocated as normative ideals for institution-building. A hybrid institution that enables interaction with elements of both the discussion and the deliberation type may be normatively preferable to both of the extreme types. The ideal-type modes of interaction are expected to be of practical value to the analyst where empirical forums come close to realising them and predictions on preference change are sought. Before an empirical assessment of the value of these ideal-types is undertaken in the following chapter, however, possible institutionalisations of each will be discussed in more detail.

4.1 Discussion

Discussion as a mode of interaction is here defined as discursive but antagonistic rather than co-ordinative in its logic. The *Encyclopedia Britannica* explains discussion as the 'consideration of a question in open and usually informal debate'. The Latin origin of the word points to more aggressive, adversary forms of interaction: it derives from '*discutere*', meaning '1. to batter; 2. to shake off; 3. to assess, to interrogate'. The last meaning highlights pressures for justification and discursiveness, which are also central to the definition here, according to which discussion is ideal-typically both public and dialogical. According to this definition, the conflict in a discussion is defined as one about factual or moral truth: interlocutors disagree about validity claims rather than about what is to be done. Where the role of actors is defined as 'expert' and the goal of interaction is correspondingly one of information, discussion as a mode of interaction is promoted. This is in keeping with the fact that discussions typically lack an explicit decision-rule: if experts do not arrive at a consensus through communication alone (they are often expected to reach consensus but typically don't), they should have no material interest in reaching unanimity by means of compromises. While discussion can improve the justification of acceptances and enable the pooling of information, preference-transformation is an unlikely outcome: the lack of co-ordinative incentives prevents compromises between practical reasons and the 'expert' fears a loss of face if he changes his acceptances.

Expert discussion as a mode of interaction seems comparatively easy to institutionalise. Forums that provide preconditions for expert discussion may be subsumed under the label 'expert commission'. The typical expert commission is a forum authorised to examine the definition of a problem, a situation, or the available alternatives with which a collective is confronted. Expert commissions are created and given responsibility by a hierarchically superior body such as the government or parliament. The typical expectation is that the commission will, through its members' superior information and judgement, arrive at explicit and rational recommendations on policies to adopt. Members usually come from different disciplines and represent different positions within single disciplines. To the public, they are presented as each of them being (one of) the best within their field.[18] The independent status of members as experts can be ensured only if the forum is established ad hoc, to confront a specific definition problem, and disbanded afterwards. Standing expert commissions tend to turn their members from disinterested specialists into civil servants.

The conflict experts are dealing with is presumed to exist in differing definitions of the situation. It is hence typically defined as factual in nature, with the joint goal of establishing the truth. Truth is regarded as the ultimate and also as the only goal in interaction. Members are expected to be entirely free from selfish goals and private interests, and there should be no 'hidden agendas'. The only aspect of the outcome that is supposed to be relevant to them is its truth, which cannot be bargained about or compromised on. The definition produced by an expert commission is expected to be consensually agreed upon, as majority decision is ruled out on the way to truth. As the object of the decision process within an expert commission is the truth of a proposition (or a set of propositions), no recommendations for action can be expected to evolve from it unless the end is explicitly defined beforehand: 'technical expertise will only suffice to justify the choice of efficient means in situations in which the goals are beyond dispute' (Scharpf 1997: 213). The idea that an answer to the question of what we *should* do can be derived from the answer to the question of what *is* the case is a naturalistic fallacy for which there is no room in ideal-typical expert discussion.

Furthermore, a forum for discussion must enable both dialogue and publicity. Dialogue reflects that experts interact as equals and is also instrumental for the thorough assessment of commitments and justifications. The fact that reasons given for commitments undertaken in factual disputes must be general and transferable strongly recommends publicity: a reason for me to accept p as true (e.g. evidence xy) is also a reason for you to accept p as true, and a reason for everyone else, even if they are not present in our discussion. Publicity is not only well justified by the nature of the conflict but also ensures that the conflict is not redefined in different terms and that non-universal, non-transferable reasons do not get the upper hand.

Around the world, there are plenty of examples of political forums in which expert discussion is institutionalised – sometimes more, sometimes less successfully. Three empirical cases will be described in some detail, as they are each representative of many similar cases.

The National Institute of Clinical Excellence, UK

The National Institute of Clinical Excellence (NICE) was set up in 1999 as an expert commission with the task of evaluating new and existing technologies to be funded by the National Health Service (NHS). NICE is intended to improve transparency, participation and quality control and to provide explicit guidance to local health trusts on how to allocate scarce resources. Formally, trusts are still free not to follow NICE recommendations. However, the positive case (funding drugs not recommended) is usually prevented by cash shortages, while the negative case (not funding recommended drugs) is likely to result in public protests. Within NICE, the 'technology appraisal committee', authorised by the Department of Health, evaluates drugs and technologies. Working with three independent chambers, the committee commissions reports from universities or research institutes before it assesses a specific treatment. Besides academic experts, practising nurses and physicians, patient representatives and representatives of the pharmaceutical industry are members of NICE. The committee aims at consensual decisions; however, the chairman can call a simple majority vote if consensus cannot be reached (cf. Landwehr 2006).

The discursiveness of the NICE expert forum is high. Discussions are at least partially public, so that private reasons and bargaining are prevented. Reports and decisions are published promptly, in both expert and lay versions, and justified extensively. In case of negative votes, patients can make use of an appeals procedure and explicitly challenge the reasons given for the decision. With regard to the criterion of co-ordination, by contrast, NICE deviates from the preconditions for ideal-typical discussion. The available option of a majority vote increases incentives for co-ordination, as all members have to bear the decision. Moreover, the fact that the committees are staffed not only with experts but also with interest-group and patient representatives increases the relevance of interests compared to medical and economic controversies, which makes compromises easier.

NICE is a typical example of many expert forums that are firmly institutionalised and have a clearly defined role in the decision-making process. These forums are not created ad hoc to be disbanded after the particular decision has been taken but permanently and thus have a continuing perspective. Institutions of this type often make recommendations or even decisions that are implemented by the government without further public debate and assessment. They tend to become part of the administrative body. In this process, members can lose their independence and the forum its publicity. Commissions of this type are often charged with decisions that require specialised knowledge and are (consequently?) rarely politicised. An extreme example of this type of expert forum is an independent central bank.

The Parliamentary Priorities Commission, Sweden

In Sweden, too, growing demands and shorter budgets increased pressures for priority-setting in the allocation of health care. In contrast to the UK, a parliamentary commission was charged with the development of a priority plan. The commission consisted of seven Members of Parliament, in proportion to the relative strength of the larger parliamentary parties, and nine experts without voting powers. In 1995, the commission presented a consensual report that was discussed in parliament. The parliament ruled that the general principles stated in the report were to be turned into an obligatory basis for concrete allocation-decisions, which, in the decentralised Swedish health-care system were to be taken at the local level (cf. Landwehr 2006).

As the commission's members were appointed in accordance with the parliamentary parties' size, certain parliamentary characteristics were transferred into the forum. Nonetheless, the commission did exhibit a high level of discursiveness. The number of participants was low, which made dialogical interaction easier. At the same time, expert involvement and public hearings kept justificatory pressures high and prevented moves towards bargaining. While the preparation of the decision in the commission to some extent countervailed the antagonistic logic of party competition (possibly helped by the strength of the norm of consensus in Swedish culture), the commission's co-ordinative capabilities were not as strong as might have been expected. The report confines itself to setting out comparatively abstract principles, which are to be converted into concrete decisions by other bodies. It seems that a consensus was possible only at the price of factoring out controversial issues. The far more potentially divisive evaluation of specific treatments and services had to be relocated to a lower level. On the whole, the majoritarian logic of the parliamentary debate seems to have prevented co-ordination after all. One main result was that a similar commission was set up to succeed the first one.[19]

Parliamentary commissions are common in many other countries as well. They usually consist of parliamentarians (typically in proportion with the parliamentary strength of parties) and experts. The latter are often, either officially or unofficially, proposed by the parliamentary members and selected on the basis of party allegiance. Parliamentary commissions often deal with topics that are ethically controversial (such as health-care rationing, genetic engineering or stem cell research) and over which political parties themselves tend to be internally divided. Like the Parliamentary Priorities Commission in Sweden, some of them have produced well known reports, but these rarely resulted in parliamentary decisions. In a sense, the function of parliamentary commissions seems to be to convey a message to citizens that an important topic is on the political agenda, even if a decision is not yet possible.

The Rürup Commission, Germany

The Rürup Commission was created by the German government in 2002 and named after its chairman Bert Rürup, a well known professor of economics and political adviser. The commission was charged with the development of recommendations for the reform of the social-security system, including pensions and health insurance reform. Although the commission was presented as an expert forum, the majority of its members were interest-group deputies rather than academic experts, including, for example, trade union representatives and executives of major corporations and insurance companies.

In 2003, the commission published a final report in which it recommended specific measures for pensions and nursing-care insurance reforms and outlined two alternatives for the future funding of health-care insurance. Subsequently, the commission disbanded. Several of its recommendations have been implemented as legislation and the alternatives outlined for reforming health-care insurance remain on the political agenda. In sum, the commission seemed to reflect the government's programme for welfare-state reform and more or less served to provide additional legitimacy for decisions that had already been taken behind the scenes (cf. Rüb 2003).

The problem with this and similar commissions that are installed by the government to deal with contemporary and highly politicised topics is that they are rarely balanced in composition but rather biased towards the government's position. This reduces their potential for the assessment of acceptances and incentives for conscientious justification of assertions. Moreover, politicisation seems to require the representation of the different interests affected in the policy area. In so far as interest-group deputies are less interested in justification and tracking truth than in preventing policies that run counter to their interests, moves towards bargaining become likely.

Obviously, neither of the three types of expert commissions provides optimal conditions for the realisation of discussion as the mode of interaction. On the contrary, contextual factors seem to prevent the institutionalisation of one pure, ideal-typical mode of interaction. Nonetheless, the examples confirm the assumption that discussion is promoted where:

- Forums are composed of academic experts rather than interest groups (or experts representing interest groups);
- Forums are not too firmly institutionalised but set up to deal with one clearly defined topic; and
- The goal of a forum is defined as one of establishing the premises for making a decision (by identifying goals, values and interests affected by it and by assessing available options for their instrumentality to reach specified goals) rather than taking the decision itself.

Only in so far as the mode of interaction comes close to the ideal-type of discussion will predictions of how this will affect actors' preferences be likely to be accurate.

The following predictions follow for forums in which discussion is institutionalised. Acceptances, as cognitive premises of preference, will be thoroughly assessed and well justified. There are limitations, however, for the revision of existing commitments. The views that experts hold are likely to be the product of previous contestations and appraisals. Within the forum, contradictory claims may well be seen as tenable and dissent viewed as legitimate. However, assuming that members of a commission have a background in different disciplines and schools, actors may gain new information and arguments for existing acceptances rather than change their acceptances. If actors possess a set of consistent and well justified acceptances when the interaction begins, there is no reason why they should not want to complement the set with new ones where these increase coherence and do not violate consistency. The resulting hypothesis is thus that interaction in expert commissions will leave actors with a more comprehensive and better justified set of acceptances rather than with a substantially different set. Convergence of acceptances may be expected in so far that assertions compatible with many actor sets will be added to all of these, so that actors with differing, but non-contradicting sets end up with identical ones.

The case is different where the volitive premises of preference are concerned. Although new information may have an effect on practical reasons, action-plans are not what is at stake in expert discussion. If interaction has an effect on practical reasons and the rules according to which they are aggregated into volitive premises of preference, this effect will be an empirical side-effect rather than a consequence of its logic. Collective goals are either presupposed (like currency stability for central banks) or not defined as a relevant aspect of the conflict being dealt with. With regard to the volitive premises of preference, expert commissions tend to provide little incentives for justification or co-ordination.

4.2 Deliberation

Deliberation is defined as the only type of interaction that is both discursive and co-ordinative. The *Encyclopedia Britannica* describes it as 'a discussion and consideration by a *group* of persons of the *reasons for and against a measure*' (emphasis added). This description comes very close to my own idea, as does the meaning of its Latin origin *deliberare*: 'to weigh, to consider, to reflect'. Compared to some explications found in the extensive literature on deliberative democracy, the definition of deliberation as an ideal-typical mode of interaction here is thus rather parsimonious. Deliberation is public and dialogical, and thus discursive, and it is characterised by strong co-ordinative incentives. These incentives are, in large part, due to the conflict being defined as a political conflict about the evaluation of alternative *measures* (i.e. policies) rather than about facts. Participants in deliberation are members of *one group* (the political collective) and thus act in the role of citizens. By comparing reasons for and against measures, citizens do not aim at tracking truth (finding the 'correct' option) but at finding a feasible, workable solution for the collective. Whether an ultimate consensus is possible depends on the exact nature of the conflict but deliberation is likely to enable compromises between fundamental values and convergence of preferences. It is thus the mode of interaction that may be expected to be most favourable to preference-transformation.

Ancient city democracies are widely regarded as the most well known, or even the only, instances of deliberation among citizens being successfully institutionalised; and they are still influential as a normative ideal. Internationally, there have since been numerous attempts to create opportunities for stronger citizen involvement in policy-formulation, driven by normative rather than strategic considerations.[20] These forums seek to provide a non-expert normative evaluation of alternatives by the addressees of legislation. Members are obviously defined as citizens, who are often selected to be statistically representative of the population at large. The conflict they are dealing with is defined as one of value. What is at stake are reasons for choosing alternative options rather than the instrumental quality of options with regard to given goals. In conflicts of value, reasons are essentially shared and transferable and disagreements exist merely about how these are to be weighed against one another and aggregated into a complete preference-order. Factual agreement and a joint definition of the choice situation is to some extent presupposed in deliberation. In its institutionalisation, this poses the question of where such information is to come from, as the average citizen is known to be rather poorly informed on political and technical questions alike.

Like discussion, deliberation requires dialogical publicity. The dialogical aspect follows from the equality of participants (the essential property of the citizen role is equality) as well as from the necessity of co-ordination. A problem in the creation of forums for citizen deliberation is that group size must be somehow be limited (empirical experience recommends 10–12 members) and that the membership should be constant throughout the interaction. The task of evaluating reasons and of aggregating them into preferences presumes a pre-defined community with a limited number of reasons motivating 'us' to choose option A 'for us'. In other words, evaluation requires personal, territorial and temporal boundaries in order to be manageable within a limited time. Nonetheless, publicity is equally essential for citizen deliberation. Where it is institutionalised, the fact that members typically do not know one another before meeting in the forum helps to ensure some degree of publicity in that it creates a pressure to name general and transferable reasons. Another way to further publicity is to leave the doors open to a wider audience, for example by television broadcasting.

Instead of discussing any of the numerous empirical attempts to institutionalise citizen deliberation, I shall briefly discuss three models for this type of forum.[21] These models, developed by social scientists, are influential in discussions about deliberative democracy and function as reference points during the creation of new forums. Most empirical cases of institutionalised citizen deliberation either follow one of the models explicitly or represent combinations of them. As we will see, each of the models has particular strengths and shortcomings with regard to its potential to enable interaction that comes close to the ideal type.

The Consensus Conference
The consensus conference model was developed by the Danish Board of Technology in the 1980s, with the goal of increasing public participation in technology assessment. It has since been applied around the world but remains particularly popular and influential in the Nordic countries.[22] Conferences have dealt mainly with technology-assessment and bioethical issues, such as genetic engineering, prenatal diagnostics and stem cell research (note that this selection is similar to the one for parliamentary commissions). These topics are controversial across social groups but, at the same time, less politicised than, e.g. unemployment or social security, which are topics that are not normally dealt with in participatory procedures.

Participants in consensus conferences are selected by randomised procedures. The size of the forum is, compared with the other models, small – between ten and 25 members. Before the conference, all participants receive briefing material with well balanced information on the topic that is to be dealt with. On two weekend meetings, they identify important aspects of the decision and prepare a list of questions they want to pose to experts. Interaction is facilitated by a moderator, who is no expert on the matter himself and refrains from substantial contributions. On a third weekend, a public expert hearing takes place. Experts are selected by lay citizens themselves and usually come from different disciplines and backgrounds. After the expert hearing, the citizen-group prepares a report with policy suggestions, which is distributed to government officials and parliamentarians.

Two features of the consensus conference model are particularly important in this context. The first is the fact that consensus is an explicit goal of the procedure, which creates strong co-ordinative pressures. If the citizen report only listed several possible positions on the issue, it would hardly receive the same attention and have the same influence as a consensual vote. In Denmark, consensus conferences have often been successful at producing a unanimous report, while in other countries, consensus was rarely achieved. Whether this is due to the specific political culture in the Nordic countries or to superior experience with the model remains an open question. The second point is the randomised selection procedure. Although an element of self-selection remains (after all, nobody can be forced to participate), the fact that participants are laypeople without much political experience rather than politically active people stresses equality and is likely to prevent moves towards bargaining.

The Planning Cell
The planning cell is one of the oldest models for institutionalised citizen deliberation. It was developed by the German sociologist Peter C. Dienel (1978, 2002) and has found numerous applications since the late 1970s, mostly in Germany. According to Dienel, application is not limited to specific topics or one political level. However, planning cells have usually taken place at a local or regional rather than national level and have often addressed administrative rather than political decisions, such as the regulation of public transport. Compared to consensus conferences, the issues dealt with in planning cells tend to be more concrete ones that affect participants in their everyday life.

A Planning Cell project involves between five and twenty independent cells with around 25 members each. Members are randomly selected and supposed to be representative of the population at large. The separate cells each deal with one aspect of the policy problem at hand. In a sense, each of the cells resembles a consensus conference (Hendriks 2005: 84–7). However, there is usually a stronger focus on group deliberation; experts, although they are involved, play a less important role. Most of the interaction takes place not in the plenum of the cell but in groups with rotating memberships of five persons. The focus on small groups is intended to enhance the dialogical quality of interaction and to prevent domineering behaviour but, at the same time, decreases publicity and justificatory pressures.

One important feature of the planning cell model is the fact that the results of deliberation within the cells are not aggregated by citizens themselves but by conveners. The resulting report, which is confirmed by citizen representatives, is usually a lengthy document that tends to be less qualified and explicit than reports of consensus conferences (Hendriks 2005: 87). To a considerable extent, this mechanism leaves challenges of co-ordination to organisers rather than participants. Another important feature is the financial reward citizens receive for participation. Although not high, it is presumed to assure participants that their contribution is valued and that they are engaging in a serious political undertaking (Hendriks 2005.).

Deliberative Polling

The method of deliberative polling was developed by political scientist James Fishkin in the early 1990s and first and most famously applied in the community of New Haven, Connecticut (Fishkin 1991). It reflects the advent of deliberative democracy as a dominant approach in democratic theory and the desire to realise its normative ideals. Deliberative polls have been used to address even more diverse topics than those that consensus conferences and planning cells have dealt with, ranging from foreign policy to electricity supply (Fishkin & Farrar 2005: 75–6). However, they tend to be more concrete than those in consensus conferences and of more far-reaching national relevance than those in planning cells. In fact, they are mostly topics that are politicised in the context of an upcoming election.[23]

For a deliberative poll, a large number of citizens is invited by means of random phone calls. However, self-selection usually produces a sample that tends to be older and more educated and less likely to have an immigrant background than the average (Fishkin & Farrar 2005: 74). The plenum can consist of up to 500 citizens (typically between 100 and 200) and is divided into smaller groups of around twelve members. Expert hearings take place in the plenum, while face-to-face deliberation is encouraged in the groups (which are not split up again as in the planning cell model). Compared to the other two models, deliberative polls are less time-consuming, as they are supposed to be carried out on a single weekend or even a single day. As in the planning cell model, citizens receive a remuneration for participation.

Deliberative polling does not aim to produce a consensual citizen vote or report. Instead, questionnaires are filled in before and after interaction in order to document preference-changes and their direction. The model is thus partly intended as an instrument to back up deliberative democracy's claim that deliberation transforms preferences and renders these more informed and more just.[24] While deliberative polls are to some extent experiments in social science, there are also political goals. In contrast to the other two models, where the production of policy advice is aspired, the foremost aim behind deliberative polls is to produce more informed voters, by sparking discussions among community members.

Obviously, these short descriptions cannot do justice to the complexity of the models and to the rich experience with them. Neither can they offer an adequate comparison of their respective advantages and disadvantages regarding inclusive democratic deliberation. One point, however, should be kept in mind where participatory procedures are discussed: all of them are connected with considerable expenses. Where they are funded by private enterprises, ministries or interest groups, some consideration should be given to motives behind the support. Where they are funded as experiments in social science, the citizen role of participants is challenged – if reports are of interest only to researchers, but not to politicians, interaction loses some of its political relevance.

The institutionalisation of discursive and co-ordinative citizen deliberation as the mode of interaction seems to be particularly likely under the following conditions.

- Consensus is an explicit goal and participants seek to produce a vote or report that constitutes an input to a political decision-making process.
- Groups are reasonably small, albeit not too small, in order to create strong justificatory pressures and a large pool of reasons to draw on (10–12 participants).
- The focus is on evaluation and weighing of reasons rather than information. This is ensured where relevant information is provided in advance and experts hearings, etc. do not play a central role.
- The citizen role of participants is highlighted. A randomised selection procedure appears important here, and financial remunerations, even if they are small, can also contribute to this.

In so far as deliberation is in fact realised as the mode of interaction, the predictions regarding preference transformation are most favourable to the promises and ideals of deliberative democracy. It may be hypothesised that the aggregation-rules by which preferences over outcomes are derived from practical reasons are likely to be so transformed as to produce a considerable degree of convergence. This effect on the volitive premises of preferences derives from the strong justificatory and co-ordinative pressures connected with the citizen role, the interactive weighting of practical reasons and the task of evaluating political alternatives. Transformation of cognitive premises appears less likely, as this task in a sense presupposes a joint definition of the situation. Where factual agreement does not obtain, however, the strong justificatory and co-ordinative pressures are likely to result in transformation of cognitive premises as well – on many matters, citizens are unlikely to be fully informed and the responsibility to be so is an essential part of the role they are playing.

4.3 Bargaining

Bargaining has been widely discussed in political science as a specific mode of interaction and communication.[25] As such it was contrasted with arguing, where bargaining was often regarded as the competitive, arguing as the co-operative mode. The ideal-type presented here, by contrast, stresses its co-ordinative aspect and identifies the lack of discursive incentives as the central characteristic of bargaining as a mode of interaction. Bargaining is defined as non-discursive because it is, while dialogical, non-public. At the same time, it is a co-ordinative mode of interaction: if no agreement on a course of action is achieved, participants will not be able to increase their utility beyond the status quo. In corporatist bargaining contexts, non-decision can result in hierarchical decisions which leave all participants worse off. Consequently, strong material interests in compromises and co-ordination may ideal-typically be assumed.

The definition the *Encyclopedia Britannica* gives for bargaining is very much in keeping with this one: '1. to negotiate over the terms of a purchase, agreement or contract: haggle; 2. to come to terms: agree'. The first meaning apparently refers to the process, the second to the product of bargaining.[26] While bargaining aims at compromises, the ideal-typical lack of discursive qualities of interaction prevents genuine preference change. As there are no pressures to justify one's preferences by reference to acceptances and practical reasons, these will not be questioned, assessed and reconsidered. Rather, participants seek to maximize their own preferences under the constraints of the other participants' preferences. While compromises in deliberation are between conflicting practical reasons, compromises in bargaining are more superficial ones between concrete action plans.

Looking at attempts to institutionalise bargaining, the first relevant aspect is the functional one: what is the task the respective institution is charged with? Ideal-typically, it is the distribution of a given sum. Unlike economic models of bargaining, the ideal-type does not entail the assumption of full information on other actors' preferences and resources. These economic models have in fact little to do with linguistic interaction. They do not describe a process, but an instance of maximizing choice under constraints (or, at most, a sequence of maximizing choices). The assumption here is that linguistic interaction does make a difference and that there is room for more or less successful co-ordination. Communication about preferences, accompanied by threats, promises and pointers to exit options enables package deals which can yield a higher overall utility than could be achieved by hierarchical allocation. The sum that is to be distributed is limited and cannot be further increased by information and problem-solving activities, but an unco-ordinated distribution may impede upon actors achieving their maximum pay-off.

The conflict in distributive bargaining is defined as one of pure interest, all reasons involved being private and non-transferable ones. Bargaining takes place at a stage when it has become clear that differences between actor preferences cannot be resolved by reference either to joint ultimate values or to empirical evidence. Members at a bargaining table are not selected for their superior expertise or to increase democratic legitimacy but for their potential to activate political veto players and block policy implementation.[27] Interaction here is non-discursive in that it is dialogical but not public. Secrecy is required because the reasons motivating actor preferences are private and non-general and hence could not be defended with regard to a common good or collective utility. As a collective decision over alternative options for collective action can only be publicly vindicated in terms of such, public notice of private, 'selfish' reasons determining it is likely to de-legitimise both the decision and the groups involved in it. The dialogical nature of the interaction reflects the equality of the members. Although not all of them are staffed with the same resources, they enjoy equal rights to speak and to be heard in the bargaining process. If an actor did not possess such rights, he simply would not be included at the table in the first place.

Well-documented empirical examples of institutionalised bargaining are the European Council and Council of Ministers (see, e.g. Moravcsik 1991, 1999), collective labor agreements and wage settlements (see, e.g. Svejnar 1986; Revel 1994) and mediation committees between first and second chambers of parliament (see, e.g. Lehmbruch 1999; Rutschmann 2002).

Parliamentary caucuses constitute a further example of forums for interest bargaining.[28] Although, depending on the system of government and institutional context, their role is a different one in different countries, their comparative secrecy and co-ordinative pressures often result in respective logics. A comparison between parliamentary caucuses and parliamentary expert commissions indicates the existence of a continuum between expert discussion and interest bargaining. In which direction interaction moves seems to depend on the topic the forum is dealing with, on its exact composition and on the interests involved.

One example of institutionalised interest bargaining shall be discussed in some more detail. It is interesting in that it deals in part with the same decisions that the Swedish Parliamentary Priorities Commission and the National Institute of Clinical Excellence are concerned with – the assessment and rationing of medical technologies. This gives rise to the question of whether interest bargaining and expert discussion are alternative modes of interaction in dealing with the same problem.

The Federal Joint Committee (Gemeinsamer Bundesausschuss), Germany

In the late 1970s, German health policy made the first moves from service expansion to cost containment. Since then, Joint Committees, in which health insurers and doctors negotiate services and remuneration, have gained in importance.[29] The move from expenditure-oriented revenue policy towards revenue-oriented expenditure policy was thus accompanied by an instrumentalisation of the joint committee for the regulation of distributive conflicts (Döhler/Manow-Borgwaldt: 584). In return for its commissioning for cost containment goals, the Committee received far-reaching instruments for its implementation (Urban 2001: 10). The Federal Joint Committee set up in 2004 merges several existing committees and covers inpatient and outpatient medical and dental care. It issues legally binding decisions and thus possesses remarkably far-reaching competences for the allocation of health care. The latest major health care reform, however, has also considerably restructured decision-making procedures.

The committee's discursive quality was substantially strengthened by the 2004 reform. The participation of patient representatives, albeit only with consultative influence and without voting rights, improves the publicity of meetings. The fact that each of the separate panels is chaired by three experts not only increases pressures for justification but at the same time reduces decision costs. Whereas previously, each party at the bargaining table (insurers vs. doctors or hospitals) practically held veto powers, majority decisions are now possible. In case of a confrontation of interests, it is the experts who dispose of the deciding vote. As a minimal winning coalition requires either expert support or compromises with the opposite side, co-ordinative incentives nonetheless remain strong. Moreover, an "Institute for Quality and Efficiency in Health Care" – modelled after the British NICE – was established to provide the Joint Committee with reports on specific technologies. Forums in the Joint Committee consider publicly available cost-benefit assessments of this expert forum as a basis for decisions.

Increasing institutionalisation and the reform of consultation and decision procedures have changed the Federal Joint Committee's structures in a way that interaction in it now significantly deviates from the ideal-type of bargaining. This confirms the view that (even limited) publicity and expert involvement countervail respective incentives. Together with the fact that in NICE, features favourable to bargaining rather than expert discussion have been institutionalised, it also indicates that complex conflicts with dimensions of fact, value and interest cannot be resolved by means of a single mode of interaction. Accordingly, institutional design seeks to realize different modes in a single forum. It remains questionable, however, whether in this case it is indeed possible to 'have the cake and eat it too'.

In sum, the following institutional features are evidently particularly important for the realization of interest bargaining as a mode of interaction:
- the task of a forum is the distribution of a given sum
- interaction takes place behind closed doors and involves only actors with bargaining resources in the form of veto powers or opportunities to interfere with implementation
- participants function as agents, but have some discretion with regard to their principal
- participants are well informed with regard to consequences of policy choices (although not necessarily with regard to other actors' preferences)
- the conflict is clearly defined as one of interest, and factual or moral dimensions either do not exist or are ignored

In so far as bargaining is indeed realised as the dominant mode of interaction, the following simple predictions can be made: actors are likely to have the same preferences post-interaction that they had pre-interaction, even if they agree on an action plan. In this package deal, which consists of several interconnected and non-separable elements, actors will have maximized their existing preferences under the constraints of other actors' preferences and resources.

4.4 Debate

The forums discussed above can all be classified as types of negotiating regimes. According to the Coase-theorem, decision-making by means of negotiation tends to enable Pareto-efficient outcomes and is in this respect superior to hierarchical decision. With regard to the collective that is affected by these decisions, however, several questions remain. It seems impossible, to begin with, to ensure that all those affected by the collectively binding norms that make up the output of political decision-making be involved in negotiating regimes. As Ronald Coase noted, transaction costs rise exponentially with the number of independent participants and will soon become forbiddingly high (Scharpf 1997: 116/7). The second important problem with negotiated solutions is that they tend to reinforce existing inequalities in resources.[30] Re-distribution of resources thus requires other forms of collective decision making, in particular majority voting and hierarchical direction.

Saretzki points out that both of the communication modes of arguing and bargaining have their place in the preparation of a collective decision but cannot replace the decision itself (1996: 29). The place where, in modern representative democracies, the collectively binding decision is taken is the plenary session of the parliament. Parliamentary decisions are of course prepared in caucuses, parties and administrative bodies as well as negotiating regimes resembling the forums discussed above. The majoritarian parliamentary decision, however, remains both the default-mode of decision making and the ultimate closing procedure for discursive interaction and preference formation. The plenum then serves two purposes: the decision itself and its justification to the electorate.

The mode of interaction that is institutionalised in the parliamentary plenum is the debate. It is defined above as both non-co-ordinative and non-discursive. It is non-discursive because it is non-dialogical: it is a sequence of monologues rather than a dialogue, and assertions cannot immediately be challenged. Because assertions cannot be challenged, the hearers (or rather listeners) are not committed to results of interaction. The *Encyclopedia Britannica* defines debate as the 'formal, oral confrontation between two individuals, teams or *groups* who *present* arguments to support *opposing* sides of a question, generally according to a set form or procedure' (emphasis added). The French origin, 'débattre', meaning 'to defeat, to strike down', (figuratively) points to the goal of participants in a debate. *Groups* (more than one!) are pre-defined, and they *present* rather than exchange arguments. While a plenary debate in parliament presupposes many co-ordinative efforts and compromises within parties and coalitions, the debate itself does not enable further co-ordination. Instead, it serves the majority to defend a decision that has been taken in advance and the minority to attack it.

The parliamentary plenum constitutes both a starting point and an end point of a circular process wherein different modes of interaction and their institutionalisations play different roles.

Figure 3.12: A cyclical model of policy-making

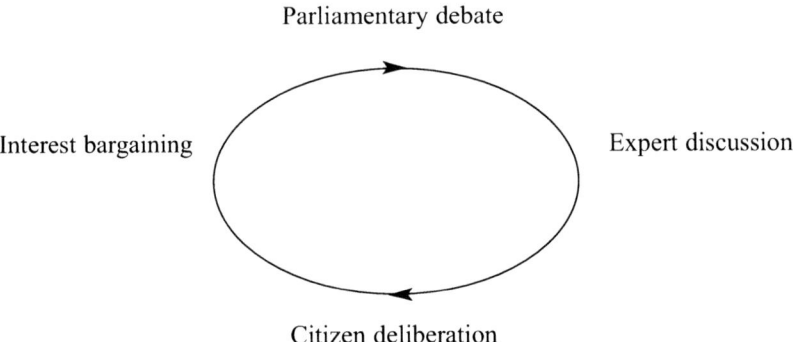

Parliamentary debate

Interest bargaining

Expert discussion

Citizen deliberation

Expert discussion is employed in situations of uncertainty in order to explore the ground for a decision by providing a definition of the situation and of alternatives for collective action. Citizen deliberation can ideal-typically be employed where consensus on situation and alternatives is presupposed, but where the respective weight of the various practical reasons involved in the conflict needs to be assessed. Where no conflicts over values remain and actor preferences are driven solely by private reasons, which are not transferable and can play no further role in justification, distributive bargaining can take place. Empirically, however, institutions normally lead to interaction that has properties of more than one ideal-type, and the different modes of interaction typically occur simultaneously rather than successively.[31]

The non-discursive and non-co-ordinative parliamentary debate is probably best institutionalised in Westminster-style parliaments, whereas presidential systems of government entail stronger co-ordinative incentives inside the parliamentary plenum. Members of the plenum are elected representatives belonging to competing parties, one of which provides the government and its head. The conflict is at this stage one about competing options for collective action. Only detailed action-plans can be introduced to the parliament for decision, and it is only on these that the plenum can decide, not on the truth of propositions or ranking of values. The conflict may either be between a new option for action and the status quo or between two or more newly proposed options and the status quo. The majoritarian decision in a way puts an end to the conflict, if only temporarily. At the time the parliamentary debate takes place, it can be argued, the eventual decision has already been taken and is ideal-typically identical with the position of the governing party.

The publicity of the parliamentary debate reflects the responsibility of the actors to the entire constituency and the necessity to justify the decision in terms of a common good by means of general, transferable reasons. To create publicity for decisions and justifications, which sparks discussion and active political participation is one of the primary functions of the parliament. What may appear less obvious is the monological character of communicative interaction in parliamentary debates. After all, speakers with competing positions take turns on the floor, where they challenge the opponent's commitments, offer alternative ones and defend these. The paramount importance of the audience, however, tends to destroy all potentials for a meaningful dialogue. Speakers do not address one another, but the audience alone, and fail to take adequate notice of each other's contributions.[32] They deliver lengthy, pre-arranged speeches which cannot be interrupted without permission. The monological quality of interaction reflects both the inequality between parliamentary majority and minority and that between the speakers and their audience. Further attempts at co-ordination are at this stage redundant, as the parliamentary majority which authorizes the decision is presumed to be already established.

Given that majority voting constitutes the default mode decision-making, the parliamentary debate as a mode of interaction seems comparatively easy to institutionalise. Its realization is most likely to be restrained where premises of decisions remain unclear or where actors with veto power can block a decision and its implementation. Predictions regarding actor preferences are that there will be neither transformation nor co-ordination in the debate. A major reason for this is that preference changes of interlocutors are seen as a defeat in the battle, so that the debate becomes the mode of interaction that is least favourable for preference-transformation. This is assumed to hold, it must be noted, for actors participating in a single debate as members of parliament (and thus potential speakers). The arguments delivered in justification of relevant options may well have an effect on listeners' acceptances and practical reasons. Moreover, members of parliament must certainly be expected to revise their reasons and acceptances in between debates. Within a plenary session (i.e. during a debate with subsequent decision), however, neither preference change nor convergence may be expected.

5. SUMMARY

In this chapter, discussion, deliberation, bargaining and debate were pointed out as politically relevant modes of interaction more or less favourable to preference transformation. Which mode of interaction is realized in a political forum depends on institutional factors. Section 1 discussed the way in which institutions constrain and enable different forms of action and interaction. Section 2 pointed out that the settings in which political interaction takes place are often deliberately chosen and designed by governments in order to fulfil specific demands. In this way, deliberation is increasingly advocated as an instrument to arrive at better decisions. Instead of outlining a normative ideal of deliberation, however, section 3 identified features of interaction that are of particular relevance for justification and co-ordination of acceptances and practical reasons: its publicity or secrecy, its mono-logical or dialogical character, the way the conflict is defined, the roles that are assigned to participants, and the task that is addressed.

On the basis of these variables, two dimensions were pointed out to be consti-tutive dimensions of ideal-type modes of interaction. Interaction was defined to be discursive where interaction in it is both public and dialogical. It was argued to be co-ordinative where the definitions of conflict, actor roles and tasks were such as to create incentives for co-ordination. In section 4, a model was proposed that regards the probability of preference-transformation as depending equally on the discursive and the co-ordinative qualities of interaction. On the basis of this model, the four ideal-type modes of interaction were identified. For each of them, empirical examples of attempts to institutionalise them were discussed. On the basis of the variables identified in section 3 and empirical experience, institution-al properties were identified that promote the realization of the respective mode of interaction. Hypotheses were stated on how each mode of interaction, to the extent that it is in fact realized in a forum, affects preferences. Only deliberation, which is both discursive and coordinative, is expected to result in a transformation of preferences. In the overall process of political preference-formation and decision-making, however, all four modes of interaction and their respective institutionali-sations play an important role, as the case study in the following two chapters will illustrate.

NOTES

1 For compelling criticism of deliberative democracy, see Sanders (1997), Przeworski (1998), Stokes (1989) and Young (2003), who draw attention to the dangers of manipulation, distorted communication and unequal access to deliberative forums, as well as Gaus (1997) and Greven (2000), who point out that deliberation cannot replace majoritarian decisions. Buchstein/Jörke (2003) point out how deliberative democrats renounce the participatory appeal of democracy.

2 See, for instance, Ackermann/Fishkin 2003 and Gastil/Levine 2005 and section 4.2 below.

3 Elster (1997 [1986]) draws attention to the problem that this 'approximation assumption' may be a fallacy: a little deliberation (like a little rationality or a little socialism) may indeed be worse than no deliberation at all. However, this point is made from a normative perspective. A little deliberation may have normatively less desirable results than none at all, but if it does not increase the probability of preference change in either direction, it would quite simply be irrelevant.

4 The Federal Joint Committee (*Gemeinsamer Bundesausschuss*) in Germany, for instance, takes decisions on whether new medical treatments are to be funded by the social insurance system which are immediately binding for doctors, insurers, and patients.

5 The 'when' -variable is also known as the moderator, the 'how'-variable as the mediator.

6 See particularly Elster 1995, 1998, Chambers 2004 and O'Flynn 2006 (ch. 5).

7 Which is not true for parliamentary committees, round-tables and caucuses, which are part of the institution of parliament but not part of the plenary debate. Accordingly, they are normally non-public. On the deliberative potential of parliaments, see below and Holzinger 2005.

8 A further interesting case are television interviews. These are public and also dialogical in that it is the interviewer's task to challenge the interviewee's commitments. However, it is not part of the interviewer's role to undertake his/her own commitments or make positive statements, which again reduces the dialogical quality.

9 The case is different for private information about people's preferences, choices and biographies.

10 The concept of publicity employed here is a purely analytical one. A forum of the kind described here may of course fall far short of the requirements of a more normative understanding of publicity which entails aspects such as legitimacy, representation, non-discrimination etc.

11 Which is an instance of 'interest reductionism' as described by Greven (1999: 28–39).

12 Chambers discusses the effects of publicity on the rational qualities of a discourse and summarizes: 'It appears as if the ideal of public deliberation pushes deliberation into two opposite directions: into the public sphere to promote the *public* nature of public reason but out of the public sphere to safeguard the rational component of public *reason*' (2004: 393). She thus assumes that secrecy may not only enable bargaining between private reasons but also ensure the reasonableness of discourses.

13 Holzinger draws attention to an empirical example in her case study, where participants took turns in proposing amounts of waste that should be expected for the future – a typical bargaining behaviour (2001: 436). As the future amount of waste is nothing within the voluntary control of the actors involved, this seems paradoxical. Goodin and Brennan (2004) argue that factual disputes can indeed sometimes be provisionally and conditionally settled

by negotiation. Where this is the case, actors agree to treat something as true for a particular purpose at hand. Holzinger's example obviously fits into this class of cases. In search of a joint premise, actors compromise to accept a proposition instrumentally, but not epistemically.

14 Economic models of bargaining consequently see no role for communication but that of signalling offers, rejections and consent. Ideal-typically, participants, under conditions of complete information, recognize immediately what the best deal they can get is and make the respective offer, which is accepted accordingly.

15 See chapter 2, section 4 for indecision as the primary risk for expert bodies and its causes.

16 See Diego Gambettas discussion of analytical and indexical conceptions of knowledge (Gambetta 1998). Where knowledge is conceptualised indexically (which, according to Gambetta, is typically the case in southern European and Latin American countries), actors are distinguished into 'knowers' and 'know-nothings'. If an actor is found to be correct in one case, he is assigned competence on other topics as well. If he is found to be mistaken, he is denied competence in the future. In consequence, actors avoid to admit ignorance and errors. This indexical conception of knowledge seems to me to apply to elected politicians in general, who are forced to present themselves as 'knowers'. The analytical conception of knowledge, which detaches knowledge from individual persons and allows for specialization and partial ignorance is more favourable for preference transformation and hence for deliberative democracy, as Gambetta points out.

17 In traditional models of the policy-making process, evaluation typically comes in as the final stage, where the success of a policy is assessed post-hoc. In the categorization proposed here, such processes would rather qualify as a definition of the new situation rather than as evaluation. The category 'evaluation' will thus be used only for evaluations of alternatives, not for post-hoc evaluations of policies.

18 Jorgensen (1995: 22) notes that panels may be composed either as balanced or as neutral. A balanced panel comprises advocates of differing schools of thought and competing views on the given topic. A neutral panel consists of experts without a stated opinion on (or particular experience in) the relevant subject. To realize preconditions for expert discussion as the dominant mode of interaction, a balanced rather than a neutral panel would be required.

19 This 'National Commission of Priority Setting' is to guarantee central control and evaluation and to ensure that concrete decisions are guided by the report's framework.

20 For an overview, see collections by Joss/Durant 1995 and Gastil/Levine 2005.

21 One example that is widely regarded as a successful realization of citizen deliberation, and in which participants' views did in fact have an effect on the eventual political decision is the Oregon Health Plan. See Gutmann/Thompson 1996, who praise it as evidence that democratic deliberation does work and Daniels 1996 for a slightly more critical view.

22 For an introduction to the model, see Hendriks 2005 as well as Grundahl 1995, Klüver 1995 and other contributions in the volume by Joss/Durant 1995.

23 Recently, Ackermann and Fishkin (2003) proposed a 'Deliberation Day', modelled after the Deliberative Poll, to be held two weeks before the general elections.

24 Fishkin and his followers use control groups to ensure that preference changes are not random and have shown significant transformations in deliberating groups. Preferences after deliberation are shown to be more informed and more structured (Fishkin/Farrar 2005: 76).

25 See Elster 1995, 1997, 1998, Saretzki 1996 and the debate in the German journal *Zeitschrift*

für Internationale Beziehungen, which is summarized and discussed in Risse 2000.

26 Its probable origin in Middle English 'byrgan' – 'to bury, to cover up' could similarly point to the latter, but may also be more or less irrelevant to the modern meaning.

27 I think it is a misunderstanding to regard interest group consultation and involvement in decision-making as a means of increasing democratic participation (see Greven 2005). Interest groups are typically involved in decision-making where their co-operation is necessary for successful implementation (e.g. insurance funds, doctors and hospitals in health policy) or where they can motivate political actors such as the second chamber (e.g. the German *Bundesrat*) or the electorate (in countries such as Switzerland, where laws can be vetoed in referenda) to block the decision.

28 For an article on bargaining in caucuses as a threat to deliberative democracy in the US, see Solomon/Wolfensberger 1994.

29 Committees of doctors, hospitals and insurers are part of a system of corporatist self-regulation in the German social insurance sector. Institutions and their competences are sanctioned by federal law, so that actors negotiate in the shadow of hierarchy. Wherever they are charged with specific tasks, they are independent and their decisions are binding. This is a notable difference in comparison with NICE, which issues only recommendations.

30 This claim is most obvious for distributive bargaining. Critics of deliberative democracy, however, have compellingly argued that the same might be true of deliberative forums. Certain groups, persons and views apparently have less of a chance to be heard and to be successful. Participation in 'deliberative' discourses also seems to require conversational skills which are highly unequally distributed in our society (cf. Sanders 1997, Young 2003).

31 This cycle of modes of interaction resembles the classical "cyclical model" in policy analysis, which has recently been criticized as empirically inadequate and therefore dated. I do not think, however, that the fact that empirical policy-making to some extent differs from the model means that it is instrumentally useless. For a defence of the cyclical model, see De Leon 1999.

32 Empirical evidence for this claim is provided in Holzinger 2005. On the effects of publicity in parliamentary settings, see also Steiner *et al.* 2005.

chapter four | case study: the German decision on the importation of embryonic stem cells

The remaining part of the book seeks to apply the theoretical framework for the analysis of modes of interaction, their institutionalisation and their effects on actor preferences to an empirical case: the German decision whether to permit the importing of embryonic stem-cell lines. The case is typical and interesting in that the conflict over the decision displayed factual and moral dimensions as well as dimensions of pragmatic evaluation and conflicting interests. What is more, though, is that several different forums were involved in the decision-making process. In these, the institutionalisation of the ideal-typical modes of interaction outlined in the last chapter was, to a greater or lesser extent, intended. The case thus illustrates how differing institutional contexts produce different modes of interaction. Most importantly, however, the analysis enables us to draw inferences about how linguistic interaction leads to preference-transformation and it can thus confirm or challenge the hypotheses developed above.

The role of this chapter is to provide background information on the stem-cell conflict in Germany (section 1), outline the controversial questions and thus the dimensions of conflict (section 2) and to give a brief survey of the way the conflict was processed through different institutions (section 3). The available data and the methods by which they were analysed are described in some detail before the following chapter immerses itself more deeply in analysis (section 4).

1. THE PROBLEM

When Oliver Brüstle, a neurobiologist at the University of Bonn, submitted an application for funding for a research project using imported embryonic stem cells (ES-cells) to the German Research Foundation (*Deutsche Forschungsgemeinschaft, DFG*) in August 2000, it became apparent that German law was not well prepared for this specific challenge produced by scientific progress. Since a law on the protection of embryos (*Embryonenschutzgesetz*, ESchG) had been passed in 1991, new findings and technology, among them James Thomson's 1998 success in cultivating stem cells from a human embryo, brought up options not foreseeable at that time.

In particular, the EschG, which is part of German criminal law, sanctioned the production and killing of embryos for research purposes but did not regulate importing embryonic stem cells produced in other countries. On the one hand, embryonic stem cells do not count as embryos according to the definition in the EschG. On the other hand, the isolation of stem cells inevitably leads to the death of the embryo, which means that the import of stem cells may encourage a practice that is illegal in Germany. Researchers thus found themselves in a situation of legal uncertainty. While there was a broad consensus in the political sphere that such uncertainty must be abolished, there was fundamental disagreement about how these new opportunities for biomedical research could and should be restricted.

In international comparison, the German public as well as major political parties are particularly sceptical towards biotechnology (Hampel *et al.* 1998). Projects in genetic engineering and plans to set out genetically modified plants had been met with fierce resistance since the 1980s. The bioethics convention drafted by the Council of Europe,[1] intended to 'prevent abuse of medical, biological and genetic techniques', was harshly criticised by associations of the disabled, feminists, churches and other social groups for being too permissive on many issues. In consequence, the German parliament failed to ratify both the convention and an additional protocol on cloning.

Where the evaluation of new technologies developed in the life sciences is concerned, ethical and moral questions apparently play a more prominent role in Germany than in other countries: 'Resistance to genetic engineering in Germany seems to be more of a symbolic act where people declare their concern about the path of technological development of their 'lifeworld' (*Lebenswelt*) than the result of a technocratic balancing of benefits and risks' (Hampel *et al.* 1998: 70). In addition to this, there seems to be a widespread perception of insufficient control of both research and industrial applications of new technologies (Hampel *et al.* 1998: 70). Memories of the German past and in particular of the atrocious experiments conducted by Nazi doctors play a considerable role in these sceptical attitudes.

The discussion in Germany over importing ES-cells was also closely linked to the simultaneous debate over pre-implantation diagnostics (PID). The 'surplus' embryos used for the production of stem-cell lines are a product of in-vitro fertilisation. In contrast to many other countries, German law does not allow more embryos to be produced than can be implanted at once (three), so that only very few embryos become 'surplus' (due to death or severe illness of the mother). If embryos were to be examined for genetic disorders before implantation, many more would have to be produced and would constitute a potential source of stem cells. Accordingly, many of the people campaigning against PID were also fiercely opposed to ES-cell research.

In the decision over importing embryonic stem cells, therefore, politicians were expected to abolish legal uncertainties as well as to achieve effective regulation and control of research and applications. The challenge they confronted consisted in a highly critical public sphere and political parties that were (and still are) internally deeply divided over bioethical questions.

2. DIMENSIONS OF CONFLICT

The purpose in argumentation, and political argumentation in particular, can be regarded as the development of an argument leading to an answer to a controversial question (Klein 1980: 10). An argument consists of assertions legitimately linked to one another. If an assertion is legitimately linked to another one and supports it, it provides a *reason* to embrace it (Klein 1980: 15). The structure of an argument may thus be illustrated as a tree, in which the top constitutes an answer to the controversial question (in Klein's terminology: the *quaestio*), the branches legitimate (inferential) links and the nodes reasons for the answer.

If we describe an argumentation, we describe the process wherein a number of actors interact in the composition of a collective product. 'In an argumentation, people try by means of the collectively valid to transfer something that is collectively controversial into something that is collectively valid' (Klein 1980: 19, my translation). A controversial question is resolved when one of the possible answers has been established as collectively valid. In order to construct an argument and resolve the *quaestio*, actors need to manage three separate tasks:

- Assertions must be successfully justified.
- Coherence must be ensured: the single assertions must be legitimately linked. The type of links regarded as legitimate may itself be questioned and require justification.
- Co-ordination of different parts of the argument (= branches of the tree) must be achieved (cf. Klein 1980: 16).

Klein distinguishes open from closed *quaestios*. Closed *quaestios* require simple yes/no answers to a decision question such as 'Are embryonic stem cells embryos?'. Open *quaestios* such as 'Why should importing stem cells be disallowed?' demand more detailed and complex answers, which is why co-ordination tends to be more complicated in this case. According to Brandom's distinction between doxastic and practical reasons, it makes sense to further distinguish doxastic (or theoretical) *quaestios* such as 'Are adult stem cells pluripotent?' from practical ones such as 'Shall we do A?'. As I argued before, all political conflicts are essentially practical ones, although they may originate from doxastic differences.

This section will provide an overview over the dimensions of conflict and controversial questions involved in the discussion of the import of embryonic stems cells as well as the reasons and arguments provided by participants in order to resolve the *quaestio*. The superordinate *quaestio* in this case is 'Shall we permit the importing of embryonic stem cells?'. The controversy over the *quaestio* has various dimensions: factual, legal, moral and pragmatic. Within the factual dimension, questions concerning empirical reality are controversial. Within the legal dimension, the laws and their correct interpretation are at stake. Within the moral dimension, the specification and weighing of norms and values requires resolution. The pragmatic dimension, finally, includes questions about feasibility.[2] While these dimensions and the controversial questions within them are relevant to the logic of argumentation, colliding interests affect argumentation at the practical level. Whether something is collectively controversial or valid, that is, depends not on argumentation alone, but equally (or in some cases solely) on the interests of actors involved.

2.1 Factual questions

The potency of embryonic stem cells. Since the law on the protection of embryos defines the embryo as 'any totipotent human cell with the capacity to develop into an individual' (§ 8, sec. 1), the question of whether embryonic stem cells could under any conditions qualify as totipotent or could be transformed into totipotent cells was a controversial one at the beginning of the debate. Most biomedical literature defines totipotent cells as cells with the potential to develop into any type of cell and thus to bring forth an entire human being. They are distinguished from pluripotent cells, which can develop into a number of different cell types but not into an entire individual. Adult, or somatic, stem cells can reproduce only cells of a specific type (e.g. blood, tissue). The cells extracted from an embryo at the morula or early blastocyst stage (which can nearly infinitely be reproduced) are usually regarded as pluripotent (cf. Beier 2002). However, there remain doubts about whether they cannot be re-programmed into totipotent cells. This question could only be experimentally resolved by implanting pluripotent stem cells into a woman's womb, which, for ethical reasons, must obviously be ruled out. Possible premises and the arguments based on them are hence:

- Embryonic stem cells are pluripotent:
- → embryonic stem cells are not embryos.
- Embryonic stem cells are totipotent:
- → embryonic stem cells are embryos.

The comparative potential of research with adult stem cells, animal embryonic stem cells and embryonic stem cells. While the potency of stem cells could, at least in principle, be experimentally established, questions about their potential are essentially probabilistic. They concern the probability that research with embryonic stem cells (ES-cells) will before very long yield a better understanding of human development in its early stages as well as new cures for life-threatening and common diseases. With regard to applied research, their potential is compared with that of adult stem cells, which are already being used to treat types of cancer and autoimmune system diseases. With regard to pure research, it is compared with animal embryonic stem cells, which have very similar properties and are ethically uncontroversial. Concerning the potentiality question, the following reasons and arguments played a role in the debate:

- The clinical potential of ES-cells is low:
- → research should focus on adult stem cells.
- The epistemic potential of ES-cells is low:
- → research should focus on animal ES-cells.

- The potential of ES-cells is uncertain:
→ research requires comparison of different cell types, including human ES-cells.
- The clinical and/or epistemic potential of ES-cells is high:
→ research with ES-cells is a rewarding route of research.

The quality of existing stem-cell lines. Another question that sometimes arose in the discussions over importing embryonic stem cells was the quality of existing stem-cell lines. The issue was relevant with regard to other questions about the necessity of allowing the importing of lines established after a specific date or even the production of ES-cells in Germany and questions about the possibility of restricting importation to existing lines. Researchers agreed that existing lines were not suitable for applied research (because they were contaminated with mouse viruses) but it was controversial whether existing ones were sufficient for pure research. Reasons and arguments were:

- The quality of existing ES-cells is sufficient:
→ import of existing lines will fulfil requirements for pure research, so no additional ones need to be produced or imported.
- The quality of existing ES-cells is insufficient:
→ new ones need to be produced inside Germany or be imported.
- The quality of existing ES-cells is insufficient:
→ demand for new ones will grow and become impossible to control.

2.2 Legal Questions
The legal status of embryos and embryonic stem cells. The law on the protection of embryos was passed in order to regulate procedures for artificial insemination. It concerns the embryo *in vitro* until its nidation in a woman's uterus. It demands that nothing happens to the embryo that does not serve purposes of preservation (§ 2, sec. 1) and interdicts the production of embryos *in vitro* for purposes other than to cause a pregnancy (§ 1, sec. 1, no. 2). Controversies concerned the status of 'surplus' or 'orphaned' embryos. In Germany, only a small number of embryos, which for reasons concerning the mother (serious diseases, death) could not be implanted, qualify as 'orphaned'. Outside Germany, however, a higher number of such embryos is produced for purposes of pre-implantation diagnostics (PID). Embryos sorted out by PID constitute a possible source for the production of stem-cell lines. They can be stored in frozen state for a very long time, although their potential to develop deteriorates with the passing of time. Given that the surplus embryos are deprived of the chance to develop into full human beings, what is contested is whether they nonetheless enjoy full rights to life and dignity. If they did, their death may not be accepted – and the production of stem cells so far inevitably causes the death of the embryo. Reasons and arguments in this context were:

- Surplus embryos enjoy full rights to life and dignity:
  → they may not be killed or employed for research purposes.
- Surplus embryos enjoy only limited rights to life and dignity:
  → they may be killed and employed for high-ranking research purposes.

The application and weighting of constitutional norms: protection of human dignity (Art. 1) and life (Art. 2, sec. 2) and the freedom of research (Art. 5, sec. 3). The constitutional norms named above as well as the questions of whether they apply to importing ES-cells and whether and how they could be weighted against one another were of major relevance in the decision. All three are part of the catalogue of fundamental human rights introducing the German constitution, which Art. 79 sec. 3 prevents from ever being changed. Art. 1, concerning human dignity, stands above all other constitutional norms and may not be weighed or graded. Other fundamental norms such as the right to life and the freedom of research may be graded if other constitutional norms stand against them. This was done in the decision on abortion, where the woman's dignity and freedom were under certain conditions rated higher than the life of the embryo. However, if no other constitutional norms compete with a basic right, it may not be restricted. The following arguments were made with regard to constitutional principles:

- Rights to life and dignity are not affected by import:
  → importing must be allowed to ensure freedom of research.
- Right to life applies, but can be weighed against freedom of research:
  → importing can and should be allowed conditionally.
- Right to dignity applies and cannot be weighed:
  → importing must be forbidden.

Criminal prosecution of researchers. Another legal question consistently appealed to was whether researchers working with embryonic ES-cells in other countries or collaborating in multinational research projects using such cells would have to fear criminal prosecution for collaboration in abuse or killing of embryos. Explicitly allowing importing ES-cells would abolish legal uncertainty, protect researchers from prosecution and prevent them from emigration:

- Researchers must fear prosecution:
  → permission to import resolves legal uncertainty, protects researchers and prevents emigration.
- Researchers need not fear prosecution:
  → interdiction does not result in legal uncertainty.

The possibility of restricting importation with regard to EU law. EU-law on the single market demands free trade and movement all goods. If ES-cells fall under this regulation, EU-law interdicts restrictions of import. However, high-ranking reasons (other than mere protection of national markets) may nonetheless make import restrictions permissible. Arguments regarding the question of whether import could be forbidden under EU-law were:

- EU-law does not permit restrictions:
→ Germany cannot forbid import by national law.
- EU-law does permit restrictions:
→ Germany can restrict import.

2.3 Moral questions

The moral status of the embryo. The status of the embryo was discussed not only as a legal, but also as a moral issue, although the arguments employed were very similar. After all, the central constitutional norms concerned were appreciated by all actors involved in the discussion. However, it is possible to make a moral claim to certain principles while admitting that it is not necessarily covered by the constitution. Moral questions concerning the status of the embryo were more closely tied to the issue of when precisely human life should be assumed to begin. Some argued that the fertilised egg was the only non-arbitrarily chosen point in a continuous process, while others pointed out that nidation (taking place approximately 14 days after fertilisation) was an equally, or more, significant point in the development of the embryo. At this stage, the embryo develops a primitive streak (thus beginning to resemble a vertebrate) and can no longer divide into multiples (thus in a sense constituting the beginning of individuality). Depending on whether human life and individuality were assumed to begin with the fertilised egg or with nidation, the following arguments were made:

- Human life begins with fertilisation:
→ embryos at any developmental stage possess full rights to life and dignity.
- Human life begins with nidation:
→ embryos at earlier stages do not yet possess full rights to life and dignity.

To back up the latter argument, it was often pointed out that the permission to use contraceptives preventing nidation (intrauterine devices) and to terminate pregnancy under certain conditions indicated that the embryo in early stages of development was not regarded as a full human being[3]:

- We allow abortion and intrauterine devices:
→ we thus acknowledge that embryos do not yet possess full rights to life and dignity.

The instrumentalisation of embryos and moral duty to save lives (ethics of healing). None of the actors involved in the discourse denied that there exists a moral duty to help desperately ill people as far as possible. What was evaluated differently, however, was whether the duty to help could justify the instrumentalisation of human beings, even in very early developmental stages. Instrumentalisation is widely regarded as a violation of human dignity. If dignity is assigned to the embryo, its destruction in order to save other human lives is thus ruled out. The question of how the duty to save lives is to be weighted in this context also depends on how the probability that ES-cell research will actually yield new cures is estimated. Arguments were thus:

- Embryos do possess only limited dignity, we have the duty to save lives and ES-cell research promises new cures:
→ we have the duty to support research with ES-cells.
- Embryos do possess full dignity:
→ embryos may not be instrumentalised for any purpose.
- The clinical potential of ES-cells is low:
→ duty to save lives does not justify instrumentalisation.

A further point that was made concerning the question of instrumentalisation was the following: German patients would benefit from methods of treatment obtained by research with embryonic stem cells regardless of whether or not Germany allowed their import and production. Since the clinical use of research findings could not possibly be forbidden even if they were obtained by ethically question-able methods, Germany should not leave research in an important field like stem-cell research entirely to other countries:

- We will benefit from ES-cell research:
→ we should contribute to such research.

The role of the embryo's parents. The informed consent of the biological parents of the surplus embryos killed to produce stem-cell lines was pointed out as a cen-tral condition by those willing to allow (restricted) importing. To those in favour of more liberal regulation and the production of stem-cell lines inside Germany, parents were 'selfless donors' contributing to the development of life-saving treat-ments. For those opposed to import and production, the parents, but in particular the women who supplied egg cells after arduous and risky hormone treatment, were at risk of becoming 'commodity providers', which would violate their dig-nity. Arguments concerning the role of the parents were:

- Parents are 'selfless donors' providing a resource with the potential to save lives:
→ we can and should make use of this resource (surplus embryos/stem-cell lines).
- Women become 'commodity providers', which violates their dignity:
→ we must protect women by disallowing production and import of ES-cells.

Demand and supply of stem cells. A further moral question that was central was whether importing stem cells would cause research institutes and biomedical enterprises (most existing stem-cell lines are 'owned' by private companies) to produce new lines, thus killing more embryos, in order to satisfy the demand. German researchers importing ES-cells would then, if not explicitly, collaborate in the destruction of embryos. Even if importing was restricted to existing lines (thus not fuelling demand for new ones), it was controversial whether it did not represent a retrospective approval of the killing of embryos. Both opponents of importing and advocates of a liberal regulatory regime pointed out that allowing the importing of ES-cells while forbidding their production was hypocritical (and indicated acknowledgment of limited rights to life and dignity of embryos). Arguments were:

- Supply follows demand and death of embryos must be prevented:
  → import must be forbidden.
- Supply follows demand and death of embryos must be prevented:
  → import must be restricted to existing lines.
- Import constitutes retrospective approval:
  → import must be forbidden.
- Import constitutes retrospective approval:
  → not only import but production should be allowed.

2.4 Pragmatic questions

Possibility and effectiveness of regulation. While the *quaestio* guiding the discussion essentially concerned political regulation (possible answers constituting proposals for regulation), the possibility of effective regulation itself was a much contested issue. Proponents of a liberal regulatory regime argued that restrictions on import of ES-cells could not be effective and would instead lead to a black market for embryonic materials. The pressure from ambitious researchers could only be controlled by giving way to it, so that at least transparency would be ensured. Proponents of a restrictive permission assigned an 'outlet function' to their proposed way of regulation, which would reduce pressure enough to permit effective control. Advocates of a complete ban on importing, finally, argued that once even minor concessions were made, there would be no alternative to further liberalisation. The latter argument is the famous 'slippery slope' argument, which comes in several metaphorical guises: the door that, once opened, cannot be closed again; the fatal and irreversible step in the wrong direction; the breach in the dyke.

- Regulation of import cannot be effective:
  → we must permit importing to enable supervision.
- Complete ban cannot be effective:
  → we must enable controlled importing to reduce pressure.
- (Self-) control can only be ensured by complete ban:
  → we must completely rule out importing.

Comparison with other countries (locational competition). Other countries inside and outside the EU are, like Germany, confronted with the challenge of regulating and restricting the opportunities opened up by biomedical research. Comparison with other countries played a role in the argumentation, in that reference to more liberal countries was regarded as an argument in favour of (restricted) import, while reference to countries banning ES-cell research was made in order to back up arguments against it. On the surface, both arguments appear surprisingly weak: nothing is right or wrong simply because others do it. However, the implication behind these assertions is a more powerful one: comparison with other countries does play a central role under conditions of globalisation, locational competition and reduced opportunities for unilateral national regulation. Since the entire conflict was primarily framed as a moral one, recourse to economic arguments tended to be frowned upon and met by categorical moral counter-arguments. Nonetheless, the fear of falling behind economically and academically is likely to be an important practical reason for many people.

- Other countries are more liberal:
→ we must allow importing in order to remain economically and academically competitive.
- Other countries are equally (or more) restrictive:
→ we can ban (restrict) importing without inflicting competitive disadvantages on the country.

2.5 Conflicts of interest
Conflicts of interest, I have argued in chapter two, must be identified where participants in an interaction have exchanged all general, transferable reasons and have only private, non-transferable reasons left. The conflict between these reasons (such as everybody wanting the largest piece of cake) cannot be resolved by further argumentation. If it is nevertheless to be regulated (rather than left to market and other forces), either bargaining or hierarchical decision is necessary. However, conflicting interests and private reasons are likely to affect argumentation at the practical level as well, and factual and moral reasons can affect bargaining. This is why arguing and bargaining cannot be strictly distinguished empirically.

Interests playing a role in the decision over importing ES-cells were particularly those of research institutes and scientists conducting research in the respective areas. While the motive named publicly was that of finding new cures for diseases (a transferable reason), personal ambitions constituting non-transferable reasons (international reputation, journal publications) cannot be ruled out as motivating preferences. The chemical and pharmaceutical industry could be expected to be in favour of a liberal regulation, too, although its interests were less pronounced in this case, as mainly pure research and not applications were concerned (in contrast to conflicts about genetic engineering of foodstuffs).

Further interests involved were those of patients hoping for new cures from ES-cell research, in particular people suffering from diabetes and Parkinson's or other degenerative diseases. Associations of the disabled played a different role in that they were strictly opposed to research with embryos. They formed a kind of coalition with women's rights campaigners who tried to draw attention to the role of women in the conflict. These three groups were widely regarded as having legitimate interests at stake in the conflict and providing new points of view for the discussion. In spite of this, their reasons have a special and at least partially private status that allows these groups to claim that others cannot fully appreciate their significance because they are not as immediately affected. 'Because I am a patient/disabled/a woman' may be a legitimate reason but is obviously not a transferable one.

3. THE PROCESSING OF THE CONFLICT AND THE DEVELOPMENT OF POLICY

Oliver Brüstle's application to the DFG for funding for a research project using imported ES-cells sparked a lively debate in the media and drew politicians' attention to the fact that further regulation was required. On 24 March 2001, the German parliament (*Bundestag*) established the Study Commission on Ethics and Law of Modern Medicine (*Enquete-Kommission Recht und Ethik in der modernen Medizin*).[4] The commission, staffed with 13 members of parliament and 13 experts named by the parliamentary parties, had been a concern of MPs specialising in bioethics since the debate about the Council of Europe's bioethics convention. That it was eventually set up in 2001 was a direct consequence of the ES-cell debate gaining salience. Only a month later, the government (effectively Chancellor Schröder) instituted a second expert commission. The National Ethics Council (*Nationaler Ethikrat*) was composed of experts and (in smaller numbers) interest-group representatives appointed by the Chancellor. In contrast to the Study Commission, the National Ethics Council was directly responsible to the government rather than to the parliament. The first task with which the Ethics Council was charged was, accordingly, the drafting of a report on the question of importing ES-cells.

In May 2001, the DFG published a statement recommending the importing of ES-cells and pointing out the importance of stem-cell research in modern medicine, thus increasing pressure on the parliament to take action. On May 31, the prime minister of the land of North Rhine-Westphalia, Wolfgang Clement, declared that his land would support the importing of and research with ES-cells. On 20 June, however, the parliament of North Rhine-Westphalia defeated a motion on the subject with the votes of both the Christian Democrats (CDU) and of the Greens, who were part of the governing coalition. On 5 July, the question of importing ES-cells first appeared on the national parliamentary agenda. With the governmental majority, the Bundestag passed a motion submitted by Social Democrats (SPD) and Green Party, demanding a 'conscientious and comprehensive assessment of the import and research with embryonic stem cells' before the Bundestag would again deal with the question within the same year.[5]

In November 2001, the Study Commission presented a comprehensive report pointing out two alternatives for regulation: a complete ban and a conditional, restrictive permission. In December, the Ethics Council published its report, also pointing out the options of a ban and of a conditional permission.[6] However, nine of the Council's 25 members were in favour of a more liberal regulatory regime and regarded the production of stem cells in Germany as ethically justifiable. During the autumn and winter months, an inter-factional group of MPs lead by Maria Böhmer (CDU), Wolf-Michael Catenhusen (SPD), Andrea Fischer (Greens) and Margot von Renesse (SPD) developed the eventually successful compromise motion. A second group led by Wolfgang Wodarg (SPD), Hermann Kues (CDU) and Monika Knoche (Greens) drafted a motion for a complete ban, a third group led by Ulrike Flach (FDP), Katherina Reiche (CDU) and Peter Hintze (CDU) a motion to permit importing.

On 30 January 2002, the Bundestag discussed the Study Commission's report as well as motions 14/8101 (Böhmer *et al.*), 14/8102 (Wodarg *et al.*) and 14/8103 (Flach *et al.*).[7] The debate was celebrated as one of the parliament's finest hours and the quality and atmosphere of argumentation were widely appreciated. The procedure chosen differed from normal legislation in several respects. First, the requirement to vote according to party policy (the whip) was officially suspended, allowing and demanding MPs to vote according to their consciences. Secondly, the motions discussed were the product of inter-party communication and decision. Thirdly, the discussion of mere motions for legislation rather than elaborated bills is not part of the standard legislative procedure, thus constituting a kind of pilot reading before the first reading (cf. Dilling 2003). About 70 per cent of MPs signed one of the three motions and voted for the motion they had signed. Two roll call votes were taken, the first on all three motions, the second on motions 14/8101 and 14/8102, which had gained the highest number of votes. In the second vote, the compromise motion 14/8102, drafted by Böhmer et *al.*, was approved.

Subsequently, the group around Böhmer, Fischer and von Renesse drafted an explicit bill in informal meetings. On 28 February, the Bundestag referred the bill to the parliamentary caucus for education and research for leading consultation and to the caucuses for legal affairs, families, senior citizens, women and youth, and the caucus for health, for further consultation. The final two opted against own consultation, while the caucus for legal affairs rejected both the bill and all amendments. Compared to the motion approved by the Bundestag on 30 January, the bill specifies a number of only vaguely stated points, in particular regarding an appointed date before which imported cells had to be produced and regarding a Central Ethics Committee which was to sanction applications to import.

The formulation of an explicit legislative bill on the basis of a motion leaving many points unspecified and contingent can be regarded as at least partially enabled by bargaining between conflicting groups and interests. Considering the cyclical model of the policy process described in the last chapter, the fact that the central parliamentary debate took place *before* bargaining constitutes an obvious deviation. However, this can be accounted for by the fact that the debate was an exceptional 'pilot reading' and the bill only drafted afterwards. After bargaining over details, few participants involved in the drafting could in the end see all their wishes and proposals realised in the bill, but each of them had their *own* reasons to approve of the result.

On 25 April 2002, the Bundestag held a second hearing on the issue of importing ES-cells. The bill on a 'law for the safeguarding of protection of embryos in the context of import and use of embryonic stem cells'[8] approved by the caucus for education and research was accepted with one amendment (proposed by von Renesse, Fischer and Böhmer), four amendments were rejected. In December 2002, the first embryonic stem-cell lines were legally imported into Germany.

In 2003, an interdisciplinary team from the Max-Delbrück Center for Molecular Medicine and the Research Centre Jülich organised a citizen conference on stem-cell research.[9] Inspired by the Danish consensus conference model, initiators of the citizen conference hoped to enrich the debate with points of view taken from citizen's 'lifeworld', which are often neglected in public debates, and to build up a picture of the variety of opinions on the topic. Beginning early in 2003, conceptualising and planning of the conference took nearly a year. In December 2003, a first meeting of the citizen conference was called; a second and third meeting took place in January and March 2004. In March 2004, a press conference was organised and the citizen report handed over to Wolfgang Thierse, president of the Bundestag. Although the citizen conference itself took place too late to have an impact on policy development and parliamentary decision, it is an interesting subject of analysis if we consider its potential and the influence it *could* have had. According to the cyclical model of the policy process, the citizen conference should have taken place after expert forums had submitted their reports and before a parliamentary decision was taken.

Reconsidering the ideal-typical modes of interaction outlined in chapter three, each mode seems to have been institutionalised in at least one of the forums involved in the decision over importing ES-cells. The table below returns to the matrix presented in section 3.4 and assigns the empirical forums to the respective

Table 4.1: Forums in the ES-cell debate

	Non-Co-ordinative	Co-ordinative
Discursive	*Discussion:* Parl. Study Commission, National Ethics Council, July-November/December 2001	*Deliberation:* Citizen Conference on Stem Cells (MDC Berlin), December 2003-March 2004
Non-discursive	*Debate:* 30 January 2002	*Bargaining:* Drafting of bill, January-April 2002

fields and types of interaction. The arrows indicate the temporal order in which the forums addressed the conflict. Before each of the cases can be assessed in detail, however, some considerations regarding the variables, methods and goals of analysis are due.

4. METHODS OF ANALYSIS

4.1 Goals of analysis and available data

The goal of analysing interaction in the different forums in which the stem-cell conflict was addressed is clear: to illustrate the effects of modes of interaction on actor preferences and to gain a first confirmation (or invalidation) of the respective hypotheses. The case study and the single observations were selected on the explanatory (independent) variable, which prevents selection biases where only a small number of observations can be analysed (King/Keohane/Verba 1994: 137). That is, instead of choosing cases on the basis of whether preference-transformation did or did not occur, a case was chosen in which the different modes of interaction that, according to the theory induce preference-transformation, were expected to be realised.

The assumed causal mechanism between institutional properties, the modes of interaction they enable, and the transformation of actor preferences runs as follows:

institutional properties → mode of interaction → preference-transformation

Data on institutional properties of a forum, such as its composition, its task or the decision rule in it, are comparatively easy to collect. In so far as data on the mode of interaction realised in a forum are available, first descriptive inferences on systematic associations between institutional properties and interaction are possible. The main goal, however, is to draw causal inferences on the effects of modes of interaction on the probability of preference-transformation in a forum.[10] If rational (reason-based) preference-transformation occurs in a setting where the theory seems to rule it out (e.g. in the parliamentary plenum), or if it fails to occur in a setting where the theory predicts it (e.g. in the citizen conference), it remains to be seen in how far this can be accounted for by an imperfect institutionalisation of the respective mode of interaction. Where specific institutional properties can be identified as preventing the realization of a mode of interaction that comes close to the respective ideal-type, causal inferences on the effects of single institutional properties are possible.

Accordingly, the questions that the analysis seeks to answer for each of the different settings are the following:
- Do the specific institutional properties serve to realise a mode of interaction that comes close to the respective ideal-type? To what extent and in what respects is the interaction that takes place in the forum discursive and co-ordinative?
- Which doxastic and practical reasons play a role? How are they being aggregated?

- *Does preference-transformation occur?* If yes, is it due to changes in acceptances or changes in practical reasons and their aggregation?
- Is the result in accordance with hypotheses generated for the respective ideal-type mode of interaction? If not, can it be accounted for by deviation from the ideal type?

Question 1 concerns the value of the explanatory (independent) variable, question 3 the value of the dependent variable. Question 2 looks at the processes and mechanisms by which the former affects the latter, i.e. it aims to illustrate causality (beyond mere correlation). Question 4, finally, seeks to confirm or invalidate hypotheses developed in the theoretical part of the book.

Obviously, a single case study and a comparatively small number of observations can hardly serve as a test for hypotheses satisfying standards of an academic survey. Although such a test would in principle be possible, it goes beyond the scope of this book. The goal of the case study is mainly to explore processes of co-ordination and preference-transformation and to illustrate the analytical value of the theoretical framework. Nonetheless, I believe that some descriptive and causal inferences are, if with less certainty, possible on the basis of the observations. Compared to other political conflicts and decisions, the stem-cell case may in fact be somewhat biased towards more preference-transformation, as the degree of uncertainty was high and as political parties and social groups were divided over the issue (which was reflected in the suspension of party discipline in parliament).

According to the goal of arriving at descriptive and causal inferences, specific methods were used in order to find answers to specific questions. The analysis carried out is mainly a qualitative one. The selection of methods depended both on the question concerned and on the type of data available. Table 4.2 provides an overview of available data and methods of analysis.

For an assessment of the discursiveness of a specific institutional setting, close analysis of transcripts of communicative interaction is desirable. A highly sophisticated instrument that has been developed to assess properties and quality of discursive interaction is the 'discourse quality index' by Jürg Steiner *et al.* (2004: 52–73). However, this index is primarily intended to assess the normative

Table 4.2: Available data and methods of analysis

Subject of analysis	Type of data	Method of analysis
Discursiveness	Transcripts of interaction, interviews, observation reports	Speech-act analysis, qualitative description and analysis
Co-ordinativeness	Transcripts, interviews, observation reports	Speech-act analysis, qualitative description and analysis
Reasons and aggregation	Transcripts, other documents, interviews, observation reports	Argumentation analysis, qualitative description, questionnaires
Preference-transformation	Interviews, questionnaires, voting behaviour	Qualitative and quantitative analysis

promises of deliberative theory, for example, that the discourse promotes justification, respect and constructive politics.

The intention here, by contrast, is to assess more basic empirical properties of interaction at the level of linguistic action, which is why the method of speech-act analysis was selected. Speech-act analysis (SAA) was first employed in a political science context by Katharina Holzinger, who employed it to provide an empirical basis for the distinction between 'arguing' and 'bargaining' as communication modes (Holzinger 2001, 2004, 2005).[11] Section 4.1 provides a brief introduction to the method.

However, transcripts of interaction were only available for two of the four cases: the parliamentary debate and the citizen conference. The lack of available transcripts with regard to the other two cases (expert commissions and bargaining) can be regarded as indicating lack of publicity and thus of discursiveness. Nonetheless, the question of whether discursiveness was obtained or not could only be conclusively answered if the data were available for comparison, which is not the case.

The co-ordinativeness of a forum, defined by the definition of actor-roles and conflict type as well as the task it is charged with, is easier to assess: official documents and statements identify members and responsibilities and provide reasons for the establishment of a new forum. Observation of proceedings, even from a distance, can thus already provide important data in this respect. However, SAA constitutes a valuable tool as well. The presence of bargaining speech acts (see below for a list), in particular, is of relevance for an assessment of the co-ordinative quality of interaction.

The reasons motivating actors' preferences could strictly speaking only be assessed if it were possible to look into people's heads. The same is obviously true for preferences and their transformation. In so far as the reasons that are to be aggregated in a communicative process need to be named and justified, though, transcripts and other documents (reports, statements, minutes of meetings, press releases etc.) provide a valuable source. Again, transcripts are only available for two of the cases, with an incomplete corpus of documents remaining for the other two.

For the Bundestag's debate, a closer analysis of arguments employed was undertaken (see 4.2 for details). The method draws on discourse and argumentation analysis. In a sense, it constitutes an extension of the speech-act analysis: where SAA remains at the level of illocutionary acts, argumentation analysis penetrates to the propositional level.[12] For the citizen conference, questionnaires filled in by participants after each of the three weekend meetings provide evidence on motivating reasons and changes in them (documented in the evaluation by Henning/Erdwien 2004).

Preference-transformation, finally, can either be inferred from people's choices and actions, such as, in the parliamentary case, their voting behaviour, or from their reports in questionnaires and interviews. As illustrated in chapter two, preference-transformation is of relevance as a rational and rationalisable process where it can be regarded as a perlocutionary effect of argumentation. Speech-act and argumentation analysis must therefore be closely linked to an analysis of actors' preferences and preference changes. Organisers of the citizen conference questioned participants at each of the meetings on their opinions and on the reasons for them, thus gaining valuable data for an evaluation of preference-change. For the parliamentary debate, some information could be gained by comparing the motions parliamentarians had signed with their eventual voting behaviour, as the vote was a roll call (i.e. information on who voted for which motion is available). In addition to this, a questionnaire was sent out to those members of parliament who had not signed any of the motions before the debate (achieving a return rate of around 20 per cent). To gain insights with regard to preference-transformation and its causes in expert commissions and bargaining rounds, interviews were conducted with participants in these forums. The data thus obtained obviously do not allow for conclusive statements but nonetheless provide valuable evidence.

In sum, the data available for the parliamentary debate and the citizen conference are much richer than those available for the expert commissions and the bargaining processes. They therefore enable more in-depth analysis as well as more far-reaching conclusions. By contrast, analysis of the latter two cases is conducted in a rather narrative style, with answers to the above questions sometimes remaining hypothetical.[13]

4.2 The method of speech-act analysis

Developed as an approach to linguistic pragmatics by John Austin (2002 [1962]) and his student John Searle (1979, 1983), speech-act theory was introduced to European philosophy and social theory by Jürgen Habermas' 'Theory Of Communicative Action' (1984). Austin and Searle drew attention to the fact that in making an utterance in a conversation, a speaker carries out an action, the speech act (see chapter 2, section 1). An empirical analysis of speech acts undertaken in an actual conversation can focus either on the locutional level, i.e. on what is actually being said and how it is said, on the illocutionary level, i.e. on what actors do *in* saying what they say, or on the perlocutionary level, i.e. on what effects speech acts have on other participants. Take the following example:

<If we don't stop global warming, many species are going to die out.>

At the locutional level, this sentence establishes a causal relationship between global warming and the extinction of species. An analysis focusing on the locutional level might ask what this sentence presupposes (e.g. that there already is global warming) or whether the if-then relation stated is correct. At the illocutionary level, the sentence, if uttered by a speaker, constitutes an assertion, or more precisely, a warning. Speech-act analysis as undertaken here focuses on the illocutionary level and asks what illocutionary acts reveal about the mode of interaction in a given situation. At the perlocutionary level, finally, the warning might act upon the hearer as a threat. If he changed his energy consumption in response to the warning, this would be a perlocutionary effect of illocutionary act.

Illocutionary acts can be grouped into categories according to different properties. The superordinate classification is Searle's (1979) distinction into assertives, directives, commissives, expressives and declarations (see section two, chapter 1). Holzinger (2005: 243) employs lists of 'bargaining' and 'arguing' speech acts in order to detect which mode of communication prevails in a given interaction. Roughly speaking, arguing speech acts fall into Searle's category of assertives, while bargaining speech acts belong to the categories of commissives and directives. Holzinger's distinction is also useful for the purpose of assessing discursiveness.

Bargaining, it was pointed out, is non-public not only in that it often takes place behind closed doors but also in that the reasons employed are private and non-transferable rather than public and transferable. Bargaining speech acts such as DEMANDING, PROMISING or THREATENING point to private resources and interests rather than generalisable reasons or arguments. Presence of bargaining speech acts thus indicates, if not secrecy, a kind of non-publicity with regard to actors' reasons. Absence of bargaining speech acts, on the other hand, may be regarded as an indicator of the publicity of reasons and arguments, which is one of the two requirements for discursiveness. The table below lists arguing and bargaining speech acts as employed for subsequent analysis (cf. Holzinger 2005: 243). In keeping with linguistic convention, verbs referring to illocutionary acts appear in small capitals.

The second requirement for discursiveness, a dialogical rather than monological quality of interaction, can be evaluated by drawing a further distinction among the public (arguing) speech acts. As noted in chapter three, bargaining is always dialogical but not normally public in the required sense. A further subdivision within the category of bargaining speech acts is therefore not relevant for an assessment of discursiveness, as they are necessarily dialogical. Arguing, by contrast, can be either monological or dialogical, which is reflected on the level of illocutionary acts. Considering the list above, several items strike as important elements of both arguing and dialogical interaction (see Table 4.4).

Not all speech acts occurring in natural conversation are captured within these lists. Further categories include rhetorical speech acts (e.g. rhetorical questions, quotations), discourse structurers (e.g. definition of topic, reference to other speakers, meta-discourse), expressives and declarations (e.g. opening/closing a meeting). Some of these types are typical for a specific form of interaction, such as rhetorical speech for public monologues. They are thus registered to further

Table 4.3: Public and non-public speech acts

Public (arguing) speech acts	Non-public (bargaining) speech acts
To CLAIM, ESTABLISH, ASSUME, ASK, REPORT, INFER, JUSTIFY/EXPLAIN, JUDGE, AFFIRM/ACCEPT (a claim), CONTRADICT/CHALLENGE (a claim), CONCEDE, INSIST, TAKE BACK (a claim), ASCERTAIN, AGREEMENT/DISAGREEMENT	To DEMAND/REQUEST, OFFER, SUGGEST (a compromise), PROMOTE (an offer), ACCOMODATE (a demand), PROMISE, THREATEN, ACCEPT (an offer), REJECT (an offer), UPHOLD (a demand), CONCEDE (to a demand), ASCERTAIN CONSENSUS/NON-CONSENSUS

Table 4.4: Dialogical public speech acts

Dialogical public speech acts
to ASK, INFER (from another speaker's assertions), JUSTIFY, AFFIRM/ACCEPT (a claim), CONTRADICT/CHALLENGE (a claim), CONCEDE, INSIST (in face of challenges and counterarguments), TAKE BACK (a claim)

illustrate differences, although the assessment of discursiveness is based on the occurrence and proportion of dialogical public speech acts.

Speech-act analysis is a very detailed analysis of linguistic interaction. A single contribution in a conversation normally consists of a number of speech acts. In most cases, one sentence can be taken to represent one speech act: an assertion, a justification, a question. In pre-prepared speeches such as those heard in the Bundestag, single speech acts are usually easy to identify. In spontaneous speech, by contrast, actors commonly start a sentence, hesitate, correct themselves, rephrase the initial sentence, repeat their utterance, and so on. Consider the following example taken from the citizen conference:

<Citizen 1: Well, on this piece of paper it is being a bit described. Until the four cell stage the cells are not differentiated.
Expert: This is the toti, the totipotency. (...) [babble of voices]
Citizen 2: Does one distinguish between pluri- and multipotency? Or is that one below?
Expert: Well, pluripotency is then even less so to say.>[14]

Citizen 1's contribution may be counted as a single speech act: he REPORTS what the descriptions says. The expert ESTABLISHES that absence of differentiation is known as totipotency. Citizen 2 ASKS whether pluripotency is distinguished from multipotency. The second part of his contribution is an explication of the first part rather than a separate question and would therefore not be counted. The expert answers the question in ESTABLISHING that pluripotency is 'even less'. The brief excerpt hence consists of four typical arguing (public) speech acts, one of which is also characteristic of dialogical interaction.

For comparison, consider the following excerpt from the Bundestag's debate, where the attribution of each utterance unit to a type of illocutionary act is noted behind the respective unit:

<Dr. Ernst Ulrich von Weizsäcker (SPD): Mister President! Mrs Dahl! Ladies and Gentlemen! [GREET] I regard all three motions as ethically well justified and motivated. [EVALUATE] Nobody who has signed one of the motions can be accused of having chosen the easy way or even for having decided on base motives. [CLAIM] Allow me to express this positive evaluation in particular for the motion carrying the name of Margot von Renesse. [EVALUATE] In the beginning, I was indeed tempted to follow the initiative. [REPORT] But what has lead me to eventually oppose the permission of an import? [ASK, rhetorically]...>

The contribution starts with a greeting, which is merely a set phrase and typical of highly formalised interaction. It carries no propositional content and has little illocutionary point. In what follows, each grammatical sentence is associated with one illocutionary act, which is another typical feature of formalised interaction and prepared speeches. Except for the greeting, all illocutionary acts in the excerpt are arguing speech acts. Only the last one, however, is a dialogical one, and a closer look at the context reveals that it has a purely rhetorical function: the speaker does not expect an answer and is in fact the only one who can answer the question.

The data used for speech-act analysis of the debate consists of the transcripts of the Bundestag's 214th session on 30 January 2002, which took about 3¼ hours. From the available transcripts of the citizen conference, a meeting of similar duration was chosen.[15] In the analysis of both the Bundestag's debate and the citizen conference, a record of the type and number of speech acts was compiled for every speaker. This allows us to detect differences between single speakers (e.g. to identify dominant participants in the citizen conference) and to draw inferences about groups of speakers (e.g. the supporters of the compromise motion compared to the supporters of the liberal motion). Because speeches and speaking time in the Bundestag are scheduled in advance, a single case in the Bundestag data set consists of a single contribution. In the citizen conference, where participants were free to contribute to the interaction whenever they liked, single contributions were much shorter, so that a case consists of all the speech acts made by one speaker in the specific meeting. In the analysis of the conference, moderators and organisers were sometimes excluded from the sample.

It may be argued that the isolation of speech acts and their classification into CLAIMING and REPORTING, ESTABLISHING and ASSUMING is to some extent subjective or even entirely contingent. This is why coding was carried out independently by two coders using the same list of types of speech acts.[16] For single cases, there was a variance of 10–15 per cent between the coders. In the aggregation (where the total number of, e.g. arguing and bargaining speech acts was to be stated), variances mostly cancelled one another out, so that on the whole, there appears to have been no bias in a specific direction. Variances mostly concerned the number of speech acts of a specific type identified in a single contribution. For example, coder 3 tended to register several questions where coder 1 registered only one that was paraphrased once or twice. Another somewhat systematic variance concerned the classification of speech acts as to EVALUATE (an arguing speech act) or to RATE (a bargaining speech act), where coder 3 identified more of the former and coder 1 more of the latter.[17] Overall, SAA may therefore be assumed to be a sufficiently reliable instrument that provides reproducible results for the analysis of modes of interaction.

4.3 The method of argumentation analysis

In linguistics and the philosophy of language, there exists a large body of literature on argumentation and discourse analysis.[18] Some of the literature focuses on the conceptual level, while another part analyses empirical instances of interaction. The goal of linguistic and philosophical research on argumentation, however, differs from the one pursued here. While these disciplines aim at generalisations about linguistic interaction, i.e. at knowledge about how discourses are structured *in general*, my concern is with specific cases and a specific conflict. The boundaries of the discourse surrounding the conflict over importing embryonic stem cells are difficult to tell: numerous actors have contributed to it and are still contributing in a number of different forums.[19] The main arguments employed during the observation period have been identified in section 2 of this chapter; a numbered list is provided in the appendix.

The goal of argumentation analysis in the present project is to establish which reasons and arguments dominate a specific institutional context. Argumentation analysis complements speech act analysis in that it turns to the propositional level and considers what is actually being said rather than what people do in saying it. The method used is thus one of qualitative identification of arguments as employed in people's speeches followed by simple counting of the arguments made. Like speech-act analysis, argumentation analysis is only possible where transcripts of the interaction are available. Some intelligence on the most relevant arguments in a forum can of course be gained from interviews with participants. As the frequency of arguments does not necessarily reflect their relevance, such information can be important for the interpretation of results. However, participant's reports are also likely to be biased in one direction or the other. As only the Bundestag transcripts provided suitable data, the quantitative analysis was carried out only for this case, while a more indirect approach was chosen for the other three (interviews for expert commissions and bargaining, secondary data analysis for citizen conference).[20]

The identification of arguments in an utterance or document may, like the identification of speech acts, be criticised as a somewhat subjective matter. At the time of the parliamentary debate, however, the relevant arguments were well known and had been outlined in the reports of the Study Commission and the National Ethics Council. It may therefore be assumed that the analyst's identification of arguments is at least in keeping with that of participants of the debate. Because central arguments were so well known, many speakers did not fully develop every argument, but rather referred to or hinted at arguments by stating either only premise or only conclusion. In this sense, the identification and classification of arguments obviously depends on familiarity with the conflict and discourse.

The list provided in the appendix (numbering arguments identified in section 2) served for the classification of arguments in the analysis of transcripts. An argument is counted as used when either premise and conclusion are stated or when only one is stated, but the other is in some sense implied.[21] Both positive arguments and counter-arguments to them (that a premise is wrong or a conclusion not valid) were counted. The former are marked with '+', the latter with '¬'. If a speaker employs the same argument more than once in a single discursive contribution, i.e. repeats or paraphrases it, the argument is only counted once. On average, speakers in the debate made between five and ten arguments each. The first contributions made by the leaders of the three motions included a greater number of different arguments than the following ones, possibly indicating that arguments only have to be repeated when they refer to particularly important reasons. However, the number of arguments made mainly depended on the speaking time, so that the concentration of arguments in, for example, five minutes speaking time, tended to be similar for all speakers.

Arguments can obviously be realised in different ways, so that the classification on the basis of the pre-defined list constitutes a condensation. Such a list is unlikely to capture all of the reasons and arguments named in a complex and lengthy discourse. Other arguments refer to premises of the listed arguments and provide justification for them. They thus aim to complete the tree structure of argumentation in downward direction and are counted as 'back-up arguments'. Further arguments remain obscure and out-of-the-way to other participants so that they are only mentioned once and not taken up or referred to again. They are thus counted only as 'other arguments'. Arguments entirely unrelated to the collective decision problem are not counted at all. What is of interest here is the processing of a conflict over collective action, not communicative by-products occurring wherever interaction takes place.

To illustrate the method of argumentation analysis, consider the following example, in which arguments are classified according to the list:

Jochen Borchert (CDU/CSU): ... According to my Christian understanding of the human being, human life begins with the fusion of the ovum and the semen. From then on, the unrestricted protection of life applies. From then on, human dignity is inviolable. [+ 7.1] If we bind the beginning of life to other criteria such as development or nidation, we can't avoid the question: is human dignity only inviolable if a person is capable of self-respect? [¬ 7.2] If we give up this boundary, then, I believe, all other boundaries will be arbitrary. [+ 11.3]...

The first argument (7.1) about human life and dignity beginning with fertilisation, is pretty straightforward and easy to classify. The next argument is a counterargument to argument 7.2, which was employed by supporters of the motion for a permission and based on the premise that human life begins with nidation. Supporters of the permission arrived at the conclusion that research with embryos is ethically defensible, whereas this speaker argues that the conclusion is wrong. Instead, he seeks to point out that what follows from the 'nidation-premise' is that we are faced with the question whether human dignity applies only to persons capable of self-respect and consequently rejects the premise. The following argument is classified as a version of the 'slippery slope'-argument (11.3) which in this context means that only a complete ban can ensure effective control and prevent the erosion of fundamental values.

The overall number of arguments employed and the frequencies with which they are referred to in the given setting indicate the degree of aggregation achieved: Have important questions already been resolved in the sense of establishing one answer as collectively valid?[22] Has the number of reasons considered relevant been reduced? The dominance of factual, legal, moral or pragmatic arguments is treated as an additional marker for the stage of argumentation and processing of conflict. Where speakers refer to counter-arguments to their own position, this indicates that they acknowledge the relevance of other reasons, but have eventually arrived at a different conclusion: the stage of aggregation must thus be an advanced one. These matters, which are of primary interest to the question of how reasons are processed in different forums within the process of collective decision-making, can be addressed by argumentation analysis in a quantitative manner. Mere counting of arguments, however, cannot be sufficient to grasp all relevant aspects of the argumentation process and only makes sense where suitable transcripts are available.

Other properties of argumentation will therefore be addressed in a more selective manner to further illustrate results. Two pragmatic phenomena described by H.P. Grice (1979) are of particular interest in this regard: implicatures and hedges. Implicatures, it was noted in section 2.5, can reveal shared reasons that do not require explicit justification. On the other hand, they can also be used for rhetorical or even manipulative purposes. Reconsider the counterargument the speaker quoted above makes to the claim that human dignity does not apply to embryos before nidation and that they can therefore be used for research purposes. If the consequence of accepting the premise that human life begins with nidation was only that we have to *ask* ourselves the question whether dignity applies to persons incapable of self-respect, the argument would be quite a weak one. However, the way the speaker puts the question implicates something about the *answer* supporters of a ban would give: he insinuates that they would be inclined to deny human dignity to persons incapable of self-respect, such as very small children, severely mentally disabled people or coma-patients.

Hedges are short phrases speakers tend to use when they feel that they are violating one of the conversational maxims. They thereby try to reassure the hearer of their co-operation and offer an excuse for the momentary disregard of a maxim. Sometimes hedges are used to draw attention to implicatures that might otherwise go unnoticed. More commonly, however, they are used to express deference. Take the following example from the citizen conference, where hedges are marked by italics:

> Now my question, you already referred to it, that one does not quite know what the function of these cells is, where one has found them, and doesn't quite know, what they are doing there, *to put it more polemically maybe*.
> This is not quite clear for me, when you say I want blood stem cells, *I say it banally now, I would say*: then you take them from the blood.

Both utterances were made in the expert hearing, where the citizens as laypeople questioned researchers and politicians. In both cases, speakers seem to make an excuse for speaking 'polemically' or 'banally', while nothing of what they say is in fact polemical or banal. Instead, the use of hedges may be seen as expressing (apparently too much) respect. In particular with regard to the citizen conference, hedges can thus reveal something about the relationship between citizens and experts and about the citizens' confidence in their own reasons, acceptances and ideas.

4.4 Semi-structured interviews

Participants in the expert commissions and in the bargaining meetings were questioned by means of semi-structured interviews. This method was chosen in order to receive comparable answers to a number of pre-defined questions relating to the hypotheses and at the same time to gain the maximum amount of information. Semi-structured interviews are directed conversations where the interviewer asks specific questions but tries not to constrain the conversation. Wherever new issues arose, interview partners were given time to elaborate on them and follow-up questions were asked. Alternative methods such as questionnaires or more structured interviews have the advantage that they yield more comparable data for the single cases. However, as the number of relevant actors (in particular in the bargaining sessions) was small and as it was of particular interest to gain insights into their respective roles and personal backgrounds, the informal context of a semi-structured interview was more suitable in this case. The following are central questions which were in this or a similar form addressed in all interviews:

- When do you remember the topic of stem-cell research first appearing on the political agenda? What were your very first feelings and opinions about it?
- How would you characterise the atmosphere and interaction in the forum?
- Did you learn anything in the forum or did you recognise new aspects as relevant for the evaluation of alternative options?
- How important was it to arrive at a consensual decision in the forum?
- Did you change your opinions or preferences in the forum?
- Do you know whether other members of the forum changed their preferences?
- Which arguments were central in the forum? How do you evaluate them?
- Which reasons were central for your decision?
- Which reasons do you think were central for the other members of the forum?
- Did you have to make any concessions with regard to the report/bill?
- Did other members have to make concessions?
- Do you think the members of the forum supported the report/bill for the same reasons or for different reasons?
- What do you think of the stem cell compromise today? What future developments do you expect?

4.5 Measuring preference-change

Preference changes, it was noted before, can be inferred either from an actor's behaviour or from his reports in surveys or interviews. Claims about preference-transformation in the expert forums and bargaining meetings are based on interviews. For the parliamentary debate, however, the roll call allowed inferences to be made from voting behaviour: it is simply assumed that those parliamentarians who voted for the same motion they had signed in advance had not changed their preferences. To those parliamentarians who did not sign any of the motions, a questionnaire was sent out (provided, with results, in the appendix). The most important questions here were whether respondents had learned any new facts from the debate (indicating change of acceptances), whether they recognised new aspects as relevant for the evaluation (indicating changes in practical reasons) and whether they had changed their preferences over the motions during the debate or knew of anyone else who had done so. Both voting behaviour and the results of the survey, as well as specific problems, are described in some detail in chapter five, section 2.

For the citizen conference, a comprehensive evaluation by Jörg Henning and Birgitt Erdwien (2004) is available. Before the first and after each of the following weekend meetings, participants filled in questionnaires on the atmosphere in the forum, on their evaluation of the procedure and on their own feelings and opinions. Henning and Erdwien's research interest obviously differs from the one of this project, so that some of the results are only of minor relevance here. However, answers to questions concerning the most relevant aspects of the topic, participants' own knowledge about the matter and the comparative evaluation of arguments for and against ES-cell research are indicative of preference-changes. Moreover, the qualitative assessment of the conference by direct observers addresses preference-changes and their direction. Where they are relevant with regard to the hypotheses, data from Henning and Erdwien's evaluation are therefore discussed at more length in section 5.4.

Obviously, a more systematic measurement of actors' preferences and their transformation would be desirable. In particular, data on precisely when, how and for what reasons transformation took place would enable valuable insights into causes for and processes of preference-transformation. However, such data can only be gained in experimental settings such as the citizen conference. Most political decision-making processes, by contrast, can only be studied after the event, and relevant actors are not rarely reluctant to answer researchers' questions.

5. SUMMARY

This chapter was intended to provide the reader with background information for the following chapter's analysis of interaction in the different forums that addressed the question of whether importing embryonic stem cells should be allowed in Germany. Section 1 described how the opening up of new opportunities in biomedical research necessitated a political decision and gave rise to a political conflict. Section 2 outlined the different (factual, legal, moral and pragmatic) questions that were controversial within this conflict and the competing interests involved in it. For each question, the most important reasons named and arguments made were stated. Section 3 described the course of events between August 2000 (when the first application for research with ES-cells was made) and March 2004 (when the citizen conference presented its report). It thus gave a brief account of how the conflict was processed by political actors and institutions in Germany.

Section 4 addressed the data and the methods used for its analysis, pointing out limitations and potential for drawing descriptive and causal inferences. In particular the methods of speech act and argumentation analysis, I think, are of relevance beyond the case that is analysed here. They constitute valuable tools for the examination of linguistic interaction (where tape recordings or transcripts are available): speech act analysis enables the identification of different modes of interaction, while argumentation analysis provides insights into how acceptances and practical reasons are co-ordinated.

NOTES

1 'Convention for the Protection of Human Rights and Dignity of the Human Being with Regard to the Application of Biology and Medicine', Council of Europe, Nov. 19, 1996.

2 I will reserve the term '*quaestio*' to the superordinate controversy, to which a number of '*questiones*', subsumed under the four dimensions are relevant.

3 Abortion is in fact illegal in Germany but exempt from punishment. The Bundestag's decision over abortion is another interesting example of a compromise solution that is inconsequent and contradictory with regard to higher-ranking principles but politically successful and now widely accepted. Like the law on importing ES-cells, the law on abortion was devised under the leadership of Margot von Renesse.

4 BT-Drs. 14 / 3011. Official documents of the German Bundestag (*BT-Drucksachen*) are available online at www.bundestag.de.

5 BT-Drs. 14 / 6551. The motion brought by the oppositional CDU/CSU (BT-Drs. 14/6314) essentially demanded the same, but named different reasons for a moratorium.

6 The report discusses four options A-D, A being the most liberal one and D favouring a complete ban. However, proponents of A also embrace option B (demanding a restrictive permission) and proponents of D also embrace C (demanding a moratorium and preliminary ban). Option B, however, is more liberal than the restrictive option proposed by the Study Commission in that it does not seek to limit import to existing stem-cell lines.

7 All BT-Drs.

8 BT-Drs. 14 /8846.

9 The concept and main results of the project are published in Tannert & Wiedemann 2004.

10 King, Keohane & Verba (1994) point out descriptive and causal inferences as the appropriate goal of social inquiry. Descriptive inferences use observations in order to learn about other, unobserved cases. Causal inferences use observations in order to identify causal effects (King, Keohane & Verba 1994: 8).

11 On speech act analysis as a tool in political science, see also Nullmeier 2003.

12 The transcripts of the citizen conference did not provide a satisfactory basis for such an analysis as arguments were only referred to rather than made in the plenary meetings. For the meetings of smaller working groups, as well as for informal discussions among participants and the drafting of the vote, no transcripts are available. As the evaluation of the conference (Henning & Erdwien 2004) shows, most substantial discussions took place in these contexts.

13 A complete list of data employed for the analysis is provided in the appendix.

14 This and further translations from the transcripts of the Bundestag debate and the citizen conference are my own. Translation, in particular of colloquial speech, is a tricky matter. Examples can therefore fulfil only illustrative purposes and surely do not fulfil demands for conscientious professional translation.

15 The specific meeting is one in which citizens discuss which the most relevant aspects of the matter are and which questions they want to pose to experts in the final hearing. It was chosen because it does not include any pre-arranged expert presentations and because it took place on the second weekend, where initial organisational problems had already been resolved. Interaction therefore seemed to come closest to the ideal-typical mode of citizen deliberation. Unfortunately, no transcripts are available of the late-night meetings in which the participants formulated their report, as interaction in this context probably came even closer to the ideal-type in that citizens actually engaged in comparative evaluation instead of in merely preparing an expert hearing.

16 The list of speech acts was jointly developed by the coders after a first explorative analysis of the material and is provided in the appendix. Transcripts of the parliamentary debate were coded by the author (coder 1) and Katharina Holzinger (coder 2), transcripts of the citizen conference by the author and Markus Lindner (coder 3). All coders were familiar with speech act analysis and two were trained linguists.

17 'To RATE' was, in contrast to 'to EVALUATE' intended to classify assessments of other speakers' offers, not of claims, options for action, or possible states of the world these would bring about. Apparently, they were more difficult to distinguish than expected in case of the citizen conference.

18 A classic is Toulmin 1958. For a collection see van Eemeren et al. 1987, for a comprehensive theory. Gallhofer and Saris (1996) link argumentation and decision theory in a political science context for an analysis of foreign-policy decision-making.

19 Linguistic analysis (e.g. Klein 1980) typically uses experimental data: a group is confronted with a real or fictional conflict or question and asked to discuss it. Boundaries of the discourse are thus drawn by the artificial setting.

20 The transcripts of the citizen conference were less suitable for argumentation analysis because a large proportion of interaction constituted meta-discourse rather than substantial discourse. Moreover, the total number of different arguments employed was too high, and the arguments too diverse, to allow for a useful classification. Information on arguments was instead gained from data collected by the organisers by means of questionnaires filled in by participants after the meetings.

21 A premise may count as implicated when it has already been discursively established (when another speaker has recently mentioned it) or when it can easily be inferred from the context. The conclusion 'import must be forbidden' follows from many premises and cannot by itself count as an argument.

22 This may also be regarded as a test of Brandom's claim that an assertion once successfully vindicated need not be justified again.

chapter | case analysis: forums, modes of
five | interaction and preference-
| formation in the stem-cell conflict

It is fortunate that, in the German ES-cell debate, institutionalisations of all four of the types of interaction identified in chapter three can be observed. Although I assume that forums of these types do play a role in most complex political decisions, they are rarely institutionalised to such a degree and nor do they usually enjoy as much public attention as in this case. The case is peculiar, however, in that the order in which the different forums addressed the conflict did not follow the normal course of legislation nor the cyclical model of policy-making. The road towards compromise was paved even while factual questions were still being fiercely debated; the parliament discussed motions to draft a bill rather than the bill itself; and a citizen conference took place long after the decision had been taken.

The forums are discussed in the order in which they were initiated. Section 1 looks at the two expert commissions, the Study Commission on Ethics and Law in Modern Medicine and the National Ethics Council. Section 2 deals with the parliamentary debate on 30 January 2002, after which the motion for a compromise was passed. Section 3 analyses the drafting of the eventual bill that took place in what I describe as a bargaining round behind closed doors. Section 4 analyses the citizen conference that took place in Berlin in the winter of 2003–4. This chronological view is supposed to reconcile the theory-driven method of analysis with descriptive accuracy and to indicate how arguments have developed over time.

1. EXPERT COMMISSIONS: FRAMING THE CONFLICT

Looking at the two expert forums that were set up to deal with the conflict, ideal-typical expert discussion was apparently more successfully institutionalised in the National Ethics Council than in the Parliamentary Study Commission on Ethics and Law in Modern Medicine. However, the intentions and expectations behind the set-up of the commission were different ones from the beginning. Study Commissions are set up by the German Bundestag to address complex ethical questions with long-term relevance. The fact that majorities in the Study Commissions reflect those in the plenum, and that experts are selected by the political parties, transfers parliamentary logics into the commission forum. Although some Study Commissions have been successful in initiating and framing debates, the majority were less effective (Altenhof 2002). Many reports were dominated by the governing parties' position, with minority votes from opposition parties. In these cases, it was easy to discard reports as products of party politics 'as usual'.

A commission on bioethics was a particular concern of MPs who were critical with regard to the consequences of biotechnological progress and worried about the protection of unborn life. The SPD, which at that time was the largest parliamentary party, had the right to name a chair for the new commission. Within the SPD parliamentary group, two MPs ran for the office. Wolfgang Wodarg was a well known and uncompromising pro-life campaigner, who later led the motion for a complete ban on ES-cell import. Margot von Renesse was a much-esteemed legal expert who also was widely seen as critical of biotechnology and ES-cell research, although less severely so than Wodarg. Von Renesse beat Wodarg by a thin majority and became chair of the new Study Commission. The other 13 MP members and 13 expert members were named by the parliamentary parties.[1] Because the conflict reached beyond party boundaries, party membership did not determine a member's position on ES-cell import. However, the MPs selecting (and selected) to join the commission were those who had been active in the field of bioethics before and were mostly on the sceptics' side. Von Renesse, who had been undecided and sceptical at the beginning of the discussion, turned out to be far more liberal and willing to compromise than some of her supporters had expected, so that a critical commission was lead by a liberal chair.

For the National Ethics Council, there exist no earlier models in German politics. Critics regarded it as an attempt to bypass parliamentary processes and to create a counterweight to the critical Study Commission. Members were named by Chancellor Schröder, who was known to take a liberal position on stem-cell research and to support importing, at least in part for reasons of economic competition with more liberal countries like Britain.[2] While the Study Commission was, according to the general opinion of parliamentarians and journalists, slanted towards a ban, the Ethics Council was slanted towards a liberal position. Of the 25 members of the council, 19 were experts (mostly university professors) and six were named as representatives of interest groups or as important political personalities, including two bishops, a patient representative, a trade unionist, and two former ministers. Among the experts, five were from the legal profession, eight were researchers in the life sciences or medicine, and six were 'experts on ethics', including philosophers and theologians as well as one sociologist. As several of the latter were known to be in favour of stem-cell research and as biomedical researchers constituted the largest group in the council, the allegation of a bias appears to some extent justified. Schröder's motivation in establishing the council may well have been to present ethically plausible arguments for permitting importing and to show that the majority of an interdisciplinary expert commission supported it.

The Study Commission, although set up with the intention to inform parliamentary decision on importing ES-cells, deviated from the conditions that serve to institutionalise expert discussion in several respects.[3] First of all, its members were not selected on the basis of expertise alone but on grounds of party membership or (in case of the expert members) partisanship. Moreover, both MP members and chair were elected by the parliamentary groups of their party and thus functioned, at least in part, as representatives. Within the parliamentary parties, the recruitment mechanism was mainly one of self-selection. The *role* ascription 'expert' was thus less distinct for the Study Commission members than for the Ethics Council members. The *conflict* that faced the two forums was multi-faceted and multi-dimensional, as outlined in chapter four, section 2. While the strong presence of legal and biomedical experts in the forums indicates that many factual questions had yet to be resolved (and the reports did indeed contribute to their resolution), the underlying moral divides and conflicts of interest were salient in both as well. How was the *task* of the two forums defined? A hope that is frequently stated in inaugural meetings is that experts will arrive at consensual recommendations for political action. As pointed out before, though, expert consensus on political action constitutes a rather exceptional case. What the two forums achieved was in fact precisely what was defined as the ideal-typical task of expert discussions: they assessed, justified and pointed out *options* for action. Figure 5.1 locates the options proposed by the Ethics Council and the Study Commission as well as the motions discussed and voted on in the Bundestag on 30 January 2002, on a continuum between a complete ban and a complete permission (of both importing and production).

The strongest congruence exists between the options presented in the Study Commission and, respectively, the ban (B) and the compromise (C) motion in the Bundestag. This is hardly surprising as several of the leaders of these motions were also members of the Study Commission. There is also convergence between the options A and B presented by the Ethics Council and the liberal motion (L) in the Bundestag. Comparing the arguments presented for each of the motions with the commission's and the council's report also shows similarities in argumentation

Figure 5.1: Options in decision over ES-cell import

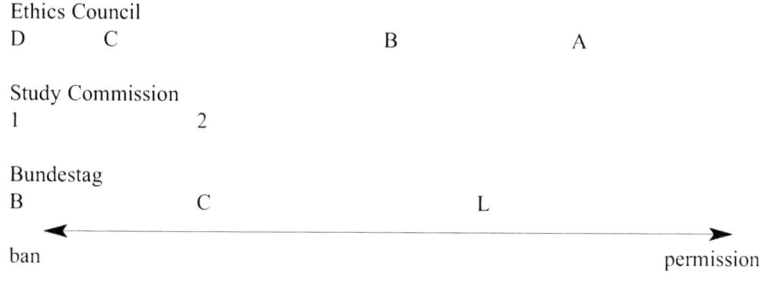

(B = ban; C = compromise; L = liberal)

and convergence of reasons.

Regarding the *publicity* of interaction, evidently neither of the forums was fully public. However, both published reports (including results of votes) and remained comparatively accessible for insiders (e.g. the commission for other MPs). Moreover, minutes of meetings and other documents of the Study Commission are available either on the internet or in archives.[4] The Ethics Council later held fully public meetings and published transcripts on the internet, albeit on different topics. Concerning the *dialogical quality* of interaction, the set-up of commission and council appears favourable. Every member was supposed to become a speaker and contribute to discussions. Numbers of 26 and 25 participants, respectively, are not too high to prevent a give-and-take of reasons and assertions. To assess the effective degree of discursiveness and co-ordinativeness of the expert forums, members of both were asked for their evaluation. In order to test the explanatory potential of the ideal-type mode of interaction, the result will be compared with the observed type and degree of preference-transformation and the way in which reasons were aggregated.

1.1 Discursiveness

Given the politicisation of the topic in the media and the public polarisation into a 'pro-life' and a 'pro-research' side, it is hardly surprising that dialogical interaction was not easy to achieve in the expert forums. At this time, fronts among experts and MPs were hardened. For the case of the Study Commission, von Renesse reports that a number of conflicts over procedural rules soured the atmosphere. It seems that the deep moral conflict within the forum was transferred to, and continued on, the organisational level, which at first seemed to render substantial discussions impossible. Representing the 'absolute minority' in the commission, she also felt fiercely attacked by other members and placed in an aggressive and charged environment.[5]

According to von Renesse, the situation began to change in spring 2001, after a minority vote on a EU directive on patents in biotechnology had deprived the commission's report[6] of its intended public attention and influence on the debate. Consequently, von Renesse began to campaign for what was labelled 'forked reports'. She saw the decision as essentially one between two options: either the commission would produce research-critical reports, in which case she would ruin it with minority votes, or it could produce comprehensive and well researched reports that stated different opinions. Only in the latter case could the commission have political influence. Whereas previously the group was effectively split into two subgroups, one of which devised the majority vote, the other the minority vote, the forum was now kept intact. The idea was to go as much of the way as possible together and then name reasons why, at a certain point, it was necessary to part. The report would thus consist of a single and coherent text that had been discussed in the plenum in every detail, including the justifications for divergent opinions and their phrasing. Knowing that forking was possible wherever divides were too deep, the commission members were able to adopt a more matter-of-fact style of argumentation and to reach consensus on several factual questions that were still controversial.[7] Although smaller working groups dealt with specific topics (e.g. potency of stem cells), all results were presented and discussed in the plenum.

The 160-page report, which provides a detailed and conscientious discussion of the scientific, legal and moral issues concerned, as well as transcripts of hearings with external experts, suggests an earnest, results-oriented style of interaction. Margot von Renesse still regards the introduction of forked reports as the key to the commission's success:

> Now all that counted were arguments. One had gotten away from the situation in which it was 'one group is in favour of human dignity, and the other against it. One group is in favour of German economic competitiveness, and the other against it.' This trench warfare, ... this religious war, was replaced by mutual respect, especially because of those forked reports. There were no more insinuations that anyone was an enemy to mankind. Or an enemy to economic prosperity ... There was a passionate discussion, but the allegation that the other is a sleazebag had gone.[8]

In the Ethics Council, the first meetings were similarly characterised by suspicions and a tense atmosphere. The way in which members were appointed, according to a formula intended to include representatives of all relevant disciplines and also proponents of both the liberal and the restrictive position, seems to have brought antagonistic logics of interaction to the forefront. Prof. Wolfgang van den Daele, sociologist and founding member of the council, describes the initial constellation as one in which everyone took a quick check on the other members' opinions on ES-cell research, which was followed by a nearly immediate polarisation. In spite of a formal politeness, the polarised groups were stalking each other on procedural matters and interaction was, van den Daele remembers, a matter of very careful strategising.[9]

Under such conditions of polarisation and mutual suspicion, it becomes particularly important to comply with procedural rules and to avoid any kind of (perceived) discrimination against or inattention to individual members. Following Grice, the enforcement of and obedience to procedural rules can be seen as a signal to interlocutors that one is sticking to the 'co-operation principle'. However, strict proceduralism can also be detrimental to dialogue and argumentative coherence. In the council, a list of speakers was rigidly followed, so that more spontaneous questions and challenges were difficult. Instead, speakers were encouraged to deliver monologues on different points, as they did not know when they would next get the chance to make a contribution.[10] This illustrates a common conflict between the equality of participants in a discourse and its dialogical quality. To make sure that all members of a forum have equal opportunities to contribute to a discussion, it may be necessary to enforce a list of speakers. This prevents spontaneous reactions and makes it impossible to immediately challenge or reject assertions, which would be required for dialogical interaction. The conflict can, to some degree, be overcome by a sufficient level of trust between participants, who grant one another the right to speak out of turn, expecting that each of the others will do the same for them. Van den Daele describes how, once the council had become more institutionalised and social contact between its members had intensified, discursive modes of interaction were easier to achieve and maintain, in spite of moral divides.[11]

Notwithstanding these initial problems, the Ethics Council, like the Study Commission, managed to resolve basic factual and legal questions. Council members who were experts on either gave short presentations to provide the others with the necessary background information. Questions were posed and answered in a matter-of-fact way and respectful ambiance. Disciplinary boundaries were respected, so that lawyers enjoyed authority on legal matters and biomedical researchers on scientific and medical matters. The first attempt was to find common 'reference lines' – to establish what the legal situation was and what was technically possible. Moreover, the Ethics Council received a draft version of the Study Commission's report before it was officially published.[12]

Although a common reference frame of joint acceptances could thus be established, the evaluation of options for political action remained difficult. In contrast to the Study Commission, the council split into two separate groups at an early stage. As soon as the legal and scientific preliminaries were settled, it was also clear that a joint position was out of reach. Each side insisted on presenting their position and arguments itself. Consequently, the intention to write the report together was given up and the two groups of liberals and opponents each worded their own part of the final document. Once the opposing groups had formed, the argumentative quality of discussions in the plenum declined. It was apparent to members of both groups that the other side would not be persuaded by their moral arguments and that differences in evaluation had become irreducible. Discussions in the plenum were more and more moved to a meta-level, while discussions in the sub-groups were characterised by results-oriented calculation on how best to present their position in the report.

This result is easily comprehensible in light of the time pressure under which the council had to prepare its report. While the Study Commission and its working groups met frequently throughout the year 2001, the Ethics Council had, after the constitutive meeting, only five further plenary gatherings. Given its polarisation, transferring the phrasing of the report to coalitions of opponents and supporters was apparently the only way to accomplish its task, albeit with negative consequences for the quality of the discourse. Instead of exchanging and assessing arguments, each group tried to make its own arguments 'waterproof'. As van den Daele notes, the drafting of the report was mainly the 'argumentative vesting of positions that had been clear from the beginning'.[13]

Evidently, both the Ethics Council and the Study Commission had problems in producing and maintaining a mode of discursive interaction. Early polarisation and a lack of trust increased antagonistic logics of interaction to a degree that renders argumentation impossible and brought procedural issues to the forefront. In the case of the Study Commission, experience and a procedural agreement to produce a forked report eventually made discursive interaction easier. In the case of the Ethics Council, an agreement to disagree (which at first sight appears to be a similarity to the Study Commission) lead to a split into two groups, which impaired the forum as a whole. Despite these caveats, the Study Commission would clearly qualify as discursive and the Ethics Council as discursive rather than non-discursive. All of the respective members had more or less equal opportunities to take the floor and challenge each other's assertions, which is central to dialogical interaction. There was also a lively exchange of relevant factual and legal arguments in both forums, which the reports document comprehensively. Finally, the reasons for and against political options that were considered in the forum are all of a generalisable, non-private kind that is suitable for public justification.

1.2 Co-ordinativeness

The co-ordinativeness of expert discussion is ideal-typically expected to be low. In fact, the forked reports of both forums set up to address the stem-cell conflict seem to confirm the prediction of indecision. For the Ethics Council, which in its composition more distinctly institutionalised the ideal type than the Study Commission, this lack of co-ordinative faculties is described by van den Daele: as soon as the different evaluations were clear, the discussion was cut short, and the members of the forum simply accepted their disagreement.[14] Most of them were renowned experts in their field who had published academically on bioethics or taken part in the lively newspaper debate on the topic. Under these conditions, a revocation in the at least partially public forum of the council could have been perceived as a loss of face. In this sense, personal interests did eventually have some relevance in the council.

At the same time, there was no clearly discernible reward for co-ordination. The council's reports had only advisory weight and had comparatively little impact, so that the material interests of its members were not at stake in its decisions. Members from both sides had strong moral feelings on the importing of ES-cells and believed that a compromise would damage rather than promote their respective positions. Van den Daele's impression was that consensus was clearly out of reach as soon as the participants realised what the composition of the forum was. The question was then how to deal with fundamental disagreements rather than how to resolve them.[15]

Although the underlying conflict was obviously one between practical, namely moral reasons, the argumentative focus in the council was on acceptances or doxastic reasons. Special emphasis was placed on logical consistency: both supporters and opponents of importing tried to deduce their position from fundamental principles rather than justifying it pragmatically. One reason that was of central importance to Chancellor Schröder, who initiated the council, was very soon discarded as untenable with regard to these principles: the criterion of economic competitiveness. While all could agree that economic considerations must be subordinated to moral ones, the opposition between moral rationales remained irreducible. Co-ordination was thus limited to coalitions between particularly active members of the council, of which one prepared the argumentation for a liberal solution and the other that for a moratorium or strict ban. An interesting detail is the fact that Therese Neuer-Miebach, who was also an expert member for the CDU/CSU in the Study Commission, was a leader of the restrictive coalition in the Ethics Council.[16] Here, the council is likely to have benefited from work in the commission, so that at least with regard to the argumentation against importing of ES-cells, the expert forums were not entirely independent of one another.

At a later stage, and after the decision on ES-cell import, when the forum had become more institutionalised, not only the discursive quality of meetings (as pointed out above), but also its co-ordinative capabilities increased. Council members began to identify with the institution and to connect its reputation with their own. Having noticed that non-unanimous votes failed to receive the desired public attention, they increasingly sought to achieve consensual reports. The first consensual report on reproductive cloning was published in September 2004. Although the topic was morally not uncontroversial within the forum either, members took the challenge to produce a unanimous report. The goal was to demonstrate to the public that the council was capable of arriving at a consensus on at least some topics. Promoting the institutional self-interest of the council in this way, however, required moves towards bargaining and compromise.

Such effect-oriented discussions, which required concessions from most members, could only take place behind closed doors. The introduction of fully public meetings (transcripts of which are available over the internet) and non-public meetings in 2003 apparently improved the discursive quality of the public ones and opportunities for co-ordination in the non-public ones. In 2001, when the Ethics Council dealt with the ES-cell import conflict, however, such co-ordinative faculties had not yet developed.

With regard to the Study Commission, the seemingly similar result – a forked report – conceals significant differences. In spite of the fact that all members stuck to their original position on the question of ES-cell import, the cornerstones of the subsequent compromise solution were laid here. Two factors were critical in enabling this. For one thing, all parliamentary parties except the FDP were internally divided over bioethical issues. The antagonistic logics of party competition that are often transferred into parliamentary commissions were thus less relevant within the Study Commission on Ethics and Law in Modern Medicine. Although a kind of fractional discipline among proponents of both the liberal and the restrictive position began to emerge, the commission members did not have to fear sanctions from their parties.

The second important factor was that the commission was aware that it was informing and preparing an impending parliamentary decision. In the motion passed after the Bundestag's first plenary debate on ES-cell import on July 5, 2001, the Study Commission's report was explicitly named as a basis for a decision to be taken within the same year. According to Bundestag by-laws, the task of parliamentary study commissions always lies in the preparation of complex and far-reaching decisions. In most cases, however, these are decisions whose time has not quite come, so that the referral to a study commission is more or less an acknowledgment of the fact that the matter is not ready for a decision yet.[17] Accordingly, commission reports rarely receive much attention beyond a small community of experts. In this case, though, things were different. The high salience of the topic, the perceived urgency of a decision and the impression that the Bundestag's decision would be path-breaking for the future of German biopolitics put the commission under particular pressure. Among MPs, its members were some of the few experts on bioethics and biotechnology and felt both an institutional and a social responsibility.

With the awareness that they were capable of shaping the outcome of a far-reaching political decision, several commission members around the chair, Margot von Renesse, and Ulrike Riedel, began to seek a more pragmatic approach. Riedel was not only an expert member for the Greens, she was also a personal assistant to Andrea Fischer, the former health minister, who was among the leaders of the compromise motion and who also drafted the eventual bill. Von Renesse and Riedel realised that there were no clear majorities either for a complete ban or for a very liberal solution. Whereas the Ethics Council focused on conflicting fundamental values, the Study Commission chose the constitution for its crucial point of reference. Although the relevant articles in the German *Grundgesetz* refer to the values of human dignity, life and freedom of research, the question of what can constitutionally be allowed or forbidden was a pragmatic rather than a moral one. The opposition between an 'ethics of healing' and the protection of life and dignity, which dominated discussions in the Ethics Council and the media, was replaced by the opposition between the constitutionally guaranteed freedom of research (Art. 5) and the protection of human dignity (Art. 1) and life (Art. 2).

The moral conflict between fundamental values remained irreducible, as no priority of one over the other could be agreed upon. The generally accepted constitutional articles, by contrast, served as guide to the contextualisation of values and restricted the set of feasible options. Only because the underlying question about the status of the embryo did not have to be touched upon, did co-ordination become possible. The consensus that any law on ES-cell import must be constitutional (and would otherwise be stopped by the supreme court) opened the way to a compromise. Between von Renesse and Riedel it became clear that there were two different rationales for limited importing that could be defended as in keeping with constitutional norms. Von Renesse wanted to enable ES-cell research but she knew that the import 'could not be implemented if a single embryo was to be sacrificed for it'. Riedel wanted to make ES-cell research dispensable in the long run, but came to believe that this required limited importing and controlled research in order to find substitutes.[19]

Supporters of a compromise motion were drawn from both the sceptics' and the liberals' side. Some of the sceptics began to see that a complete ban might not be constitutional and that a restrictive permission might better promote their goal of preventing and reducing ES-cell research than the unrestricted permission that was likely to ensue otherwise. Supporters of a liberal solution, particularly within the coalition parties, had to accept that there was no parliamentary majority for a permissive law. Chancellor Gerhard Schröder, who was known to be in favour of ES-cell research and to have a particular eye on German economic competitiveness, was persuaded by von Renesse to support the compromise motion, although he later campaigned for a more liberal solution.

The Study Commission's co-ordinative achievement was thus to initiate the formation of a third group in a polarised context. Supporters of this 'third way' had made pragmatic concessions with regard to their favoured option because they realised that it was not feasible either with regard to the constitution or with regard to the given preference constellation. Regarding the hypotheses developed for institutionalised discussion, it is surprising in itself that the commission managed to produce a report of which only a single page in over 150 does not enjoy the consent of all its members (and even the phrasing of this forked statement was agreed upon in the plenum).[20] What is more, two of the motions voted on on 30 January 2002 were developed here, including the one that was eventually successful.[21] At the same time, it seems that the Study Commission could only develop these co-ordinative faculties because its organisation and composition, unlike that of the Ethics Council, enabled interaction that significantly deviated from the ideal-type mode of discussion among experts.

1.3 Preference-transformation and aggregation of reasons

The hypotheses about the effects of discussion as a mode of interaction on preference-transformation suggest that actor preferences are unlikely to change within respective forums. Members are selected for their noted expertise in the field. It may thus be assumed that they are all well informed and aware of relevant counter-arguments. Their preferences will be based on stable acceptances and reasons. If acceptances have to be reconsidered in the light of new information, this will not alter the effective reasons on which their preferences are based. Moreover, there are no incentives to reconsider their own position, so that indecision is the result to be expected.

Looking at the Study Commission and the Ethics Council, there is indeed little to indicate that preference-transformation has taken place. The Study Commission's report lists names of the members who support a complete ban (option A) and those who support a compromise solution (option B).[22] Among the supporters of option B are mainly the same people who, earlier in the same year, had passed a minority vote against the commission's negative assessment of the EU biopatents directive.[23] Apparently, although the two groups of sceptics and liberals had accomplished a remarkable co-ordinative effort in the commission, actor preferences remained unaffected by it. Only Ulrike Höfken, representative of the Greens within the commission, did not join the minority vote on the biopatents directive but later promoted the compromise solution in the Study Commission as well as the parliamentary motion. It seems that, particularly among those MPs who were fiercely opposed not only to ES-cell research but also to prenatal diagnostics and biopatents, a kind of camp discipline had replaced party discipline as a group dynamic. Many of them had been active in an 'alliance for human dignity' that had formed in the debate about the biopatents-directive. They regarded themselves as representatives not so much of their party but of other MPs who sought to prevent importing.

In the Ethics Council, too, none of the participants seem to have revised their original preferences. Although the report provides only the numbers, not the names of the members who voted for each of the four options identified, opponents and supporters of ES-cell research can easily be identified.[24] Judging from their positions as stated before the establishment of the Ethics Council, none of the 15 voters for the liberal option (A and B or B) and 10 voters for a moratorium (C or C and D) revised their preferences during the Council's discussions. As Wolfgang van den Daele points out, neither side was under the impression that proponents of the other one could be persuaded by arguments:

> I never had the illusion that I could convince a single one of them! I tried to disprove single arguments. ... In such things it is difficult to imagine that one can convince other people. Well, one could at least convince them to focus on arguments that cannot be reached with reasons, like the attitude to life and death. That is, to convince them not to focus on false arguments.

The early split into two subgroups to some extent also prevented exposure to counterarguments and social contacts with the other side. Only in the early stages, when technical and legal matters were addressed in presentations, some of the members had to revise legal and factual acceptances on the matter.[26] However, this amounted merely to a correction of misunderstandings that was largely irrelevant to actors' motivations. In the subgroups, reasoning was less about what political actions should be taken than about how the respective options could best be presented. The discussions about argumentative coherence and stringency were thus decoupled from the motivational level and took on a purely strategic character.

With regard to preference-transformation, both forums hence confirm the hypotheses stated for discussion as a mode of interaction: the reasons effective for the decision remain intact and new or revised acceptances do not lead to a reconsideration of preferences over political options. Also in keeping with hypotheses, both forums achieved a clarification of factual matters and contributed to an aggregation of reasons within the overall conflict. At the beginning of the debate, proponents of both the liberal and the restrictive side justified their position partly with arguments that were later regarded as untenable. It seemed that each side tried to present as many reasons as possible, no matter whether these were good ones, bad ones, or no reasons at all. For instance, pro-lifers insisted (contrary to all evidence) that ES-cells were totipotent and could still develop into full embryos, while liberals claimed that stem-cell research could in the very near future provide a cure for Alzheimer's (which researchers vehemently denied).

In the Ethics Council, factual disagreements gave way to the underlying conflicts over fundamental moral values. In the Study Commission, legal and pragmatic considerations took centre stage. The expert forums thus enabled an aggregation of reasons that, in the subsequent parliamentary procedures, lead both sides to focus on a smaller number of arguments. It is difficult to say whether these were also the best and most convincing ones. Given that the reasons dominating the subsequent debate were mainly moral and pragmatic ones, however, it seems that they are likely to represent the motivating ones that were effective in the decision. The commission's report, in particular, successfully disentangled the different dimensions of conflict and provided a useful frame of reference for the further debate.

While communication obviously had little effect on preferences within the two expert forums, their reports as well as discussions initiated in them (especially in the Study Commission) had notable consequences for the preference-formation and -transformation of other MPs. In a survey, over 65 per cent of MPs claim to have read the Study Commission's report, and over 50 per cent to have read the Ethic Council's report (Dilling 2002: 134).[27] Of those who had read the reports, 20 per cent said that the Study Commission's report had influenced their vote either decisively or significantly and over 50 per cent said the same for the Ethic Council's report.[28] The group at which attempts at persuasion were directed at this stage, and whose preferences changed most noticeably, were parliamentarians who were confronted with the topic for the first time and had little previous knowledge about it. In contrast to the experts both within and outside the parliament, whose preferences were based on a stable moral rationale, this group felt insecure about weighing competing values and thought that an assessment of the complex factual questions involved was asking too much of them. Many of them had the feeling of a taboo where biotechnological questions were concerned, a sentiment that is widespread in the public as well (Hampel *et al.* 1998). Margot von Renesse says that, before the parliamentary debate and vote on 30 January 2002, she mainly spoke to sceptics who regarded modernisation and the life sciences as a process of commodification that threatened the community.[29] Andrea Fischer (Greens) similarly addressed the opponents of importing but, according to her own impression, less successfully.[30] Maria Böhmer, too, argued with the strong group of Catholics in her party, who opposed ES-cell research for religious reasons.

In quest of support for the compromise motion, the group around von Renesse thus followed a rule pointed out by Gutmann and Thompson, that 'in justifying policies on moral grounds, citizens should seek the rationale that minimizes rejection of the position they oppose' (1996: 84–5). The aggregation of reasons in the expert forums, and particularly in the Study Commission, prepared the ground for the subsequent parliamentary debate, which has been much praised, though more for its quality and atmosphere than for the result of the concluding vote.

2. PARLIAMENTARY DEBATE: THE BUNDESTAG'S FINEST HOUR?

Compared with normal legislative procedures and plenary debates in the German parliament, the Bundestag's debate over the importing of ES-cells is surely an exceptional case. Party discipline, which usually prevails in parliamentary systems, was suspended to allow MPs to treat the decision as a matter of conscience. In contrast to ordinary decisions, in which experts within the parliamentary groups determine the way to go, this one depended on the votes of lay parliamentarians. Accordingly, parliamentarians were under intense pressure in the formation of their opinions and preferences as well as under unusually intense public surveillance. Three options were presented and each of them had been assessed and extensively justified by experts. In the terminology of Gerald Gaus, all three qualified as 'publicly justified' but neither of them as 'conclusively justified' and correct beyond serious doubt (Gaus 1996, chapter 11). The parliamentary majority hence had to function as an 'umpire' (Gaus 1996, chapter 11). As most of them regarded the outcome of the decision as entirely open, MPs felt a particular institutional responsibility. It seemed that a 'sidereal hour' was indeed required to accomplish the task of responsibly taking a decision on such a complex and important matter and that the debate and decision would reflect the Bundestag's capacity to meet future challenges.

With regard to the debate as an ideal-typical mode of interaction as defined in chapter three, the Bundestag's debate on 30 January 2002 is less of a deviant case. The *conflict* at this stage was clearly one over political action. Although all speakers referred to moral reasons, it was evident that the debate and decision would not resolve the underlying moral disagreements to indicate what was objectively the correct way to go. Rather, the result of the vote would be binding by virtue of the fact that it was arrived at democratically, by a procedure that was regarded as legitimate.[31] The *task* the forum was confronting was a collective decision in which the members of the forum (the MPs) saw themselves in the *role* of representatives of their constituencies and the population as a whole. The parliamentary debate over importing ES-cells was also fully public and, in a sense, more so than ordinary debates. Although all meetings of the Bundestag's plenum are accessible to the public, this one enjoyed particular attention, was broadcast live on television and analysed by a number of journalists. For the individual speakers as well as for the institution as a whole, much reputation and esteem depended on the performance on this occasion. Nonetheless, and in keeping with the ideal-type mode of interaction, the debate in the Bundestag does not qualify as discursive according to the definition in chapter three. As the results of the speech-act analysis that was carried out on the transcripts plainly demonstrate, the plenary debate falls short of the criterion of dialogical interaction.

2.1 Discursiveness

The debate in the Bundestag was peculiar, in that the logic of party competition, which normally dominates parliamentary debates, had been abandoned for the highly sensitive topic of ES-cell importing and research. On the index of discourse quality developed by Steiner *et al.* (2004), the debate would certainly score highly for its style and atmosphere. The level and coherence of argumentation was high, personal offence was avoided as much as populist appeals, and the presentation of personal arguments prevailed over abuse of opponents. Throughout the debate, the institution of the Bundestag celebrated itself: on average, every speaker spent about a third of his or her speaking time to praise the quality of deliberation, the conscientiousness of parliamentarians as well as the obvious level of mutual fairness and consideration.

Despite the extraordinary high *quality* of argumentation, the underlying logics of interaction and the procedural requirements in this setting effectively prevented dialogue and thus discursiveness. Speaking time in the parliament is assigned according to the number of signatories for the motion and the list of speakers is determined in advance. This creates a division of the forum into speakers and listeners, for whom it is well nigh impossible to become speakers themselves – if not by means of interruption. The key to the impossibility of discursive interaction, however, lies in the purpose of the plenary debate, which is not the development and assessment of options for action but their public justification. Contributions to the debate are of a justificatory nature and constitute results of a deliberative process. Although argumentation takes place, it represents a *product* (argumentative text) rather than a *process* (a give-and-take of reasons). Most speakers have their contributions prepared in advance and, at the procedural level, a rigorous list of speakers and limited speaking time have to be enforced. While these characteristics are more or less obvious at the first glance, the ideal-typical features of interaction are even more clearly reflected in the microanalysis of single speech acts.

The effect of publicity on interaction is, at the illocutionary level, reflected in the dominance of argumentative speech acts as well as, at the propositional level, in the fact that references to non-generalisable, private reasons are avoided entirely. Table 5.2 displays the frequency of different types of speech acts in the debate.

Arguing speech acts make up more than three-quarters of the total number of speech acts. Bargaining speech acts, which are non-public, only account for 2 per cent. Even where bargaining speech acts occasionally occur, the speaker's intention is rhetorical rather than co-ordinative. For instance, where a speaker PROMISES that the abuse of new technologies will be prevented, this utterance has to be

Table 5.2: Types of speech acts in parliamentary debate

Type of speech act	Number	Percentage
Arguing	1061	76%
Bargaining	32	2%
Rhetoric	41	3%
Discourse structurers	226	16%
Expressives	36	3%
Others	0	0%

counted as a bargaining speech act although it is not entirely clear whether its essential conditions (that the speaker can and intends to prevent it) are fulfilled. The publicity and justificatory nature of communication also explain the non-negligible number of purely rhetorical speech acts and expressives, where the latter may again be classified as a particular type of rhetorical speech act.

An interesting point is the high number of discourse structurers, which include references to other speakers, markers for the beginning and end of a speech (address, thanks) and definitions of the situation, the question and the speaker's own position. One reason for the apparently high demand for discourse structuring can surely be found in the extreme formalisation of interaction: when speakers have no opportunity to react to the assertions of others immediately, they need to state more explicitly to what they are referring when their turn has come. Another relevant reason at the level of argumentation analysis may be that speakers were trying to reframe the decision in order to place it in a different light. Proponents of a complete ban, for example, tried to point out that what was being decided was not whether to permit the importing of ES-cells but how the status of the embryo *in vitro* was to be defined in future. This kind of redefinition of the situation and question at hand moves argumentation to a meta-level and thus evades challenges on the substantive one. The necessity to define the speaker's own position and the exact content of the motion supported, finally, is immediately related to the task of the forum – taking a decision – and to the purpose of communication – justifying it to the public.

With regard to the criterion of discursiveness, it is the proportion of dialogical speech acts among the arguing speech acts that is of central relevance. With only 16 per cent, it makes up less than a fifth of the total. That this percentage is strikingly small, however, only becomes apparent when comparing it with the result for the citizen conference, at which more than half (56 per cent) of the arguing speech acts were dialogical (see Figure 5.3).

The type of arguing speech acts dominant in the parliamentary debate are

Figure 5.3: Types of speech acts in parliament and citizen conference compared

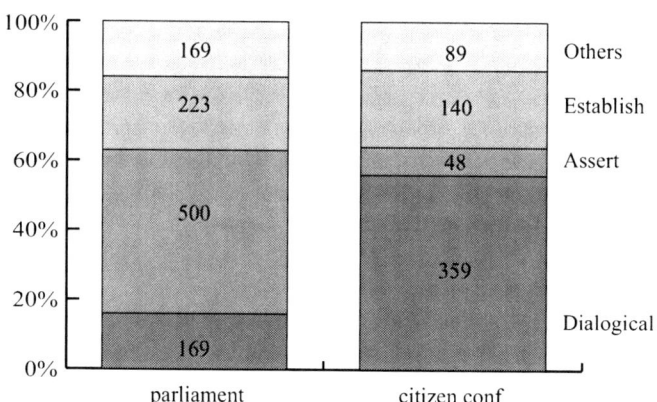

clearly 'to ASSERT' and 'to ESTABLISH'.[32] Many contributions indeed consist merely in an enumeration of assertions. It is the very specific situation of a public monologue that makes this possible. In dialogical interaction, assertions can and will be challenged and it is far more difficult to treat assumptions as taken for granted. The possibility of challenge is likely to deter speakers from controversial assertions unless they are able and willing to defend them.

A closer look at the types of *dialogical speech acts* occurring most frequently in each of the two forums is equally revealing (Table 5.4).

Table 5.4: Dialogical speech acts in parliament and citizen conference compared

Speech act	Parliament	Citizen conf.
Ask	0	67
Take back	0	1
Insist	1	17
Concede	16	6
Contradict	25	66
Agree	11	48
Infer	52	22
Justify	64	132

In the parliamentary debate, inferences and justifications are clearly dominant. In the citizen conference, the proportion of justifications is similar but a far higher percentage is made up by other dialogical speech acts. Again, this indicates the product character of argumentation in the parliamentary debate in contrast to the process character of argumentation in the citizen conference. Although inferences and justifications can and should be counted as dialogical speech acts, they are equally constitutive of the product as of the process of argumentation. To ASK, INSIST, CONTRADICT or AGREE, by contrast, is more typical of the process than for the product: they indicate where further justification is necessary. It should be noted, moreover, that the total number of justifications and inferences is much lower in the debate than in the citizen conferences. Given the justificatory purpose of parliamentary communication, this seems surprising. The alternative explanations that suggest themselves are either that only assertions that are truly controversial are being justified or that only those assertions for which public, generalisable and convincing reasons are available are being justified. An answer to this kind of question is not possible at the level of speech-act analysis and is therefore sought in a closer examination of arguments used. In particular, the argumentation analysis is expected to be illuminating on the degree of co-ordination realised in the forum.

2.2 Co-ordinativeness

In its ideal-typical institutionalisation, co-ordination is neither possible nor necessary in the debate.[33] The Bundestag's debate on importing ES-cells deviates from the ideal-type in this respect. Neither of the three motions had a sufficient majority behind it, and only three-quarters of the MPs had signed a motion at all. To achieve an absolute majority, proponents of the three motions therefore still had to gain support for their option. In a sense, the decision between three options still had to be reframed in a binary yes/no manner. Given the antagonistic institutional logics and the non-dialogical mode of interaction, however, it seems dubious whether such co-ordination was possible in the setting of a plenary debate. At the argumentative level, co-ordination could be reflected in the emergence of a joint dimension for the evaluation of options and in a focus on those practical reasons that effectively motivate preferences over options. The analysis provides no evidence for this, though.

The explanatory statements for the three motions briefly reproduce the argumentation developed for each of them in the expert forums.[34] Neither focuses on a single relevant reason. Rather, they all try to be as comprehensive and to name as many reasons as possible. Most speakers rephrase these arguments, which leads to a considerable degree of redundancy. Notably, one point that was entirely consensual at this stage, namely that stem-cell lines are not embryos, was repeated several times by both speakers for the compromise and for the permissive motion – it is an important premise for the conclusion that a (complete) ban on importing was unconstitutional. This appeal to allegedly consensual reasons and acceptances (albeit different ones!) is another typical feature of justificatory communication. It is probably motivated by the insight that appeals to already accepted reasons are most likely to be successful in making these effective in preference-formation (cf. chapter two, section 5). Although most speakers make different types of arguments, moral ones are clearly the dominant type (Table 5.5). This reflects the nature of the underlying conflict as it had come to be perceived, as well as the fact that a number of factual controversies could actually be resolved beforehand. At the same time, it indicates a general emotionalisation and politicisation of the conflict, the causes for which may be suspected both in the publicity and in the immediately impending decision.

Although speakers for all three motions used a number of different arguments to defend their positions, certain arguments occurred particularly often. Among the supporters of a complete ban, four reasons were clearly dominant: that human life and dignity begin with fertilisation (7.1); that human life may under no conditions be instrumentalised (8.2); that research with adult stem cells was more promising anyway (2.1); and that even restricted importing would constitute a step on to a slippery slope, after which regulation would become impossible (11.3). Supporters of the permissive motion focused on the ethics of healing (8.1); and the argument that life begins with nidation rather than fertilisation (7.2); as well as on the contradiction arising from the fact that abortion and intrauterine devices are allowed in Germany but ES-cell production is forbidden (7.3, see Table 5.5).[35]

What is interesting is that speakers for the permissive motion completely avoided reference to arguments about economic competitiveness (12.1), which had been central to earlier discussions. Probably influenced by discussions in the Ethics Council, they had apparently realised that these arguments were detrimental rather

Table 5.5: Frequency of arguments in parliamentary debate

No.	Ban		Compromise		Permit		Total	
	pro	*con*	*pro*	*con*	*pro*	*con*	*pro*	*con*
1.1	-	-	4	-	2	-	6	-
1.2	1	-	-	-	-	-	1	-
2.1	**10**	-	2	-	-	1	13	1
2.2	1	-	-	-	-	-	1	-
2.3	-	-	7	-	1	-	7	-
2.4	-	3	-	1	2	-	2	4
3.1	-	-	1	-	-	-	1	-
3.2	-	-	-	-	1	-	1	-
3.3	3	-	-	-	-	-	3	-
FactTot	15	3	14	1	6	1	35	5
4.1	2	-	2	-	-	-	4	-
4.2	-	-	-	-	1	-	1	-
4.3	-	**4**	6	-	-	-	6	4
4.4	-	1	3	-	1	-	4	1
4.5	4	-	-	-	-	-	4	-
5.1	-	-	1	-	-	-	1	-
5.2	-	-	-	-	-	-	-	-
6.1	-	-	-	-	-	-	-	-
6.2	-	-	-	-	-	-	-	-
LegTot	6	5	12	-	2	-	20	5
7.1	**8**	-	4	-	-	1	12	1
7.2	-	1	-	1	**5**	-	5	2
7.3	-	2	-	-	**4**	-	4	2
8.1	-	**6**	-	-	**6**	-	6	6
8.2	**8**	-	1	-	-	-	9	-
8.3	5	-	-	-	-	-	5	-
8.4	-	1	**6**	-	2	-	8	1
8.5	2	-	-	-	-	-	2	-
9.1	-	1	-	-	2	-	2	1
9.2	1	-	-	-	-	1	1	1
10.1	1	-	-	-	-	-	1	-
10.2	-	-	**6**	-	-	-	6	-
10.3	4	-	-	4	-	-	4	4
10.4	-	-	-	-	1	-	1	-
MorTot	29	11	17	5	20	2	66	18
11.1	-	1	-	-	1	-	1	1
11.2	-	-	1	-	-	-	1	-
11.3	**16**	-	1	4	-	1	17	5
12.1	-	**10**	-	-	2	-	2	10
12.2	1	-	1	-	-	-	2	-
PragTot	17	11	3	4	3	1	23	16
0.1	-	-	-	-	-	-	-	-
0.2	2	-	2	-	1	-	5	-
OthTot	2	-	2	-	1	-	5	-
Total	69	30	48	10	32	4	148	44

than useful to their position. At least in this context, reference to questions of economic competitiveness gave rise to the suspicion that speakers were guided by interests rather than morally motivated. For both motions seeking to depart from a complete ban, the appearance of being morally motivated was of particular importance. The arguments used for the compromise one were more diverse than those used for either the ban or the permission and also more fact-related than those for either of the others. The most frequent argument was that the comparison between adult and embryonic stem cells was particularly important to pure research and that it should therefore be enabled (2.3). Other repeated arguments were that freedom of research had to be safeguarded (4.3, 4.4); that importing existing stem-cell lines would not increase the demand for new ones (10.2); and that Germany should contribute to the development of new treatments for diseases as it would benefit from these anyway (8.4).

Compared with the expert forums, the reasons presented in the Bundestag debate were of a practical rather than doxastic kind. In the Ethics Council (where interaction came closer to ideal-type discussion), particular emphasis was placed on consistency, which is a central criterion for acceptances but impossible for practical reasons. In anticipation of the decision the focus was moved to practical consequences and feasibility considerations, which had been more important to discussions in the Study Commission. It seems to have become apparent that the specification and contextualisation of moral principles requires more than a consistent deduction.

However, speakers needed not only to consider positive arguments for their own position; their rejections of other speakers' arguments are equally, if not more, revealing. In criticising the compromise motion, supporters of the two radical motions reverted to categorical logic. The following quote from Monika Knoche (Greens) illustrates how these try to reframe the decision in a binary manner:

If we are honest, we realize that there can only be a decision between Yes and No.... There is no dilemma. There is no conflict. We do not need a middle way. The solution – if we want to stick to these firm values – is to confirm the status quo.

Speakers behind either of the more extreme motions were probably aware of the attraction of a middle or third way to undecided and less informed parliamentarians.[37] They sought to counter this tendency by insisting on the requirements of consistency and corollary. Ulrike Flach (FDP), speaking for the permissive motion, thus tried to convict the compromise motion of inconsequence and irrationality and point out that it fails to draw the necessary moral conclusions:

In your motion, you correctly state that human embryonic stem cells are not embryos, because they cannot develop into a complete human being. From this it follows that the protection of fundamental rights does not immediately apply. If you establish this, Mrs von Renesse, then research with embryonic stem cells is not only permissible, but morally demanded.[38]

Accordingly, speakers for the compromise motion attempted to avoid the semantics of compromise and the impression of concessions to either side. Instead, they sought to establish an interpretation of successful *Verständigung*. Against the rhetorically powerful picture of a slippery slope, they tried to set pictures of bridge-building, of a winding road or of a well guarded gate:

> More often than not, it's the winding road that leads to the way out. ... The motion is not the result of a compromise, but of a process of reaching understanding.[39]

> A strict No is as wrong as an unconditional Yes. Dear colleagues, do not blindly fling the gates open and do not block them up blindly either, but save those gates![40]

The argument that was most frequently rejected, however, was one that nobody actually made. As noted before, neither the supporters of the compromise nor those of the permissive motion argued that importing should be permitted to ensure the economic competitiveness of Germany (12.1). Nonetheless, the rejection of this argument was, besides slippery-slope arguments, the point most often made by the proponents of a complete ban. Without explicitly accusing the other party, it successfully conveyed the implication that supporters of the liberal motion were motivated by economic rather than moral considerations.

With regard to both extreme positions, certain arguments had proved particularly successful in the discussions preceding the Bundestag's decision. These arguments had knockout qualities and were particularly difficult to argue against. The slippery slope-argument (11.3) made strong by supporters of a ban has exceptional suggestive power and is also very difficult to disprove. The 'ethics of healing' argument (8.1) made by supporters of the permissive option is similarly difficult to counter. It weighs the life and dignity of a frozen embryo against that of a born human being and implicitly takes for granted that ES-cell research will indeed save lives. A typical implicature in this case was the analogy with organ transplantation, where parts of a dead person's body save a living person's life. A (perhaps more adequate) representation that weighs potential life against potential cures yields a far less obvious result.

The compromise motion, by contrast, had neither categorical logic nor knockout arguments at hand. Speakers therefore stress the quality and inconclusiveness of the debate and express their particular respect for those who feared detrimental social consequences once the status of the embryo was touched upon. As noted before, this was the group they especially sought and hoped to convince. The motive behind these apparently, in Habermas' understanding, merely 'conversational' contributions – in which communication is an end in itself rather than a means to co-ordinate action plans (Habermas 1984: 438) – could have been twofold. First, the fact that, despite the high-quality debate, justification remained inconclusive is evidence of the fact that a consensus was beyond reach and that a political *decision* was inevitable:

further communication will not reveal the one correct solution but rather reinforce the moral divisions. Secondly, it appeals to the capability of politics, and of the parliament in particular, to effectively regulate social reality, and hence to the role-ascription and self-esteem of representatives.

However, the arguments that promised to be most persuasive and successful do not necessarily represent those reasons that actually motivated the speakers' preferences. The argumentative success of reasons need not, as Habermas presumes, reflect their motivational power, as they may be more useful for justification and rationalisation than influential for motivation. In this particular debate, speakers were confronted with a dual task. On the one hand, they competed for the votes of members of the Bundestag who were still undecided and had signed neither of the motions. On the other hand, and in spite of the fact that the vote was over motions rather than bills, they had to fulfil the parliament's task to justify their decision to the public. For neither of these tasks was co-ordination, which would have necessitated compromises in practical reasons, possible.

The frequent appearance of two arguments in particular backs up the hypothesis that rhetorical persuasion and justificatory reason-giving prevailed over communication about motivating reasons and thus the co-ordination of action plans. The first is the frequent rejection of arguments about economic competitiveness by those members speaking for a ban. The pragmatic means of implicature is here used to make a rhetorically effective imputation to the opponent, denying the other moral integrity and authority on the matter. Charging opponents with dishonestly stating reasons other than the ones motivating a decision in this way is clearly a rhetorical rather than a co-ordinative move. A second one is the high frequency of slippery-slope arguments. As mentioned before, these arguments have a strong suggestive appeal and are difficult to disprove. While a matter-of-fact discussion of possible consequences and of questions about how uncertainties are best dealt with is conceivable, the picture of a door once opened that cannot be closed again is simply irresistible. As van den Daele points out, such scenarios may serve to cover up non-generalisable reasons in a public debate (2005: 36–7). In a secularised society that acknowledges the plurality of fundamental norms and moral attitudes, certain religious arguments (referring to the will of God or the proper order of His creation) and conscientious reasons are rejected as merely personal attitudes. To justify their position in public, speakers may thus try to present a decision that is in fact based on what Max Weber called *Gewissensethik* (ethics of conscience) as one motivated by what he named *Verantwortungsethik* (ethics of responsibility), and thus demonstrate its connectivity on the political agenda. In the ES-cell conflict, religious motives were influential both among members of the Bundestag and in the public but were hardly made explicit in the debate. Where such important practical reasons are absent from communication, co-ordination is obviously difficult to achieve.

2.3 Preference-transformation and aggregation of reasons
In the ballot succeeding the debate on 30 January, members of the Bundestag had

five options for expressing their opinions. They could vote for either of the three motions (ban, compromise, permit), vote 'no', explicitly abstain from the vote, or make their vote void, e.g. by failing to enter their names. As the vote was a roll call, all members who were not excused as sick or for important other obligations had to appear in the plenum and make a vote that was to be registered under their name and constituency. Over 75 per cent of the members had signed one of the motions. This is a high proportion compared with ordinary decisions under normal party discipline, in which motions or bills are typically supported only by the governing coalition parties or only by opposition parties. Considering the fact that aggregation processes in the earlier debate and expert forums had yielded three well-worked-out motions that were aligned along a single dimension, however, the percentage seems low. One quite practical reason for this may have been the fact that the groups collected signatures for their motions in the weeks around Christmas, when many members were absent.

The compromise motion, in particular, was written comparatively late in December and after the other two motions had already found stable groups of supporters. Margot von Renesse recounts that the motion was presented to the SPD parliamentary group in a meeting about two weeks before the debate, where it gained most of its signatories.[41] Accordingly, the number of SPD members on the compromise motion is disproportionately high. Another likely reason for some parliamentarians' reluctance to sign one of the motions is that, in spite of the fact that party discipline was suspended, they were unwilling to vote against the majority of their own party. The post-communist party PDS, for instance, was extremely divided over the issue. Some of its members, who also signed the motion for a ban, were strongly opposed to ES-cell research and saw it in a line with euthanasia and discrimination against disabled people. Others, more in a technocratic socialist tradition, were less concerned about ethical questions and strongly supported the importing and production of ES-cells. Although they voted for it, members of the latter group did not sign the relevant motion nor speak for it in the debate, possibly because it was primarily developed in the party they regarded as their extreme opposite in many other regards, the neo-liberal FDP.

Both time pressure and party dynamics may have restrained some parliamentarians from signing one of the motions. Nonetheless, the number of undecided or even uninformed members was considerable. Forming an opinion on such a complex and explosive topic was asking a lot from laypeople in all parties. In contrast to business-as-usual decisions, they had no clear guidance from experts within their own party, as these were internally divided.[42] As the 138 members who had signed neither motion could, in principle, swing the vote towards either the ban or the compromise (the permissive motion had too few signatures in the first place), the outcome of the decision was regarded as more or less open both by parliamentarians and commentators. Accordingly, and in contrast to other debates, there seemed to be room for preference-formation and -transformation *during* the debate. At least with regard to stated preferences, the result of preference-formation is available by virtue of the open ballot.

The hypothesis derived from the ideal-type model was that preference-transformation is near impossible in the setting of a debate. Since interaction is not discursive, opportunities for a transformation of acceptances are lacking: neither a speaker's own assertions (and acceptances) nor those of others can be challenged and extensively justified. Since incentives and pressures for co-ordination are lacking, practical reasons and rationalisations are reinforced rather than compromised: where the coalition required for a decision already exists, alternative rationales can easily be discarded. With regard to the last aspect, the debate over importing ES-cells deviated somewhat from the ideal-type – but with what consequences?

The clearest evidence for preference-transformation in this setting could be provided if parliamentarians voted for a motion other than the one they had signed. In this case, exposition of arguments would obviously have been effective on preferences, despite the otherwise unfavourable conditions. However, a look at the results of the open ballot quickly rebuts this possibility. With a single exception, none of the 460 members who had signed a motion voted for a different one in the first round.[43] This result is little surprising: with their signature under one of the motions, parliamentarians state that they have formed their opinion in awareness of the relevant arguments.

There is, of course, the possibility that some signatories were indeed shaken in their preferences by the debate but stuck to the motion they had signed for fear of a loss of face. A notable peculiarity in the open ballot points in this direction. In the first round, 21 members of the Bundestag failed to enter their name and constituency on their ballot paper and thereby rendered it void. Among these 21, at least 15 had signed a motion. Before the second round, the President of the Bundestag reminded the members that the ballot was open and that they had to submit their names with their votes. In the second round, 20 parliamentarians who were not registered for the first ballot voted; one spoiled ballot paper remains. Comparing these numbers with the results of earlier open ballots in the Bundestag highlights their peculiarity: in all open ballots between 1949 and 1999 a total number of 59 spoiled votes occurred. Typically, only one or two votes were void in a single ballot.[44]

Leaving aside for a moment the possibility that 21 parliamentarians simply forgot to put their names on the ballot paper, the number of spoiled votes suggests the debate did indeed shake some members' preferences. Nevertheless, of the 20 members more who voted in the second round, none voted against their originally stated preferences: 13 voted for the motion they had signed, two, having signed the no-longer-available permissive motion, voted for the compromise and 5 had not signed either of the motions. Although the surprisingly high number of spoiled votes suggests that the debate made some parliamentarians less sure about their preferences, clear evidence for preference-transformation remains missing.[45]

Attention consequently has to shift to those 138 members of the Bundestag who had not signed any of the motions. Being predominantly laypeople on the issue, their acceptances were probably more open to revision and the practical reasons behind their preferences less certain. The speakers' attempts at persuasion were directed

Table 5.6: Subscribers and non-subscribers of the motions by party

Party	Ban	Compromise	Permit	Abst. or no	Total
SPD	64 / 13	129 / 40	4 / 7	0 / 2	197 / 62
CDU / CSU	111 / 25	23 / 16	39 / 9	0 / 0	173 / 50
Green	26 / 4	11 /3	0 / 0	0 / 0	37 / 7
FDP	0 / 1	0 / 0	37 / 1	0 / 1	37 / 3
PDS	15 / 3	0 / 3	0 / 9	0 / 1	15 / 16
Independent	0 / 1	-	-	-	0 / 1
Total	216 / 47	163 / 62	80 / 26	0 / 4	459 / 139

at these 'undecided' members rather than at the proponents of either of the other motions. Table 5.6 below shows how signatories and non-signatories were distributed over the three motions and over the parliamentary parties (the first number in each field is the signatories, the second non-signatories, e.g., 64 SPD members who had signed the motion for a ban as well as 13 SPD members who had not signed it voted for this motion).

The number of members who did not sign a motion prior to the debate is high in the two big parties, lower for the Green Party and the FDP, and, for reasons stated before, particularly high in the PDS. As all parties except the FDP were split over the issue, party membership is no indicator of the original preference-distribution among undecided members. In fact, the eventual voting behaviour may be more revealing with regard to the debate's influence on their preferences. Table 5.7 indicates that the number of those voting for the ban was particularly high among signatories while the column showing the number of those voting for the compromise motion was particularly high among the non-signatories. The first states the total number and percentage of members who voted for each of the motions, the second one the distribution of signatories over the motions, the third one the distribution of non-signatories. The rightmost column indicates the proportion of votes each of the motions gained or lost in the ballot in comparison with its number of signatories.

Compared to the null hypothesis that the votes of non-signatories are as equally distributed over the three motions as the votes of signatories, the compromise motion clearly gains while the ban motion clearly loses. Does this indicate that the debate has swayed preferences towards the compromise motion? Although this

Table 5.7: Voting behaviour of signatories and non-signatories

Motion	Number (%)	Signed: number (%)	Not signed: number (%)	
Ban	263 (42.62)	217 (47.17)	46 (33.33)	- 13,84 %
Compromise	225 (36.46)	163 (35.43)	62 (44.92)	+ 9,49 %
Permit	106 (17.17)	80 (17.39)	26 (18.84)	+ 1,45 %
Abst./no	4 (0.66)	0	4 (2.89)	
Total	598 (100)	460 (100)	138 (100)	

interpretation would be favourable for the parliament's capability as a deliberative forum, and although it is supported by leaders of the compromise motion, plausible alternative explanations are available. One is the aforementioned tendency of non-expert parliamentarians to seek a middle way rather than adopt an extreme position on a topic they are unfamiliar with.

Another is the fact that the group advocating a complete ban had formed much earlier and in a different context from the one developing the compromise: the parliamentarians forming the 'alliance for human dignity', who also devised the motion for a complete ban, had been campaigning against the EU bioethics convention, against prenatal diagnostics and, in part, against abortion, for many years. Accordingly, they knew well enough whom to ask for their signatures. Pro-lifers, whose preferences were often based on religious reasons, had particularly stable preferences on the matter and had taken their stance very soon after it had appeared on the agenda. As most of its potential supporters had already signed the motion for a ban, it could not gain as many additional votes as the other two in the ballot. The unexpected success of the compromise motion by comparison with the number of its signatories is thus only a very ambiguous indicator for preference-transformation during the debate.

Therefore, and in order to find out more about the preference-formation of those parliamentarians who had not signed one of the motions, a survey was undertaken among them. In anonymous questionnaires, they were asked about when they formed their opinion on the matter and how it was affected by the debate. Of the 138 'undecided' parliamentarians, 26 (19 per cent) sent back the questionnaire. Given that the decision over importing ES-cell was nearly four years previously to the time of writing, the low return rate is hardly surprising. Two general elections had taken place in the meantime, so that the majority were no longer members of parliament and had retired from political life; three members had died. To assess whether the sample was representative of the whole, participants were asked to state their sex and whether they belonged to the governing or opposition parties. The results show that respondents were disproportionately male and belonged to the opposition parties.[46] This deficiency in representativeness and the small number of respondents forbid us to draw far-reaching conclusions from the survey. Nonetheless, some extrapolation is possible and provides clues to the possibility of preference-transformation in parliamentary debates.

Asked whether they had dealt with the topic prior to the Bundestag's debate, 21 out of 26 replied either 'yes, intensively' or 'yes, a bit'. Twelve claimed that they participated in discussions in one of the caucuses or within their own party, although 24 stated that they were not regarded as experts on the topic. Ten say that they had a firm opinion at the beginning of the plenary debate, nine reply 'rather yes' and seven with 'rather no', so that truly undecided members are evidently in the minority. Asked whether the debate helped them to resolve open questions (which would indicate transformation of acceptances), 16 reply either 'no' or 'rather no'. With regard to practical reasons, the picture is similar: 14 reply 'no' or 'rather no' when asked whether they recognised new aspects as relevant for the evaluation. In this case, however, six members give a clear positive answer and further six reply 'perhaps'.

Despite the fact that both acceptances and practical reasons did not remain entirely unaffected by arguments in the debate, there is only a single case of manifest preference-transformation in the sample: one respondent indicates that, originally supporting a complete ban, she was persuaded to vote for the compromise motion. This transformation of preferences over the available options seems to have been driven by changes in both acceptances and practical reasons – she states both that the debate resolved 'some' open questions for her and that 'yes', she discovered new aspects as relevant for the evaluation. Apart from this case, seven respondents state that they know of a member who has changed their preference during the debate, while 19 are not aware of any changes in preference. Of course, those who distinguish preference-transformation in others could all be thinking of the same person. However, as they are distributed over governing and opposition parties, it is more likely that some of them know of different cases. Extrapolating from the sample to the total number of non-signatories, it seems reasonable to assume that between five and ten members of the Bundestag (1–1.5 per cent) did in fact change their preferences as a result of the debate.

While these data fail to confirm the hypothesis that preference-transformation is impossible in the setting of a parliamentary debate, there is considerable evidence against the contrary assumption – that it is easily possible – as well. First of all, the estimated number and proportion of forum members who changed their preferences is very small. In whatever direction their preferences were transformed, it would not have affected the outcome of the decision. Secondly, members of the group of 'undecided' non-signatories, in which preference-transformation occurred, were listeners rather than speakers in the forum. Stuck in this passive position, they were subjected to the speakers' persuasive attempts without guidance from their party. The special conditions of suspended party discipline, a decision framed as a matter of conscience, and an open ballot were maximally favourable for preference-transformation among undecided parliamentarians. If even under these conditions, there is no evidence that more than one or two percent of parliamentarians actually changed their preferences, the hypothesis that the debate as a mode of interaction prevents preference-transformation may be upheld.

Contrary to the impressions of many parliamentarians and even of some of the leaders of the successful compromise motion,[47] the result of the ballot was thus more or less foreseeable before the plenary debate. Taken together, the permissive and the compromise motion had 26 more signatories than the motion for a ban, which had the highest number of signatories. After the first ballot, which the permissive motion clearly lost, its supporters adapted their preferences to the new choice-set. Assuming that preference-orders were single-peaked within the ban–permission dimension, the prediction is that they should prefer allowing the importing of existing stem-cell lines over no importing at all. Accordingly, nearly all of those who voted for the permissive motion in the first ballot voted for the compromise in the second.[48] Only if the ban motion had gained significantly more of the non-signatories than the other two taken together would a different result have been within reach. The fact that, at least at an informal level, the coalition for (restricted) importing was already very strong also highlights the justificatory function of the plenary debate. It appears reasonable to assume that speakers aimed first at the justification of their position to the public and only in second place at the persuasion of other parliamentarians.

Although the plenary debate thus left little room for preference-changes, the formation and transformation of preferences on the issue was by no means completed after the decision on 30 January. In the three months it took to devise a bill on ES-cell importation on the basis of the successful motion, the compromise gained further support. In the ballot over the bill on 25 April 2002, 360 members voted 'yes' (compared to 339 for the motion); only 190 voted 'no' (compared to 274 against the motion). One reason for this may have been the continued persuasive attempts of the proponents of the compromise motion. Another reason may have been that the compromise came to be valued as such while the extreme positions and categorical argumentations lost influence once the decision had been taken.

The effect of time and possibly also of accommodation to the status quo on actors' preferences also became clear when the stem-cell law was recently put back on to the parliamentary agenda and revised. On April 11, 2008, the sixteenth German Bundestag ruled with a majority of 346 against 228 votes to shift the cut-off date from 1 January 2002 to 1 May 2007. While this shift in opinions towards a more liberal regulation may partly be due to the fact that many of the Bundestag's present, especially younger, members, were not in the fourteenth Bundestag, several of the 'old' members have indeed changed their stance on stem-cell research, too: The motion for a new cut-off date (BT-Drs. 16/798) was lead, among others, by René Röspel, who was one the leaders of the motion for a complete ban in 2002.[49]

After the Bundestag's decision on 30 January 2002, the eventual bill on importing ES-cells was drafted in the less formal round that began to form in the Study Commission. Analysis of this forum shows that many of the details left open in the motion could only be settled in a bargaining process.

3. BARGAINING: WHAT TOOK PLACE BEHIND CLOSED DOORS

After the compromise motion had won a majority in the Bundestag ballot, further discussion and the development of a bill on importing ES-cells were officially transferred to the Bundestag caucus on education and research. The caucus met regularly during the following three months, invited comments from 18 experts and led intense discussions. In the Bundestag's decision on 25 April, the caucus presented a bill based on a draft by four of the leaders of the compromise motion and won a large majority for it. Although the caucus constituted the official forum for the drafting of the bill, this group of four was the informal circle in which important details were decided. Margot von Renesse (SPD), Andrea Fischer (Greens), Maria Böhmer (CDU) and Wolf-Michael Catenhusen (SPD, a junior minister in the ministry responsible for education and research) had been in close contact since autumn 2001 and had written the relevant motion together. Between November 2001 and April 2002, the group held a number of rather intimate meetings behind closed doors, which may with some justice be characterised as a bargaining forum.[50]

While much aggregation and co-ordination had taken place before the decision on 30 January, the motion was vague on, or left open, several relevant points. In part, the drafting of the bill consisted merely of a translation of the intentions stated in the motion into a legal text and in linking new regulations with existing paragraphs. These were issues that could, without many problems, be dealt with in the respective caucuses and ministries. In fact, the amendments to the draft that the caucus for education and research proposed concerned mainly the precise wording of paragraphs and not their content. However, three rather substantial and controversial points were still open at this stage, which was also reflected in the caucus discussions.

One issue was the cut-off date before which imported cell lines had to be produced; another the commission that was to decide on importation applications; and the final issue was whether the production of ES-cells by Germans abroad was to be treated as a criminal offence. With regard to the cut-off date, it was clear from the motion that no date later than 30 January 2002 was possible. A cut-off date chosen by US President Bush – 9 August 2001 – was favoured by those who were in principle opposed to ES-cell research and accepted importing only reluctantly.[51] Between these two dates, though, there remained a number of conceivable compromise options. The establishment of an 'interdisciplinary' Central Ethics Commission was mentioned in the motion, too, albeit without details on membership and institutional affiliation and responsibilities. Obviously, research-friendly supporters of the compromise supported a commission close to the ministry of education and research, in which biomedical researchers were strongly represented. Sceptics preferred a stronger representation of ethicists, jurists and theologians and an agency controlled by the parliament. The latter group also insisted that the production of ES-cells by German researchers abroad should be prosecuted in Germany, whereas research-friendly actors sought to prevent this. If a consensus on all these matters had been found before the Bundestag debate, the motion could have been more explicit on them. As I will argue in this section, however, the central actors were still divided over these matters after 30 January and could only achieve consensus on a bill through mutual concessions and compromise.

The members of this informal bargaining forum represented both the three largest parliamentary parties and different fundamental positions on ES-cell research. Wolf-Michael Catenhusen was the most liberal of the four. Similarly to Chancellor Schröder, he wanted to enable ES-cell research in Germany but knew that a majority for a very permissive solution was not to be found. SPD-member

Margot von Renesse took a similar stance. However, while she highlighted the freedom of research and was sympathetic to the demands and troubles of researchers, she was particularly keen to avoid a status definition of the embryo *in vitro*. Von Renesse, who is famous as an expert in the creative interpretation of law, seems to have been the one who was most interested in a compromise solution as such. Accordingly, she has justly come to be described as the 'mother' of the ES-cell compromise. Maria Böhmer and Andrea Fischer were known as believing Catholics and were strongly opposed to consumptive ES-cell research. Doubting whether a complete ban was legally possible, they hoped that progress in pure research would render it dispensable when a limited number of cell lines was made available. Böhmer also represented a group of mainly religious CDU members who were willing to accept a compromise but very concerned not to make too many concessions. Fischer, who had resigned as Minister of Health in January 2001, knew that her party, the Greens, had not listed her for the next election, so that she would not serve another term in parliament. Consequently, she was comparatively free to pursue her own course without special consideration of her own party.

Bargaining as an ideal-typical mode of interaction requires that participants, in the role of interest representatives, deal with a conflict of interest. Their individualistic preferences are predetermined and they seek to maximise their utility, under the constraints of other members' preferences, through compromises and package deals. In the cyclical model of the policy-making process, the role of the bargaining is seen as the distribution rather than the production of welfare. The sum to be distributed cannot be increased by gaining further information or through deliberation but remains constant. In the absence of compensations, gains to one player thus constitute losses to other players. Because the actors' practical reasons are private and non-generalisable, interaction is equally non-public and takes place behind closed doors. At the same time, participants at the bargaining table must have equal opportunities to take the floor, so that the mode of interaction is also dialogical. Because new information is neither sought nor relevant and because practical reasons are not transferable to other speakers, preference-transformation is ruled out and action plans are only adapted to constraints.

Given the fact that the four members of this circle represented different parties, different religious denominations and, among the supporters of a compromise, the restrictive and the liberal sides, they did in some sense assume the *role* of representatives of different interests. Although the underlying *type of conflict* remained a moral one, competing interests were involved. For instance, Catenhusen, as a junior ministering the ministry for education and research, had some institutional interest in enabling and promoting ES-cell research in Germany, while Maria Böhmer had to gain and keep the confidence of influential members of her party. The distributive *task* of this forum is, of course, less evident and can – if at all – only be made plausible if one adopts a wide understanding of the distribution of goods. In this sense, what was to be distributed was the regulation of points left open in the motion. It could not be increased because the motion had already passed the Bundestag and a bill that contradicted it would not stand a chance of winning a majority. Nonetheless, the claim that bargaining did in fact take place still needs to be vindicated by assessing the discursive and co-ordinative properties of the forum.

3.1 Discursiveness

With regard to the mode of interaction in this informal bargaining forum, it can certainly be assumed that it was dialogical. In a group of four without listeners (except three personal assistants), monological interaction would be plainly pointless. Also, the forum was obviously informal and non-public, so that there were no external pressures to avoid reference to non-generalisable reasons. The question, however, is whether the absence of such pressures actually induced interest politics and advanced bargaining. Considering its members' intentions as stated, namely to draft a bill that was as close as possible to the text of the motion passed on 30 January, co-ordination could have been simply instrumental to this joint goal. In this case, private reasons should have been ruled out. In this case, the mode of interaction might, despite the closed doors and contrary to the ideal type, qualify as discursive.

The joint goal of reaching consensus on a bill that promised to win a large majority in the Bundestag was indeed particularly strong in this forum.[52] Nonetheless, each of the members had practical reasons for their preferences (regarding the open points in the motion) that were not transferable to the other members. Some of them were reasons of interests in the narrow sense, while others were moral and religious reasons that were not shared in the group. For example, Maria Böhmer's quest to maintain the support of her own party was less important to SPD-member Catenhusen, whose intention to ensure German competitiveness in biomedical research was not accepted as a reason by Böhmer. As noted before, however, empirical research has shown that bargaining and arguing are not exclusive modes of interaction. Rather, threats, offers and promises in bargaining situations always require argumentative defence, so that both public (arguing) and non-public (bargaining) speech acts will occur (Holzinger 2004). The point that bargaining did take place is hence based not so much on the assumption that there were *no* generalisable arguments in this forum but on the one that there were *not only* generalisable arguments.

While the different reasons motivating the four members of the forum will be described under the aspect of its co-ordinativeness, the concern here is the contextual effects at the level of linguistic interaction. Since, due to the circle's privacy, no transcripts of the meetings are available, conclusions can only be drawn from the participants' own perceptions as stated in the interviews. Böhmer, Fischer and von Renesse in unison praise the atmosphere and quality of the discussions. Fischer recalls:

Without doubt this was my most gratifying political experience, the process of reaching understanding with these two women. First, because I have a high personal respect for both of them, and then because it was just great to see how three people move towards each other in steps, and it is clear that they want to come closer to the other, because it was about something so important, and still hesitated, took a step to the side and so on.[53]

While both Fischer and von Renesse try to present interaction as the quest for *Verständigung* (reaching agreement) rather than compromise, several other statements indicate that bargaining processes did play a role and demanded concessions from the members of the forum:

Catenhusen himself as a research politician had an interest in having the door ajar rather than completely closed ... Catenhusen somehow represented the supporters, and with him we negotiated the details. And he in turn was wise enough to know: to open up the package once more now, to back out so to say, that's a bad idea. Catenhusen is a much too experienced a politician to do something like that.[54]

As a junior minister in the Schröder government, Catenhusen represented those liberals in the SPD who supported ES-cell research but were pragmatic enough to see that there was no majority for a very liberal solution. A likely bargaining threat that could easily be disguised as a warning (and thus a public speech act) is that these liberals would seek to undermine the compromise if they were not satisfied by the bill. If the bill had been too restrictive in their opinion, for example the cut-off date too early or the ethics commission staffed only with theologians and ethicists, they might have preferred to oppose it and allow researchers to make use of the present legal loophole that permitted the importation of stem cells. They were somewhat more likely to have initially accepted the bill but jumped at the first chance to start a debate about a revision of the law – which is what Schröder did in the election campaign in 2005.

The following statement by Margot von Renesse illustrates how the members of the circle had to assure one another of their honesty and trustworthiness:

And of course we also had problems, I remember this one meeting, ... before which there were three weeks without sessions. ... And there had been interviews in between ... And the rubble of possible misunderstandings had piled up. It was about the composition of the Central Ethics Commission ... And it took us nearly an hour to get rid of this rubble ... This means, among the three of us, we kept having problems locating the other, we had to assure each other of our sincerity. That we did not set snares or pull a fast one on the other.[55]

If the purpose of this forum had been purely epistemic or instrumental to a joint goal, i.e. production rather than distribution, the question of trust would have been less important. Although any kind of meaningful linguistic interaction requires a minimal consensus and basic level of confidence in the other speakers' intentions, the persuasive power of arguments does not depend on trust. In bargaining situations, by contrast, it is essential that players are either fully informed about the others' preferences and capabilities or that they trust one another's authenticity. In a – more realistic – situation of imperfect information, where actors do not display their preferences authentically but strategically fake preferences they do not hold, undue compensations may be granted. The resulting suspicions may prevent a consensus or even lead to a complete breakdown of communication.

The topic around which, according to von Renesse, the 'rubble' of possible misunderstandings had accumulated concerns was, not surprisingly, one of the points left open in the motion: the membership of the central ethics commission. The trouble had been generated by utterances which the four members of the forum had made outside their informal circle and that probably violated the maxims of secrecy and confidentiality that are essential for bargaining. Once misunderstandings had been resolved, von Renesse continues, a consensual solution was soon found. This result is reminiscent of the later development in the Ethics Council. After the council had become more institutionalised and social contacts between its members strengthened, compromises and thus consensual reports were possible. This indicates both that the antagonistic logic of an expert forum can be overcome by moves towards bargaining and that familiarity and trust are beneficial for bargaining. As postulated in the theory, consensus is not possible without concessions on both sides, and bargaining does not take place in open space but within a social and political context.

Despite the fact that its members highlight the trustful nature of interaction in the forum and the agreement with which results were achieved, it can nevertheless justly be characterised as a bargaining forum. Bargaining is typically regarded as a highly competitive, even aggressive type of interaction and normatively disapproved. This characterisation and conclusion is apparently inadequate for some cases. Where preferences are stated authentically, mutual respect obtains and every actor's claims are accepted as justified, the pursuit of a consensus through compromises may well be experienced as a fruitful and rewarding undertaking. In this sense, understanding the reasonableness of the other's reasons produced an awareness of ethical pluralism and enabled mutual tolerance (cf. Forst 2003: 600).

3.2 Co-ordinativeness

While the motion passed on 30 January set the frame for distributive bargaining between Catenhusen, Böhmer, Fischer and von Renesse, communication and co-ordination among these four began much earlier. Catenhusen had been in contact with CSU-member Horst Seehofer over a compromise since spring 2001. When Seehofer fell seriously ill in autumn 2001, Böhmer signalled her willingness to represent her party in a compromise motion.[56] As members of the coalition parties with a strong interest in bioethical questions, Fischer and von Renesse had been in contact since the year 2000, when Fischer was still Minister of Health. In March 2001, they published a co-authored newspaper article in which they set out their shared as well as their differing positions on pre-implantation diagnostics and ES-cell research.[57] They jointly criticised the former practice and rejected the production of embryos for research purposes. At the same time, however, they indicated that their positions differed on whether the use of ES-cells should be permitted for the purposes of pure research – von Renesse obviously supported this while Fischer remained sceptical.

A look at von Renesse and Fischer's respective speeches in the first debate on importing ES-cell in the Bundestag on 5 July 2001, shows how far apart their positions still were at this time. They both made use of the categorical moral logic that is typical for the two extreme positions and which is entirely abandoned in the compromise motion they drafted six months later. Margot von Renesse points out:

> Given the case that we do not avoid the hypocrisy of not producing stem cells in Germany and at the same time ban the import, will we one day rule out the import of knowledge as well, will we forbid this as well? ... Why is the status of an orphaned embryo higher than that of a miscarried or aborted foetus, of which nobody claims that it is not a research object?[58]

She even refers to the argument of German competitiveness, which was later regarded as untenable from a moral point of view and avoided even by supporters of the permissive motion:

> If we want to remain consistent ..., Germany can only be a location for research and enterprise on a morally and ethically straight way.[59]

Andrea Fischer, in the same debate, makes use of slippery-slope arguments, which proponents of the compromise motion urgently sought to rebut in the debate on January 30:

> If we take this political decision, we must be aware that we are thereby taking an irreversible step. ... We will not stop at the few allegedly surplus embryos. The next step will rather be to actively get into the production of embryos.[60]

Although Fischer and Böhmer grew increasingly supportive of the idea of a compromise originating from the Study Commission (chaired by von Renesse), they first tried to draft separate motions within their own parties. Seeing the similarities between these drafts, they decided to develop a joint motion in autumn 2001. Böhmer describes the differences to be overcome for a joint motion (2005: 165). She and Fischer were against a cut-off date after the Bundestag's decision, while von Renesse favoured the day on which the law was to become effective. Von Renesse also supported a time limit on the new regulation, while Fischer and Böhmer sought to avoid future discussions. Days before the decisive debate and ballot in the Bundestag, Fischer points out that she supports the compromise motion only for pragmatic reasons:

If I nonetheless vote for a strictly limited import of already existing stem-cell lines, I do this only because the strict position probably cannot be implemented in a legally compliant way.[61]

Von Renesse similarly presents their joint motion as building a bridge between two divergent positions (the one held by herself and SPD-members like Catenhusen and the one held by Fischer and Böhmer) rather than a consensus:

One side would like to go further where research with embryos is concerned, but sees that this cannot be culturally integrated and is thus politically not enforceable. And the second position is: we would like to ban the import, but we see that the constitution does not 100 per cent permit this.[62]

Apparently, concessions were necessary on both sides even before the successful compromise motion could be drafted. At this stage, however, action-plans were adapted to what were perceived as external constraints: parliamentary majorities and public opinion on one side; constitutional restrictions on the other. Only after their joint motion had gained a majority in the Bundestag, and when the bill was to be worked out, did constraints come to be represented by each other's preferences and loyalties, so that not only co-ordination but bargaining took place.

With regard to the three important points left open in the motion – the cut-off date, the Central Ethics Commission and crimes abroad – all four were reluctant to acknowledge compromises. The cut-off date, on which both sceptics and liberals kept an eye and which was much discussed in the caucus for education and research, plays no significant role in the memories of Fischer and von Renesse.[63] Von Renesse presents the eventual date – 1 January 2002 – as the result of purely pragmatic considerations upon which the group agreed. She wanted to avoid the latest possible date, which would have raised suspicions, but also a very early date, which would have frustrated researchers. 1 January could, she hoped, become a European rather than solely German reference date.[64] Nonetheless, it seems revealing that the eventual date is significantly closer to the 30 January 2002 (the latest possible date) than 9 August 2001 (the Bush-deadline and the earliest date discussed).

Although none of these possible cut-off dates could have encouraged the production of new ES-cell lines, the result is definitely a comparatively research-friendly one. And despite the fact that von Renesse's reasoning is appealing, a rationale for an earlier date was also available: the Bush-deadline (or an even earlier one such as 5 July, when importing ES-cells was first discussed in the Bundestag) could have signified that no cell lines produced after the beginning of the debate about ES-cell production and research were to be used in Germany. Catenhusen was at first in favour of a later cut-off date, which would allow the importation of stem-cell lines that already existed (for a specified time) when an application to undertake research with them was filed. Such a ruling, it could be argued, would not provide incentives for the production of new lines. As

Catenhusen saw that no majority was to be won for this proposal, he supported a fixed date in the motion.[65] It is plausible to assume, however, that he tried to avoid a too early date when the bill was drafted.

Of the three topics, most public attention was directed to the composition and institutional affiliation of the Central Ethics Commission to be established and this was also intensely discussed in the caucus for education and research. It seemed at this stage that decision-making power would be passed on to the new forum and that the future of ES-cell research in Germany would depend on its members.[66] Most of the experts whose comments were invited by the caucus mentioned the commission and they typically demanded a stronger role for their own profession. Further demands were for parliamentary control, equal representation of men and women as well as quick and transparent decisions. The membership of the commission was a source of potential misunderstandings in the group of four as well. Andrea Fischer remembers disagreements as to what the 'interdisciplinary commission' mentioned in the motion should look like and particularly which academic disciplines should be represented in it.[67]

Apparently, the dissent concerned not only the composition of the commission but also its task. For most biomedical researchers as well as Catenhusen and von Renesse, who were the more research-friendly members of the bargaining forum, this task was to *discuss and evaluate* whether the intended project was high-ranking enough to warrant the use of ethically controversial materials. Accordingly, they wanted as many different disciplines and research fields within the life sciences to be represented as possible:

> Among the scientists we needed as many disciplines as possible. Even with five scientists, I have not covered everything. But at least I need to have people who can think into those disciplines as bridgeheads and who know whom they could ask. That means, I could not have enough scientists.[68]

The role of ethicists and theologians, in this view, is merely to spark reflection and encourage deliberation by asking the right questions. Thus, a single ethicist would be sufficient in a forum but several experts would be needed to answer these questions:

> Ethicists or theologians in a body are for ethical reflection: why do I think this, and why does another one think that, and why can I justify my arguments to him and spark reflection. They are not the ones who represent ethics, or the right thing. ... The idea that ethicists are for what is right and scientists for purely scientific matters, that's nonsense.[69]

In the eyes of sceptics, by contrast, the main task of the commission was to *take decisions* about importing ES-cells. The uneven number of members, which was soon agreed upon, implicitly acknowledges this role as well as the necessity of reducing decision costs by enabling majority decisions. However, there were also arguments for parity between ethicists and researchers, for a representation of various social groups ('stakeholders') in the forum and for a high degree of transparency and accountability.

The commission as it was eventually outlined in the bill and subsequently established is subordinated to the ministry of health and has nine members. Five of these, and hence a majority, are experts from the life sciences (biology and medicine), two are theologians (one Protestant, one Catholic), and two are philosophers. Although Fischer adopts von Renesse's justification for a strong representation of biomedical researchers and claims to have been convinced by it, the pivotal role of non-ethicists in an ethics commission is likely to constitute a concession to the liberal side, represented by Catenhusen and von Renesse. Their goal was a 'manageable law' that would enable ES-cell research in Germany at least for purposes of pure research and to reduce the dissatisfaction of biomedical researchers.[70]

If, in addition to the restriction of importing to existing cell lines, the majority of the commission's members had been critical with regard to ES-cell research, these goals might have been missed entirely. Researchers might have opted for illegal imported material rather than making a costly application that was unlikely to succeed. Nor would German economic and academic competitiveness, which was of primary importance to SPD members such as Schröder and Clement, have been helped by a research-critical commission. In the end, Fischer and Böhmer may have accepted concessions in this case because they knew that a commission that was likely to effectively prevent importing altogether would result in the topic being put back on to the political agenda before long.

The third topic that was controversial in the group of four was whether the production of new ES-cell lines, and research with them by German researchers abroad, should be prosecuted in Germany. This final detail attracted less public attention than the other two topics but was of central importance to all four. Von Renesse and Catenhusen wanted to abolish all legal uncertainties for researchers and to enable them to take part fully in international exchange and co-operation. Moreover, they had problems with the concept of an *Auslandsstraftat* in itself: prosecuting an action that is legal in the country where it is carried out.[71] To Böhmer, by contrast, a situation where it was not illegal for German researchers to produce ES-cell lines – and thus to kill embryos – abroad, was against the spirit of the compromise motion, which decidedly condemned consumptive research with embryos. The case reflects a fundamental difference between Böhmer and von Renesse with regard to the role of politics and law, which is voiced by Böhmer:

> In a very fundamental way, Margot von Renesse – that's how I see it – starts off from the question: what may the legislator in a democratic, pluralistic society forbid? My question ... is rather: what may the legislator, with the duty to protect human dignity and life, in ethically highly sensitive matters allow? (Böhmer 2005: 161).

In addition to this, supporters of the compromise motion in the CDU/CSU parliamentary group were on average more sceptical than those in the SPD and Green party and they often had religious motives. They were thus particularly likely to vote against any bill that did not condemn the production of ES-cells clearly and unambiguously. Böhmer confronted fierce criticism in her party and was concerned about losing the majority for the law (Böhmer 2005: 166). The critical attitudes in the CDU/CSU parliamentary group definitely constituted a warning to the bargaining round not to make too many concessions to the liberal side. In fact, they may have been used as a powerful bargaining threat by Böhmer, who was the most sceptical of the four. The first draft of the bill did not entail the offence of an *Auslandsstraftat*. In the end, von Renesse conceded the prosecution of German researchers for producing ES-cells abroad, allegedly because she knew that such a law was 'a tiger without teeth', unlikely ever to be applied in practice.[72] She joined Fischer and Böhmer in a motion for an amendment of the bill to this effect presented to the Bundestag on 25 April.[73] Catenhusen, by contrast, insisted on his rejection of such a paragraph and voted against the amendment.

With this exception, co-ordination on all three of the major points left open in the motion was thus successful in the informal circle of four. Despite the fact that its participants insisted on the result being a consensus rather than a compromise and praise deliberation and agreement in the forum, there is significant evidence that bargaining took place. While the four players refuse to confirm this view, it can be argued that a comparatively late cut-off date and research-friendly commission were traded for a more restrictive ruling on offences abroad.

At the same time, the prevalent negative view of bargaining needs to be corrected. The members of this forum definitely had at least partly different and non-transferable reasons to support the motion – which necessitated compromises and concessions. What took place between them, nonetheless, was presumably *mainly* arguing: explaining and justifying positions by reference to one's own experiences, motives and loyalties. This must be contrasted with the antagonistic logics of interaction in the Ethics Council, where emphasis was on truth, morality and argumentative consistency.

Böhmer, Catenhusen, Fischer and von Renesse did not seek truth or morality when they drafted the bill together. Each had reasons to support the compromise that could not (entirely) be shared by the others. However, such reasons were respected as authentic and well founded by the others, which allowed an atmosphere of trust to develop that was essential for bargaining and compromises:

> In the beginning it was a scanning ... We were never unaware of the fact that she was deeply Catholic and I deeply Protestant, that I was deeply SPD and she was deeply CDU. We accepted that we were different. We came together from separate ends.[74]

The compromises accomplished in the drafting of the bill appear to be merely pragmatic details with regard to an underlying conflict that was not so much about interests as about deep moral convictions. In the sense that the compromise was a moral one, it may also have reflected compromises between conflicting reasons at the individual level, which would account for the actors' experience of reaching agreement. In this case, however, practical reasons for preferences would have been affected and preferences would have been transformed – something the ideal-type of interest bargaining rules out.

3.3 Preference-transformation and aggregation of reasons

Comparing early statements on ES-cell research with later accounts by the members of the 'biopolitical quartet',[75] it seems that at least Böhmer, Fischer and von Renesse did indeed change their opinions on the matter and that against the hypotheses, preference-transformation took place. This would be surprising, given that the forum was, at least in part, functionally defined: the participants were bioethical experts within their respective parties and they represented their parliamentary groups as well as the more research-friendly and the more sceptical side. Statements in interviews and elsewhere, however, indicate that, with regard to the underlying moral conflict about the status of the embryo, all four stuck to their original positions. Margot von Renesse points out: 'If I could have had my way, I have a far less sacred idea of the embryo than the Catholics.'[76]

Andrea Fischer, too, makes clear that her feelings and moral convictions on bioethical questions were not affected by the compromise:

> I don't want abortion. I don't want stem-cell research, I don't want prenatal diagnostics, I don't want abortions of children because they are disabled, and I could continue this list. This is my deep personal conviction. And I could have a discussion with you on why I think this correct. But whether I can prescribe these convictions to everybody, I am not so sure.[77]

This quote indicates that what changed were not preferences over research with embryos (i.e. over states of the world in which this research is practised or not practised) but opinions about what was legally and politically feasible. What happened was thus an adaptation of preferences to the preferences of other players (the politically feasible) and to what was acceptable in society at large.

The way in which the members of the quartet value the compromise as such, the democratic decision, and the Bundestag's as well as their own role in it, is less extraordinary than it may seem at first glance. As noted before, bargaining and compromise unjustly have a bad public reputation in many contexts. Moreover, players are responsible to the groups or parties they represent and have to avoid the impression of having made too many concessions. Consequently, they try to present compromises as win-win solutions and emphasise gains rather than losses. At the same time, however, the four seem to value the compromise *because* it gained a democratic majority and enjoyed public support. In this sense, they prefer a state of the world over others not (only) because of its properties but (also) because of the way it has been brought about, namely democratically.

When the stem-cell law returned to the parliamentary agenda in 2008, Böhmer, Fischer and von Renesse published a joint statement against a revision that would shift the cut-off date from 1 January 2002 to 1 May 2007. The proponents of the revision saw the new regulation as an 'update' of the original law that was in keeping with its logic, a position that is consonant with Catenhusen's, who had campaigned for more liberal regulation before.[78] The three 'mothers' of the stem cell law, however, including von Renesse – known to take a more liberal position on stem-cell research – pointed out that with the revision, the logic of the stem-cell law would break down.[79] Their defence of the old stem-cell law, it seems, was not so much a defence of the law itself as of the way it was brought about through compromise and *Verständigung*. If the law was to be replaced, they argued, the new law should be based on new information and would require new reasons and justification – it cannot be rationalised as a mere 'update' of the original legislation.

While these later developments indicate the degree of *Verständigung* achieved between the leaders of the compromise motion in the bargaining forum (and outside it as well), none of the actors seems to have changed his or her preferences on importing stem cells during the period when the bill was drafted. Instead, both the more liberal and the more restrictive sides had to make concessions. The biopolitical quartet may thus be adequately described as a forum of interest bargaining and confirms the hypotheses proposed in this respect.

The compromise that evolved in a cross-party coalition in the Bundestag and which was cast into a bill in this informal circle constitutes the result of the politicisation of a moral conflict about the status of the embryo. The earlier attempt to de-politicise the conflict by transferring it to the expert forum of the Ethics Council had not been successful at producing a unanimous vote (or a large majority) and a convincing rationalisation for allowing importing. As Bogner and Menz (2002) have argued, such split votes by expert commissions also serve to demonstrate the necessity of a political decision and its authority. While the proponents of the compromise motion argued that theirs was the only legally passable option, the two alternatives were entirely feasible as well. It is far from certain that the German supreme court or the European Court of Justice would have ruled against either a complete ban or a permission. Even if they had, there would have been political ways available to achieve either. The political decision was contingent rather than without alternatives and was so perceived by the public and by parliamentarians.

4. CONSENSUS CONFERENCE: DELIBERATION AFTER THE DECISION

About two years after the expert forums of the National Ethics Council and the Study Commission had dealt with the importing of embryonic stem cells and one and a half years after the Bundestag had passed the bill that permitted restricted importing, a citizen conference dealt with the same topic. The forum, in the style of Danish consensus conferences, was organised by a co-operation between the Max Delbrück-Center for Molecular Medicine (MDC) and the Research Centre Jülich and funded by the Ministry of Education and Research.[80] In a lead time of nearly a year, three weekends of citizen meetings were prepared and 20 participants

Table 5.8: Time schedule for citizen conference on stem-cell research in Berlin 2003/2004

Weekend 1	Introduction; information; organisation
12.12.2003	Reception; identification of important questions on stem-cell research; work in small groups and presentation of results; reflection.
13.12.2003	Compilation of mind maps on stem-cell research; presentation by a technology writer; discussion; summarising of results and reflection.
14.12.2003	Analysis of mind maps and identification of focal topics; formation of working groups on these topics; work in groups and presentation of results; outlook on weekend 2 and reflection.
Weekend 2	**Preparation of expert hearing**
30.01.2004	Collection of important aspects for final report (citizen vote); clustering of aspects; expert presentation by and discussion with ethicist (demanded by participants).
31.01.2004	Group work on focal topics; presentation of results; development of a list of questions for expert hearing on weekend 3.
01.02.2004	Discussion on the list of questions; group work and presentations; selection of experts to be invited; discussion about procedural aspects of hearing.
Weekend 3	**Public expert hearing; drafting of citizen vote; presentation of vote**
12.03.2004	Public expert hearing; part 1; reflection.
13.03.2004	Public expert hearing; part 2; reflection; scheduling of next day.
14.03.2004	Discussion about vote; group work; drafting of vote.
15.03.2004	Presentation of final vote to the president of the Bundestag; Wolfgang Thierse, in a public press conference

recruited. The entire event was extensively documented with tape and video recordings, the meetings were chaired by independent moderators and the procedure was evaluated by a team of external observers. For the first three-day weekend meeting in Berlin in December 2003, 17 citizens turned up. From this original forum, five members had dropped out when the group presented its vote to the president of the Bundestag in March 2004. The rough schedule for the three meetings is summarised in Table 5.8.[81]

The motivation behind the organisation of forums for citizen deliberation on bioethical topics is often a twofold one. On the one hand, there is a hope that participatory procedures will contribute to a vitalisation of democracy, inform political decisions with new perspectives from the 'lifeworld' of participants and improve citizens' knowledge on complex matters. Sometimes, there is also an implicit expectation that discussion with experts will reconcile opinions with controversial new technologies such as ES-cell research.

On the other hand, the social scientists organising citizen forums often have a vivid interest in the ways participants interact, in the way they perceive the procedure and in what they gain from it. Such an evaluation is of importance for an assessment of the potential of citizen forums in political decision-making and of relevance to democratic theory, in particular to theories of participatory and deliberative democracy. As noted before, the normative and regulative idea behind most forums for citizen deliberation that are organised is the much-idealised model of ancient city democracies. In modern reality, the institutionalisation of citizen deliberation is notoriously difficult to arrange. The choice of institutional and procedural details is likely to be driven by theoretical inclinations and can have a decisive effect on results, so that general conclusions on citizen forums are difficult to draw.

For the conference on stem-cell research that is discussed here, the deliberate choice of a label was already indicative of the procedure as a whole. Although the forum was modelled after Danish consensus conferences, the organisers preferred to call it a 'citizen conference' to avoid the implication of unanimity that, in their opinion, could not reflect the likely reality with regard to stem-cell research (ben Salem/Tannert 2004: 106). The renunciation of the goal of consensus points towards a different *task* for the conference from that which would be required for an institutionalisation of ideal-typical deliberation. While the ideal type assumes that participants seek a joint evaluation of different options for action, this alternative rationale implies that the function of the forum is to achieve an adequate reflection of social reality and public opinion.

At the same time, the decision not to expect consensus shows that the *conflict* over ES-cell research had come to be regarded as more or less irreducible. It was clear that further factual information could not resolve it and that at the heart of it was a moral divide rather than a clash of interests. A political decision on the matter had already been taken and a new one was not impending. The choice of the term 'citizen' instead of 'consensus' conference thus constitutes an attempt to acknowledge moral plurality that is not in conformity with the ideal-typical function of the forum. However, it also provides a clear *role* ascription to participants. A problem with regard to the participants' role as citizens consists in that participation was evidently not instrumental to a generally binding decision but, in a sense, an end in itself. This situation is likely to induce members of the forum to relapse into the roles of consumer or private individuals (cf. Niewöhner 2004: 70).

The ideal of the citizen role is nonetheless more than apparent in the organisation of the conference. Particular emphasis was placed on the representativeness of the citizen group, which was to be ensured by a sophisticated system of random sampling. In spite of this, university graduates were over-represented among those who declared an interest in participation as well as in the eventual citizen group. What is more, drop-outs during the process increased the imbalance as the exit option was predominantly selected by members with lower formal education levels. The opportunity of an easy and more or less costless exit is a further caveat with regard to the citizen role: participants cannot be forced to live up to expectations and fruitfully deal with conflicts in a deliberative process. The evaluation and analysis of transcripts in fact shows that, throughout the process but particularly on the first weekend, participants were confused about the goal and task of the forum as well as their own role in it. One participant even uttered the suspicion of being part of an 'experiment in manipulation' (Henning/Erdwien 2004: 31) – a suspicion that, given the intense interest of social scientists in the procedure, is not without cause.

Concerning the public and dialogical qualities of interaction, the organisers took pains to ensure both in the choice of procedural details. A part of the conference, the expert hearing, was fully public and attended by a number of interested citizens. During the plenary meetings, an audience of observers as well as the tape recording of proceedings constituted publicity to some degree. Work in smaller groups, by contrast, took place behind closed doors. In this case, a logic of publicity was kept up only in the sense that the product of interaction, the citizen vote, was to be presented and justified to a wider public. The dialogical quality of interaction was enabled by the comparatively small size of the forum and encouraged by the moderators. One of the rules set up for the conference was that 'troubles had priority': whenever a member was unhappy with the course of the discussion or the procedures in general, this dissatisfaction was dealt with immediately. The clear intention in the procedural rules and set-up of the forum was that each of the citizens should be at liberty to speak whenever they wanted and that consideration for others should evolve naturally. The extent to which discursiveness and co-ordinativeness, which define the ideal-type of citizen deliberation, were realised in this instance will be assessed in somewhat closer empirical analysis.

4.1 Discursiveness

As the results of the speech-act analysis illustrated in Figures 5.3 and 5.4 show, interaction in the citizen conference was clearly dialogical. Compared to the setting of the parliamentary debate, dialogical speech acts are far more frequent. In particular those dialogical speech acts that are indicative of the process rather than the product of argumentation, such as to ASK, TAKE BACK, INSIST, AGREE or CONTRADICT, occur with comparatively high frequencies. A more qualitative reading of the transcripts as well as the evaluation (Henning & Erdwien 2004) confirm these results. At all stages of the conference, participants made use of the opportunity to contradict assertions or demand justifications, and frequently demanded changes in procedure when they felt that important aspects were being neglected. Even in the expert hearings, citizens confidently lead the inquiry on a basis of equality with the experts and avoided being pushed into the role of mere listeners, as the following example illustrates:

Weekend 3, day 2 (13.03.2004)
Em12:
... And I don't consider this alternative particularly reasonable. We must struggle together to achieve the highest possible level of agreement.

Bm5:
May I ask a question here? I understand that you see the reason for these dif-
ferences in the first place in the fact that there is a different history of norms.
That is, that norms have formed societies accordingly.

Em12:
I would speak of principles here rather than norms and also of corresponding
attitudes...[82]

The expert offers a normative evaluation of the situation, for which a citizen
demands further explanation. In his question, he proposes an interpretation to be
confirmed, to which the expert replies with a clarification.

Regarding contributions in the plenum, there were significant differences
between the single members of the forum. Considering the transcripts of day two,
weekend two (31 January 2004), which were used for the speech-act analysis, the
number of speech acts per citizen speaker varied between six and 220. Three participants clearly dominated the discourse with more than 100 speech acts each.
Another group of five had 17 or fewer speech acts each and a middle group of
seven had between 31 and 59 speech acts. Of the dominant trio, two were lawyers
(a man and a woman) and the third was a (male) former police superintendent. In
the bottom group were a trader, an unemployed painter, a college student, a laboratory assistant and a retired engineer. Three members of this bottom group
dropped out between the second and third weekend.[83] However, participants were
aware of this imbalance, as the following quote shows:

Bw2 (14.12.2003):
I feel an uneasiness here, that is, I get the impression that some people can
rhetorically express themselves very well, but others can't, and I would want
more of a balance to be established here. I want to hear more clearly the people who do not talk so much otherwise and find a way that those participants
express themselves, too.

One of the more assertive members, a lawyer (Bm5), acknowledged his domineering behaviour and expressed the intention to change it. Despite these efforts, several participants indicated discontent with their own contribution to the citizen
vote and the procedure as a whole in the final evaluation. This result appears even
more relevant considering that dissatisfaction was probably a cause of the five
drop-outs during the conference.

The citizen group as a whole showed confidence towards the moderators and
organisers of the forum as well as towards experts. In the expert hearings, citizens
frequently insisted on their questions and arguments and are in some cases hard to
satisfy. Nonetheless, it is notable that particularly in the expert hearings, a comparatively high number of 'hedges' (cf. 4.3) occurred. Interestingly, dominant
members with higher formal education levels used hedges more often than other

members. A possible explanation, in keeping with a diagnosis by Bogner and Menz (2002; 2005), is that these people were particularly keen on being accepted as equals by the experts. Towards the end of the conference and in the citizen vote, it becomes apparent that the dominant members adapted to the expert discourse and more or less reflected it, instead of offering alternative views.

There are moments where it becomes clear that some other, non-expert styles of argumentation tended to be regarded as inadequate by the majority. Take the following example, in which a 52-year-old citizen training as an alternative practitioner relates a story about recipients of donor organs developing some characteristics of the donor:

> Bw7 (13.12.):
> ... And now the following happened: the patient did, after he had tolerably recovered with his donor organ, that is the heart, suddenly acquire characteristics of the other patient. Has anyone considered that?
> Em20:
> Well, that is completely new to me, I must say. LAUGHS.

The significance of the contribution in the context of ES-cell research is entirely clear: the speaker fears that patients treated with such products might lose their own personality as a result of the donation. The expert obviously feels uncertain how to react to this unorthodox concern and feigns ignorance. At the same time, his laughter expresses unwillingness to deal seriously with the story.

The example is revelatory of a conflict between the goal of informing citizens and enabling an unprejudiced assessment of a new technology and the intention to enrich a discourse with 'lifeworldly' perspectives. The former looks at the desired output of participatory procedures – an active, well informed, supportive citizenry – whereas the latter looks at their possible input to political decision-making. The dominant members of the citizen group shared with the experts as well as the organisers of the conference criteria for the evaluation of reasons and arguments according to which the above quote is esoteric. The final vote of the citizen group points out:

> The religious attitudes and biographical experiences of single persons cannot be generalized. For a fruitful conversation, information on the topic, an exchange of ethical arguments and their structuring are important. This includes the effort to justify the intuitive evaluation with rational arguments.[84]

While the quote is indicative of a self-conception of enlightened citizenship (as most models of deliberative democracy presuppose), it also reflects a restriction of the discourse and of the positions that can legitimately be held within it. If the aim is to ensure a rational discussion and produce a report that is easily accessible to the media and political actors, the failure of esoteric arguments in the citizen conference can be welcomed. However, if the aim is to represent the diversity of different opinions and experiences and to co-ordinate these, it must be seen with a more critical eye.

Another problem that becomes apparent in practice concerns the publicity of the forum. While the organisers took pains to ensure publicity and transparency, the citizen group was apparently surprised to find an audience of observers and disturbed by tape and video recordings and camera flashlights. One participant even dropped out because she could not cope with the frequent observation. Suspicions of being guinea pigs in an experiment undermined the participants' citizen role and, at the same time, served as an argument against publicity, which is essential to it. On the first weekend, the group decided that for half an hour on every day, they wanted to be amongst themselves without the presence of either the moderators or other observers. On the second weekend, however, they often demanded work in the plenum where the organisers had planned work in small groups. There was a strong feeling among participants that important questions had to be addressed by the entire forum and could not be decided in subgroups. The idea behind this was apparently that the proper assessment of arguments required the larger forum and that decisions required the consent of all its members. When drafting the vote on the last weekend, citizens again decided to do without the presence of a moderator, although they wanted organisers to be available for advice.

A final constraint of the discursiveness of the forum consists in the time pressure that became increasingly apparent on the second weekend. Although discussions among citizens were always topical, the goal of producing a vote and thus the necessity to decide often faded into the background. In order to keep up with the schedule and timetable, the moderators felt compelled to somewhat authoritarian interventions. This enforcement of structure and procedure was clearly in conflict with an open discourse but apparently necessary to achieve more than merely information and discussion. In a sense, it seems to reflect a more general conflict between discursiveness and co-ordinativeness of interaction – between the quest for truth and the necessity to decide.

4.2 Co-ordinativeness

At least two aspects might have been expected significantly to reduce the co-ordinativeness of the citizen conference compared to the ideal-type of deliberation. One is the organising committee's aforementioned intention to reflect the plurality of opinions and values rather than actively to pursue consensus, which is also reflected in the rejection of the 'consensus' label. Another is the fact that, at the time the conference took place, the Bundestag had just taken a decision on the matter, so that any results produced by the citizen conference could not be immediately relevant to a political decision.

It is therefore interesting that, at the level of speech-act analysis, the comparison between the parliamentary debate and the citizen conference yields the following results. The debate is an instance of almost pure arguing: bargaining speech acts, where they occur, are of a rhetorical rather than illocutionary nature.

Table 5.9: Types of speech acts in citizen conference

Type of speech act	Number	Percentage
Arguing	636	70%
Bargaining	135	15%
Rhetoric	1	0%
Discourse structurers	103	11%
Expressives	25	3%
Others	8	1%

In the citizen forum, by contrast, bargaining speech acts were surprisingly frequent (compare Figures 5.2 and 5.9).

As noted above, there were some restrictions on publicity in the citizen conference, which could in principle have increased incentives for bargaining. Considering that participants had no material interests in the results of the procedure and that exit was easily possible, however, bargaining in the classical distributive sense appears unlikely in this setting. Moreover, the total percentage of arguing speech acts is only marginally higher in the debate than in the citizen conference (76 per cent compared to 70 per cent), so that bargaining does not seem to have impaired arguing.

A closer look at the instances in which bargaining speech acts occur shows that they are found mainly in a context of procedural meta-discourse. Bargaining takes place over when to reassemble on the next day, over the ordering of cards on the flipchart or over whether to discuss a topic in small groups or in the plenum. Most of the bargaining speech acts are proposals or appeals; threats or promises do not occur. At the same time, the distinction between meta-discourse and substantial communication is difficult to draw. Discussions about which experts to invite, which questions to ask them, and in which order, were in many cases resolved by means of bargaining or even voting rather than argumentation. Nonetheless, procedural conflicts also reflected disagreements at a substantial level. For instance, participants with a rather critical attitude towards ES-cell research (who were in the majority) gave preference to 'ethical' over 'scientific' experts and sought to focus the hearing on moral and social aspects rather than factual ones.

On the whole, the transcripts show a more or less profound insecurity, on both the organisers' and the participants' sides, where the necessary degree of co-ordination is concerned. The organisers and moderators had an apparent (even material) interest in the success of the conference. Criteria for such a success were adherence to the schedule; no or only a small number of drop-outs; and, most importantly, a presentable result in the form of a citizen vote. At the same time, they had to avoid any impression of authoritarianism or unjust influence on participants' opinions. On the citizens' side, the strong desire to learn and to do justice to all relevant aspects of the topic distracted attention from the goal of a joint (if not consensual) vote and report.[85]

However, the group was quite perceptive of these problems and did not fail to

discuss them. After the discussion with a technology writer on the first weekend
had helped to resolve many factual questions and misunderstandings, a shift of the
focus towards ethical questions also sparked reflection on members' own role as
citizens and the role of political decisions in society. On the first day of the second weekend, a participant addressed the question of how to deal with consensus
and disagreement in the vote:

> Bm5 (30.01.):
> Well, I think one should state the majority situation, because I think that if the idea
> is to make an input to politics with which they have to deal, then there is no point
> in telling them that there are different opinions. Because, they know that anyway.

This citizen clearly had more ambitious goals for the conference than the organisers. Far from deeming it sufficient to reflect the well known plurality of opinions
and moral conflict, he regarded its results as an important input to political
processes. More than that, he recognised that only a clear majority or consensus
was likely to give politicians reason to rethink their position.

Already on the first weekend, participants had broached the issue of their own
role in relation to the experts. One citizen pointed out:

> Bm1 (14.12.):
> ... I think, we can hear people who all have their own opinions. But the one
> expert who tells us, this is what's right, we won't find. Well, that's what we
> have to do for ourselves. ...

Despite the participants' desire to learn and be adequately informed, which sometimes prevented results-oriented communication, there is thus an awareness of the
contingency of evaluation and the necessity of a political decision: the citizens
politicise their decision. The following dialogue points in the same direction:

> Bw4 (14.12.):
> What I don't like is that what comes out in the end is referred to as a report.
> Because report, that sounds a bit/well, in the presentations here it's always
> called vote, and I like that because –

> M1m:
> Let's call it vote, yes.

> Bw4:
> Because, report sounds a bit expert-like, and I mean, the idea is just that we
> give a vote and not that we presume to write a report.

> Bw6:
> And we won't be experts – [babble of voices]

Bw4:
Yes, exactly, and to express that, that what we're doing here is something different from what the experts are doing on the topic.

The citizen criticises the use of the term 'report' for their product and prefers it to be referred to as a 'vote', arguing that their task differs from that of experts. On the second weekend, she elaborated further on the issue:

Bw4 (31.01.):
... That's more or less the general expectation. Citizens ask experts. Here is the citizen, and the expectation, to begin with is, he has no idea, and rightly so. And now he asks the expert. And what does he do in his awe? He asks the expert on a topic on which the expert has been named to him as such. ... But the citizen is in his own way an expert in matters that concern these fundamental questions.

It must be noted, however, that this participant was also the dominant speaker in the forum: a well informed lawyer with few problems in adapting to expert discourse and with well justified and sophisticated opinions. Other, more diffident and insecure members may well have felt differently.

Nonetheless, another indicator of the politicisation of the forum is the discussion about which experts to invite to the hearing on the third weekend. The citizens were presented with a list of academic experts from different disciplines but expressed a wish to invite representatives from interest-groups such as ATTAC and Greenpeace. The organisers reacted with reluctance and pointed out that this was not what they had in mind. Eventually, two of the 13 experts invited to the hearing were not researchers: Margot von Renesse and Stephan Kruip, chair of a self-help group for people with cystic fibrosis. In both questionnaires and discussions on the last weekend, participants complained that too much time was consumed by the expert hearing and its preparation, which could have been better used for the drafting of the vote – and thus for co-ordination.

On the whole, it seemed that the dynamics within the citizen group countered the contextual factors that were less favourable to co-ordination. One thing that is likely to have contributed to this is the high degree of trust and mutual respect within the group (cf. Henning & Erdwien 2004: 37). Although some more extravagant or esoteric arguments were not taken up in the forum as they apparently failed to comply with discourse standards (see above), narrative elements and emotional utterances were fully accepted. On the first weekend, one participant tells the group about her grandmother's suffering from Parkinson's and breaks out in tears. The others react compassionately and take her utterance as an argument in favour of an 'ethics of healing'. Summarising her experiences of the day, another member points out:

Bw4 (14.12.):
... And I did not get the impression that that was an embarrassing situation in

any way. That is, that one can show everything. And also is not restricted to the rational discourse. In conversation, it is often a purely rational discourse. But rather, that one can say things here that go beyond that without the feeling/ or that one can give a lot from oneself, without others doing something mean. And I think that is a good experience ...

Note that her point is not that emotions and non-generalisable experiences can replace rational discourse but that they are permitted 'beyond' it and that other members do not exploit weaknesses. Even where rational discourse is concerned, though, there is less emphasis on consistency and deductibility than in the expert forums analysed before (especially in the Ethics Council). In particular, citizens do not pick each other's arguments to pieces in order to secure esteem. Rather, they present doubts and objections in a tentative, considerate manner.

When the time came to formulate passages of the eventual vote, citizens refused moderation and tape recordings. A smaller group of particularly active members met outside the official forum to discuss controversial topics and draft comments on them. Nevertheless, co-ordination remained difficult, so that at some stage the goal of a presentable vote became a distant prospect. In one situation, the moderator started to call votes on single passages, against which the citizens protested.

The final vote has remarkable similarities with the reports by the Ethics Council and Study Commission.[86] There are consensual passages on factual basics and on aspects for evaluation but, in the evaluation itself, the group divided into fractions. Concerning the status of the embryo, a majority of eight participants held that the embryo develops as a human being from the moment of fertilisation, while the remaining four members thought that human life begins with nidation. Among the eight critical members, three believed that the killing of embryos cannot be justified by an ethics of healing, two wanted to await new developments in clinical research before taking such a decision, and three thought that protection of the embryo should be gradual and increase with the stage of development. Consensus existed only with regard to a preference for research with adult stem cells as the ethically unproblematic technology and in the rejection of ES-cell production for research purposes. Neither of these points was actually controversial in the German debate, even the extreme position of the FDP parliamentary group saw only 'surplus' embryos as a legitimate source of stem cells.

Judging from their respective reports, the co-ordinative faculties of the consensus conference forum appear little stronger than those of the Ethics Council, in which the ideal-type of expert discussion was approximated. Nonetheless, the co-ordinative achievement of the citizen conference must be rated more highly than that of the council. Most of the council members were acknowledged experts on either ethics or stem-cell research and fully informed about relevant aspects of the matter, which had been discussed at length in quality newspapers. There was thus less need to resolve factual matters. After some legal and technical questions had briefly been addressed, the expert forum split into groups of advocates and proponents of ES-cell import, which formulated their respective parts of the report. Again, as professional academics they were used to and confident in the phrasing of such a document.

By contrast, the citizen group had little previous knowledge of ES-cell research and most members were also less familiar with technical terminology. Accordingly, the largest share of the time scheduled for the conference was used for information and preparation of the expert hearing. Given the resulting shortage of time, the degree of co-ordination achieved is non-negligible and it may well be hypothesised that an additional weekend would have increased consensus. Moreover, not only is the consensual part of the report larger, but agreement was also achieved on procedural matters, such as whom to invite and what questions to ask.

Reconsidering the fact that interaction was both highly dialogical and characterised by moves towards bargaining, a conclusion that suggests itself is that dialogue enabled co-ordination at the price of permitting non-public speech acts. If consensus had been treated as the primary criterion of success in the first place, and if the group had been given more time for co-ordination (instead of being overtaxed by organisation), a unanimous vote might have been within reach. Given the already high number of drop-outs, however, it must be expected that the co-ordination process would have further reduced the size of the group. Such frequent use of the exit option by disagreeing, disadvantaged and dissatisfied members casts a further shadow on the already limited democratic legitimacy of consensus conferences.

4.3 Preference-transformation and aggregation of reasons

The members of the citizen conference, in contrast to those of all the other forums discussed here, entered the procedure with little previous knowledge of the matter and, in particular, undetermined preferences on it. On the first weekend, several participants indicated that they had not yet formed an opinion on ES-cell research and required further information and reflection to form one:

Bm3 (14.12.):
... As I said, at the moment my stance is a bit: yes and no. ... I am willing to compromise, I actually seek a compromise, what one may do and where one should really say, stop, this is the end of the rope, here we put the brakes on, here we need to have legal regulations, which absolutely interdict this ...

Bw3 (14.12.):
Yes, I see this similarly, ... for me, I would say, pro and cons are evenly balanced, that of course I have a tendency, which surely everyone has, to which he tends more after all.

Another citizen not only points out that her opinion remains unstable but also refuses to make it known in the forum, for fear of being restrained in changing it:

Bw1 (14.12.):
Well, what has confirmed my opinion or not, I don't necessarily want to reveal
my opinion, because I think, that I would thus deprive myself of the chance to
decide differently, if I now say I am in against or in favour. I just don't want
to be pigeonholed and simply just that people don't know what I think and I
will leave it open for me how I will develop further.

She thus expresses a fear of loss of face through preference-transformation, which
is a common problem in all public settings. While the refusal to state a position
can be interpreted as a rejection of the citizen's role and as a failure to recognise
the political nature of the problem, it may at this stage actually be normatively
adequate. The citizen is aware of her own uncertainty and lack of information and
wants to engage in a rational discourse before she expects to be able to live up to
the ideal of an informed citizen. Such a forbearance from personal biases and
reliance on rational discourse is part of the normative ideal in deliberative models
of democracy. It prevents untimely coalition-building, restrains rhetorical action
and allows for learning processes. At the same time, it betrays a rather technocratic understanding of politics and may conceal irreducible conflicts of interests.

The technocratic understanding of politics both among the organisers and
among some 'insufficiently emancipated' participants, which Niewöhner (2004)
points out in a very critical assessment of the conference, was at least partly overcome by citizens themselves, though. On the one hand, evaluation by independent
observers came to the conclusion that the citizens' expectations from the conference were mainly 'to increase knowledge on the matter' and 'to get to know new
points of view', while 'to actively engage in public discussions' and 'to make a
contribution to political decision-making' rank much lower (Henning & Erdwien
2004: 24).

A majority also confirms a strong expert influence on their opinion-formation
(Henning & Erdwien 2004: 64). Immediately after the hearing, about half the citizens stated that it had rendered them more sceptical (Henning & Erdwien 2004:
57). It has to be kept in mind, however, that the citizens themselves selected the
mostly critical experts, which reflected a critical tendency at an earlier stage.
Qualitative assessments by Niewöhner (2004) and Bogner & Menz (2005) stress
that citizens largely adopted the expert discourse by assuming the role of 'active
recipients' (Niewöhner 2004: 70), so that the vote amounts to a narrative reproduction of expert statements. When drafting the vote, citizens sought the organisers' advice in order to avoid 'gross factual blunders'. According to this reading,
preference-transformation in the citizen conference amounts to a transformation
of acceptances, not practical reasons. Such a result would contradict the ideal-typical hypotheses for institutionalised citizen deliberation and question its potential
for the evaluation of options for political action.

At the same time, however, transcripts and evaluation indicate a certain development away from factual towards ethical and political questions. One question
asked by the evaluation team concerned the aspects participants deemed important

for an evaluation of ES-cell research. While in the control group, the ranking of relevant aspects remained stable between the dates for the first and third weekend (Henning & Erdwien 2004: 26), the ranking in the citizen group changed significantly over the three weekends (Henning & Erdwien 2004: 25). 'Ethical aspects' rank highest from the beginning; 'social aspects' first lose but eventually gain in importance; and 'political aspects', which ranked very low on the first two weekends, gained considerably in importance on the last weekend. 'Health aspects', which were in second place on the first weekend, significantly lost relevance in the citizens' opinion, similar to 'economic aspects'. 'Religious aspects' ranked low from the beginning, whereas the relevance of 'scientific aspects' was stable at a high level.

The change in aspects considered relevant for the evaluation indicates changes in the weighting of practical reasons and hence preference-transformation on the volitive, and not only the cognitive, side. The fact that social and political aspects have, compared to economic and health aspects, gained in importance suggests a politicisation of the forum.[87] Although 'scientific aspects' (a somewhat vague term) remain important, the citizen group has apparently seen through the rhetoric of an 'ethic of healing' that, among liberals in politics and the media, often intentionally confuses the potential for a cure with the actual cure.[88] Information on the factual state of research (only pure research and no applications in the near future) as well as critical voices from patient representatives in the hearing induced first a change in acceptances and subsequently one in the weighting of practical reasons.

One reason that was particularly important in all other forums and effective for the Bundestag's decision, but met with less resonance in the citizen conference, was the constitutionally guaranteed freedom of research. At first, participants apparently failed to understand its relevance in the given context and regarded it as secondary to moral reasons. Margot von Renesse's persuasive contribution in the expert hearing seemingly induced them to address the argument in the vote. Although the text of the vote embraces the constitutional status and moral relevance of freedom of research, it does not look as if it has affected the evaluation as a practical reason.

Taking the group as a whole, it is not only apparent that preference-transformation did take place and originated both on the volitive and the cognitive side, but also that preferences have changed in a similar direction: contrary to the hopes of science politicians and researchers in technology assessment, citizens have become more critical with regard to ES-cell technology (Erdwien 2004: 136).

The results of this analysis of institutionalised citizen deliberation should be considered in light of the ideal-type as well as in light of the normative ideals and hopes connected with it. While the renunciation of the consensus goal and the fact that no political decision on the matter was impending are characteristic only of this specific case, some other aspects have more general relevance. These concern 1) the lack of information among participants; 2) the too-easily-available exit-option; and 3) the under-determined role of citizen forums in the political decision-making process.

Lack of information

That citizens are inadequately informed about new technologies is a widely acknowledged empirical fact and an important motive for the initiation of citizen forums. In the ideal type of citizen deliberation described in chapter three, it was assumed that participants have already obtained and processed the relevant information and have achieved a far-reaching consensus at the factual level. This counter-factual assumption is necessary to regard the conflict that is dealt with as one of value, concerning evaluation of consequences of feasible and justifiable options for political action. In reality, most forums and most topics will require the resolution of factual questions before evaluation and co-ordination of action plans become possible.

Although in the case analysed here, a lack of factual knowledge among the citizens was evident in the first place and necessitated a strong informative element in the procedure, preference-formation more or less followed the course described in chapter two. In a first phase, state-of-the-art information on ES-cell research was gained and a sufficient degree of consensus on its potential for new cures and possible dangers in application (cancer, infections) reached, albeit at the cost of several drop-outs. During this stage, acceptances were formed and transformed, so that the cognitive premises of preferences were stabilised.

In a second phase, aspects for the moral evaluation of ES-cell research were assessed and weighted. Whether the volitive premises of preferences eventually stabilised or whether the picture gained from the vote and the third weekend's evaluation (see Henning & Erdwien 2004) is merely a momentary snapshot in preference-formation is hard to tell. Nonetheless, it is clear that volitive premises changed only after cognitive premises had stabilised. In fact, citizen forums could be improved by increasing the extent to which deliberation as an ideal-typical mode of interaction is actually institutionalised in them. If a first weekend meeting could include an expert hearing and help to resolve a number of factual questions, so that two further weekend meetings could be devoted to evaluation and the drafting of a vote, achieving a higher level of co-ordination seems possible. Even if a consensus remains out of reach, individual preferences would be given a chance to stabilise, so that the vote could definitely reflect more than a momentary snapshot of opinions.

Costless exiting

Besides a strong element of self-selection, the availability of a costless exit is a more or less inevitable problem of citizen forums. Drop-outs of less eloquent members or members whose opinion runs counter to the forums' mainstream threaten the heterogeneity and representativeness of the group and devalue its report. Burow & Kühnemuth go so far as to propose to renounce the goal of representativeness to a large extent and to make work more effective by delegating it to self-selected sub-groups (2004: 123–5). Homogeneity could, in this case, replace incentives and pressures for co-ordination and promise a smooth process. At the same time, the proposal sacrifices the idea of the citizen conference as mirroring the society at large. If participants can no longer be expected to come from different backgrounds and to have different experiences and opinions, their citizen role in the forum becomes highly dubious.

A report from a group of citizens who share a particular interest in and position on, for example, stem-cell research, effectively amounts to nothing more than an interest-group statement. More promising strategies to avoid drop-outs and maintain heterogeneity could be to pay citizens for their participation (as in the planning-cell model) but to disburse the award only after the conference, or to require them to commit themselves to attending the conference from beginning to end. If participants were selected in a lottery from the whole population and they were told that their task required commitment and a sense of responsibility, they might be more likely to regard this as an honour, as many lay assessors in courts do. Although neither strategy could prevent drop-outs altogether, they would make exit more costly.

Under-determination of the role of citizen forums
While the Berlin citizen conference on stem-cell research was a clear case of 'deliberation after the decision' and without any effect on the political decision-making process, the role of citizen forums in general is under-determined in both theory and practice. Most of their proponents adhere to participatory models of democracy, in which participation is regarded as an end in itself and valued independently of its results. The informative and activating effects of participation are given precedence over effects on policy output. Even in singular cases such as the Oregon Health Plan, in which participatory procedures apparently had a significant effect on political decisions (cf. Daniels 1996), it is unclear whether the effect is due to the citizen forums' results or to the general politicisation of an issue. Far from sharing the organisers' participatory understanding of democracy, however, the citizens in the Berlin conference clearly expected their vote to have an effect on future decisions over ES-cell research. They also demanded more citizen participation in bodies such as the Central Ethics Commission (which assesses applications to import for ES-cell lines).

Obviously, the vote of a citizen conference cannot legitimately have binding consequences for political decisions. Nonetheless, where the institutionalisation of citizen deliberation is attempted, forums should, like other non-democratic forums (particularly expert commissions), be assigned a clear role in a decision-making process in which the parliament has the final say. In Denmark, where the original consensus conference model was developed and where a large number of conferences have already taken place, reports are distributed to all members of parliament and broadly covered in the media (Grundahl 1995: 38). Politicians are interested in the results because they reflect potential voters' views on the matter (Grundahl 1995: 38.). In effect, the consensus conference thus assumes a role somewhere between an opinion poll and an advisory body. Although this role may yet fall short of participants' expectations, it enables more than symbolic participation and maintains the democratic accountability of elected politicians.

5. SUMMARY

Soon after the topic of ES-cell import had reached the political agenda in Germany, opinions in the media, the public and among the members of the Bundestag polarised into a group of radical pro-lifers and a group of liberal supporters who refused to acknowledge ethical problems connected with importing stem cells. The conflict was a fundamental as well as multi-dimensional one, comprising both factual and moral disagreements and uncertainties as well as clashing interests. Several different forums were, accordingly, charged with addressing the conflict. Interaction in these forums can reasonably be compared to the ideal-types developed in chapter three. The use of these ideal-types as reference points of analysis has served to demonstrate their heuristic value and allows for conclusions about the potential of respective forums in democratic decision-making processes. What is more, however, a look at how the communicative focus of interaction moves from one dimension of conflict to the next illustrates how different modes of interaction fruitfully help to disentangle the dimensions of a controversy.

In the case of the decision over importing ES-cells, the expert forum of the National Ethics Council seems to have been the least successful of the forums involved. The interview partners, some possibly out of institutional self-interest, denied that it had any impact on the debate and decision. The split vote, which theory and ideal-type predict, was publicly regarded as indicating the failure of experts to identify a rational solution. Nonetheless, although the communicative focus on argumentative consistency and deducibility prevented co-ordination in what was essentially a moral conflict, the Ethics Council served to assess arguments and to provide comprehensive rationales for different options. For instance, the argument about German economic and research competitiveness, which was an important reason for the advocates of importing, was found to be untenable and subsequently replaced by the 'ethics of healing' argument.

The Parliamentary Study Commission, although it also had advisory functions, had less in common with an institutionalisation of ideal-typical expert deliberation than the Ethics Council. Only half of its members were experts (chosen on the basis of party partisanship), the other half were representatives of the parliamentary parties. The election of lawyer and SPD member Margot von Renesse as chair of this forum had important consequences for its development. The communicative focus of the forum moved away from the moral conflict over the status of the embryo *in vitro* and towards aspects of constitutionality and feasibility. Sceptics were presented with the argument that a complete ban on importing would violate the constitutionally guaranteed freedom of research while liberals were confronted with the fact that a parliamentary majority for unrestricted importing was out of reach. Although, not surprisingly and quite like the Ethics Council, the Study Commission did not arrive at a unanimous vote, its forked report had considerable resonance among members of parliament. Although parallel contacts regarding a compromise were established between the CDU/CSU (Seehofer/Böhmer) and junior minister Catenhusen, it seems that the basis for the compromise motion was laid in the Study Commission between von Renesse and expert member Ulrike Riedel (also personal assistant to Andrea Fischer, Greens). Despite the fact that there is little to suggest that members of the commission changed their opinion in the forum, its report and the discussions carried over into parliamentary groups had a significant effect on the preference-formation of parliamentarians.

During the weeks before the Bundestag's debate and ballot on 30 January 2002, the leaders of the compromise motion managed to convince liberals in the SPD that the motion for unrestricted importing would not win a majority, and to convince some (but fewer) sceptics that a ban would not be constitutional. The debate itself, which, due to the suspension of party discipline, was somewhat exceptional in the German parliamentary system, can still be seen as an institutionalisation of debate as an ideal-typical mode of interaction. While the argumentative quality and atmosphere have justly been praised, interaction followed institutional logics that promoted monological contributions and rhetoric. Speakers presented the *product* of argumentation rather than engaging in a *process* of argumentation, and the communicative focus was clearly on the public justification of the respective options. Predictably, only very few previously undecided parliamentarians changed their preferences during the debate, so that the result of the ballot – a clear success of the compromise motion in the second round – was not surprising and the function of the debate evidently lay in the justification of a decision and its alternatives. In addition to this, however, the debate also served to reinforce trust in the parliament's ability to regulate controversial matters and to prevent the abuse of new technologies effectively.

Following the success of the compromise motion, its leaders – Böhmer, Catenhusen, Fischer and von Renesse – established a more informal forum. Behind its closed doors, several relevant details left open in the motion were negotiated and the eventual bill was drafted. Although all four sought to maintain the 'spirit' of the motion and the law on the protection of embryos (*Embryonenschutzgesetz*) in order to win a large majority for their bill, they also had individual goals and interests. The communicative focus in this forum was on manageability and enforceability of the law but co-ordination was not achieved through communication alone. Rather, compromises had to be found on several details, which justifies the classification of this round as a bargaining forum. Preferences apparently did not change at this stage, despite the fact that all four praised the process of reaching agreement and rejected both the interpretation of it as bargaining and the term 'compromise'.

The citizen conference on stem-cell research in Berlin 2003–4 took place after the matter had been decided politically and thus had little resonance among representatives. It deviated from an institutionalisation of ideal-typical citizen deliberation in that the goal of consensus was renounced and in that there were strong informative intentions. The communicative focus was at first mainly on information and only later moved to the evaluation of options for political decision. The result is little more than a snapshot of lay opinions, after comprehensive information but incomplete deliberation and co-ordination. Nonetheless, the analysis confirms the hypotheses derived in chapter three in that the citizen conference is the only forum in which actors' preferences changed significantly. Moreover, changes took place in both the cognitive (initially) and the volitive (subsequently) premises of preferences. Regarding the direction of change, it should be noted that participants held more critical views on ES-cell research after the conference than before it.

Table 5.10 below summarises the results of the analysis of the different forums and indicates that the ideal-typical forums have served as a useful heuristic and tolerably good predictor of preference-transformation:

Table 5.10: Summary of case study results

	Communicative focus	Co-ordinative result	Preference-transformation
Nat. Ethics Council	(moral) consistency, deducibility	split vote	no
Study commission	constitutionality, capability of winning a majority	forked report	little or none
Parliamentary deb.	justification, persuasion	majority decision	little or none
Bargaining	manageability, feasibility	compromise	little or none
Citizen conference	information, evaluation	forked report	yes

The law on importing stem cells enjoys strong public support in Germany and has pacified the moral conflict. When the topic was put back on the political agenda in 2008, a revision took place with (regrettably) less public attention but also in a less confrontational atmosphere. Although the fact that the decision was partly prepared in the nondemocratic forum of the Ethics Council and partly resolved through bargaining may induce charges of delegation and 'expertocracy', its democratic quality is actually high. The more influential forum of the study commission was legitimated by the parliament and so were the leaders of the compromise motion in drafting the bill. Also, the debate was accompanied by a broad media coverage and public debate and the eventual decision prepared and taken in a highly transparent manner. The alternatives to an extensive preparation of the decision in different forums would have been either indecision (effectively enabling importing by a legal loophole) or a narrow majority decision for a ban, which might have proved unconstitutional and would have intensified rather than pacified the conflict. The result, which has been criticised as morally contradictory, is in fact a well balanced political response to an irreducible antagonism.

NOTES

1 Respectively, five MPs and five experts by the SPD, four by the CDU/CSU, two by the Greens and one each by the FDP and the PDS, as well as deputies for all members. An interesting

detail is that Therese Neuer-Miebach, professor of social work and health, was an expert member of both the Study Commission and the Ethics Council.

2 During the debate in 2001, Schröder did not publicly promote a liberal solution, although he was known to support it. In the parliamentary vote on 30 January 2002, he spoke and voted for the compromise solution, probably because he wanted to maintain coalition peace and knew that a more liberal option could not be successful. In a TV duel with his challenger Angela Merkel on 4 September 2005, he openly demanded that 'red biotechnology' and therapeutic cloning be legalised in Germany.

3 Cf. the ideal types developed in chapter three, section 4.

4 The Study Commission also held an online discussion forum on 15 November 2001. Although citizens' contributions had no repercussions in the report (which was published less than two weeks later), the commission thus tried to justify its verdict to a broader public.

5 Interview with Margot von Renesse, 14.11.2005 in Bochum.

6 BT-Drs. 14/5157.

7 Interview with Ingrid Schneider (SPD expert member of the Study Commission), 15.08.05 in Hamburg.

8 Interview with Margot von Renesse, 14.11.2005 in Bochum. This translation and all following ones from interviews and documents are my own.

9 Interview with Wolfgang van den Daele, 23.01.2006 in Berlin.

10 Interview with Wolfgang van den Daele, 23.01.2006 in Berlin.

11 Interview with Wolfgang van den Daele, 23.01.2006 in Berlin.

12 Interview with Wolfgang van den Daele, 23.01.2006 in Berlin.

13 Interview with Wolfgang van den Daele, 23.01.2006 in Berlin.

14 Interview with Wolfgang van den Daele, 23.01.2006 in Berlin.

15 Interview with Wolfgang van den Daele, 23.01.2006 in Berlin

16 Leaders of the liberal coalition were van den Daele, Bettina Schöne-Seifert, Peter Propping, Ernst-Ludwig Winnacker (president of the German Research Foundation) and Volker Gerhard (cf. interview with Wolfgang van den Daele, 23.01.06 in Berlin).

17 BT-Drs. 14/6551.

18 Interview with Margon von Renesse, 14.11.2005 in Bochum.

19 Interview with Margot von Renesse, 14.11.2005 in Bochum.

20 BT-Drs. 14/7546, which is in fact the commission's intermediate report on ES-cell research. The commission published a final report on its work in the fourteenth legislative period in May 2002 (BT-Drs. 14/9020).

21 The third, least restrictive motion was effectively a motion by the parliamentary group of the FDP.

22 BT-Drs. 14/7546, p. 102.

23 BT-Drs. 14/5157, p. 15.

24 A German newspaper questioned members of the council on their position on ES-cell import shortly after the forum was established and received eleven replies (*Süddeutsche Zeitung* 30.05.2001, S.17/18). A Bavarian group of hardliners campaigning against the importation of ES-cell (and related matters) published portraits of its members, including information on their stated or likely position on bioethical questions ('Interessengemeinschaft kritische Bioethik Bayern', www.nationaler-ethikrat.de).

25 Interview with Wolfgang van den Daele, 23.01.2005 in Berlin.

26 Interview with Wolfgang van den Daele, 23.01.2005 in Berlin.

27 The survey had a return rate of approximately 30 per cent among MPs (N= 217).

28 This result is somewhat surprising because the Ethics Council was widely regarded as lacking the parliamentary legitimacy of the Study Commission and because the latter was better integrated into parliamentary processes. One possible explanation may be the fact that the council's report was far shorter than the commission's and focused on moral arguments, while the commission tried to factor out moral questions where they were not tied to constitutional ones.

29 Interview with Margot von Renesse, 14.11.2005 in Bochum.

30 Interview with Andrea Fischer, 26.01.2006 in Berlin.

31 In fact, some parliamentarians (and commentators) questioned the legitimacy of the procedure and argued that a different voting scheme would have yielded a different result. In their eyes, the motion for a complete ban should have been successful as it had the highest number of supporters behind it. This argument is untenable, however, as it refuses to see that preferences on the matter were single-peaked within a single dimension. If a relative majority had been sufficient, proponents of the liberal motion would have promoted the compromise motion in the first place. If voting had been in pairs, they would equally have supported the compromise against the complete ban. Under the given preference constellation, the success of the compromise motion was thus entirely predictable.

32 The distinction between the two is based on the assumption that assertions are claims that the speaker acknowledges to be still controversial while establishments presuppose agreement, that something is taken for granted (e.g. 'As we know...'; 'As has been shown...').

33 In presidential systems, it must be noted, the debate as an ideal-typical mode of interaction is less likely to be institutionalised in the legislature. Rather, some kind of co-ordination will always be required.

34 BT-Drs. 14/8101, 14/8102; 14/8103.

35 The table is accessible with help of the list of arguments provided in the appendix. For each of the motions, instances in which the arguments were positively made (pro) and instances in which they were rejected (con) are noted. Numbers in bold print highlight the arguments with the highest frequency.

36 Monika Knoche, Plenarprotokoll 14/214, p. 21198.

37 As von Renesse points out (interview, 14.11.2005, Bochum): 'The parliament in general seeks to avoid extreme courses of action. One always tries to remain somewhere in the middle.'

38 Ulrike Flach, Plenarprotokoll 14/214, p. 21197.

39 Margot von Renesse, Plenarprotokoll 14/214, p. 21195.

40 Carola Reimann, Plenarprotokoll 14/214, p. 21225.

41 Interview in Bochum, 14.11.2005.

42 Interview with Andrea Fischer, 26.02.2006 in Berlin. Wolf-Michael Catenhusen (interview, 24.07.2006 in Berlin) takes a somewhat different view: he estimates the number of undecided parliamentarians to be less than 10 per cent and believes that the outcome was clear from the beginning of the debate.

43 This exception is Heinz Wiese (CDU/CSU), member for Ehingen, who signed the compromise motion but voted for the ban in the first round. In the second round, which was a

run-off ballot between the ban and the compromise motion, he voted for the compromise. Possible explanations are that he accidentally ticked the wrong box, that he was convinced in informal conversations between the ballots or that he was unsettled by the debate but then regained confidence in his preference.

44　Only two decisions in 1985 were passed with a comparably high number of void votes. One concerned the development of new nuclear power stations (8 votes void), the other a treaty with the Netherlands about co-operation on the borders (10 votes void) (Source: Schindler 1999). In the open ballot over the bill on ES-cell import on 25 April 2002, for which party discipline was again suspended and a roll call in place, there were no spoiled votes.

45　With regard to the high number of spoiled votes, Margot von Renesse insists that it could only be due to the fact that the votes were not counted properly (interview, 14.11.2005 in Bochum). Andrea Fischer regards it as more likely that the voting procedure was too complicated and that people forgot to enter their names (interview, 26.01.2006 in Berlin).

46　Which may be due to the fact that men and members of the CDU/CSU or FDP were more likely to still be members of parliament and therefore easier to contact. Moreover, many ministers and junior ministers in the coalition did not sign a motion at Chancellor Schröder's instruction that 'the cabinet keep out of the matter' (interview with Wolf-Michael Catenhusen in Berlin, 24.07.06). These may have been less likely to reply, too.

47　Interviews with Margot von Renesse and Andrea Fischer. Catenhusen takes the opposite view.

48　Members of the FDP, where the motion was essentially devised, voted in a body for the compromise, a move that was probably decided in advance. Some members of the CDU/CSU who had voted for the permission in the first ballot voted "no" or abstained in the second – possibly because they rejected the compromise (as inconsistent or too little), but also possibly because they regarded it as the government's motion.

49　In the debate on 11 April 2008, four motions were discussed and voted on: 16/7982 for a liberalisation of stem-cell importation, 16/7983 for a complete ban, 16/7985 for keeping the law passed in 2002 and 16/7981 for shifting the cut-off date (all BT-Drs., see also Plenarprotokoll 16/155). The motion for a new cut-off date was led, besides Röspel, by Ilse Aigner, who voted for the ban in 2002, and by Jörg Tauss, who supported the compromise in 2002. A majority of the SPD and FDP members voted for the new cut-off date and a majority of Green members against it, while CDU/CSU and LINKE (successor of the PDS) members remained divided. Maria Böhmer, Andrea Fischer and Margot von Renesse publicly took a position against the revision in a newspaper article ('Die Logik zerbricht', in: *Die Zeit*, 10/04/2008, p. 13).

50　Three of the four (Böhmer, Catenhusen and Fischer) were accompanied by personal assistants but nobody else had access to this forum.

51　The cut-off date fixed by Bush concerns not the general permission for importing and production but state funding for it. Research projects using ES-cells produced after 9 August 2001 thus require private funding but are still possible.

52　Interviews with Andrea Fischer, Margot von Renesse and Wolf-Michael Catenhusen.

53　Interview with Andrea Fischer, 26.02.2006 in Berlin.

54　Interview with Andrea Fischer, 26.02.2006 in Berlin.

55　Interview with Margot von Renesse, 14.11.2005 in Bochum.

56　Interview with Wolf-Michael Catenhusen, 24.07.06 in Berlin.

57 'Niemand hat das Recht, über den Lebenswert eines Menschen zu entscheiden', *Frankfurter Allgemeine Zeitung*, Number 53, 03.03.2001, p. 11.

58 Plenarprotokoll 14/182, p. 17965.

59 *Ibid.*

60 *Ibid.*, p. 17968.

61 'Menschen sind mehr als die Summe ihrer Gene' Interview with Andrea Fischer and Ernst-Ludwig Winnacker, *Welt am Sonntag*, No. 4, 27.01.2002, p. 5.

62 'Bei uns glaubt man, Forscher verkauften ihre Seele dem Teufel' Interview with Margot von Renesse, *Der Tagesspiegel*, 29.01.2002, p. 4.

63 Interviews, 26.01.2006 in Berlin and 14.11.2005 in Bochum.

64 Interview with Margot von Renesse, 14.11.2005 in Bochum.

65 Interview with Wolf-Michael Catenhusen, 24.07.06 in Berlin.

66 The eventual role of the commission is, hardly surprisingly, evaluated differently by sceptics and liberals. The latter regard it as comparatively insignificant, while some of the former criticise it as biased because, even for the places for ethicists and theologians, research-friendly people were appointed. By November 2005, the commission had discussed 19 applications, of which 16 were evaluated positively (ZEK-Tätigkeitsberichte, www.rki.de).

67 Interview with Andrea Fischer, 26.01.2006 in Berlin.

68 Interview with Margot von Renesse, 14.11.2005 in Bochum.

69 *Ibid.*

70 Interview with Wolf-Michael Catenhusen, 24.07.06 in Berlin.

71 Interviews with Margot von Renesse, 14.11.2005 in Bochum and Wolf-Michael Catenhusen, 24.07.2006 in Berlin.

72 Interview with Margot von Renesse, 14.11.2005 in Bochum.

73 BT-Drs. 14/8876.

74 *Ibid.*

75 Schwägerl, C.: 'Das biopolitische Quartett', in: *Frankfurter Allgemeine Zeitung*, 25.04.2002.

76 Interview with Margot von Renesse, 14.11.2006 in Bochum.

77 Interview with Andrea Fischer, 16.01.2006 in Berlin.

78 Contributions at the conference 'Bioethik im Kontext von Recht, Moral und Kultur' in Berlin, 14.16.09.2005.

79 Böhmer, Maria, Andrea Fischer and Margot von Renesse: 'Die Logik zerbricht. Warum der Bundestag das Stammzellgesetz nicht ändern sollte. Ein Plädoyer für das geltende Recht' *Die Zeit*, No. 16, 10.04.2008, p. 13.

80 The procedure, results and evaluation of the project are documented in Tannert & Wiedemann 2004.

81 Information on the citizen conference is based on the evaluation of the conference by external observers (Henning/Erdwien 2004) and the author's own reading of transcripts that were kindly made available by the MDC.

82 For the transcription pattern, see appendix. E stands for expert, B for citizen, m for male (w for female), and the number allows identification.

83 For a list of participants, including information on age, sex, religion and occupation, see appendix.

84 The citizen vote is reprinted in Tannert & Wiedemann 2004: 139-151 (here p. 150).

85 For instance, several citizens expressed the wish to visit (adult) stem-cell researchers in their nearby laboratories in Berlin-Buch. The moderators and organisers try to take this wish seriously but it becomes clear that they fail to see how a visit to a laboratory could be relevant to the evaluation of ES-cell research.

86 It must be noted, however, that the citizen group knew those reports, which may have motivated imitation.

87 In the control group, 'ethical aspects' ranked highest, too, followed by 'health aspects', 'legal aspects' and 'scientific aspects'. Social, political, religious and economic aspects ranked low.

88 Which is not to say that the potential for a cure is not a strong argument. However, advocates of ES-cell research often tried to create the false impression that cures for, e.g., Alzheimer's and Parkinson's diseases were within reach and have thus played on the hopes of many sufferers.

conclusion

The starting point of this project was the observation that the presently dominant approach in democratic theory – the theory of deliberative democracy – has important problems. In particular, it so far lacks an empirical theory of preference-transformation and systematic ideas on how institutional contexts affect interaction and enable or prevent meaningful deliberation. The intention of this book was thus to make proposals on how these gaps in deliberative theory could be filled. This was not to be accomplished either by a thorough analysis of the broad literature on deliberative democracy or by an original contribution to the normative part of the theory (on, for example, how central concepts such as justice, equality or citizenship are to be explicated and specified). Instead, the goal was to deductively derive a positive theory from the fundamental empirical and analytical assumptions of the theory.

These central empirical and analytical assumptions of deliberative democracy, I have argued in the introduction, concern first, its concept of rationality and second, the role and effects of communication in decision-making. The concept of rationality applied in deliberative theories is typically not limited to instrumental rationality but extends to cover the choice of ends as well as that of means. The role and effect assigned to communication is that it enables the co-ordination of opinions and action plans. What follows from this is that political preferences are conceived of as endogenous to a political decision-making process, that is driven by linguistic interaction. If rational decision is understood as reason-based decision and if political preferences are understood as preferences over alternative political programmes and policy strategies, the formation and transformation of political preferences in communicative processes can be rationalised and accounted for by an external observer.

Many people have pointed out the way in which democratic polities do or do not enable rational and just decisions or do or do not fail to realise the ideals of equality and participation. This book does not contribute to this debate. Instead, it aims to explore and explain, by the development and application of a theoretical framework, how communication and rational preference-transformation help, if not to resolve, at least to accommodate conflict in political decisions.

In contrast to epistemic models of deliberative democracy, the project was based on the assumption that political decisions are essentially contingent decisions. It is assumed, that is, that there exists no such thing as the one rational, objectively 'correct' decision. At the same time, it is not normally the case that any one decision is as good as any other, as it is for questions of pure co-ordination such as whether to drive on the right or left side of the street. Rather, there are in most cases several options that can be justified and rationally preferred. Rational preference-formation and -communication are important to decide how to decide between these or to find compromises between them. However, while I believe that rationality and communication can potentially accommodate conflicts, it is also important to keep in mind that rationality requirements can also be despotic and communication manipulative.

Chapter one pointed out the analytical value of a concept of rationality as reason-based decision and the way in which preference-formation can be reconstructed as such. It was argued that political preferences are best understood as being defined over alternative political programmes and strategies rather than over alternative states of the world. From this understanding, it follows that political preferences are based on cognitive as well as volitive premises. The cognitive premises political preferences are based on, concerning, in particular, the availability of options and their instrumental quality, were described as *acceptances*. The volitive premises of political preferences, which comprise goals, interests, values and commitments, were described as *practical reasons*. I have tried to illustrate that the proper way to conceptualise and analyse the formation and transformation of preferences is via the rationalisation of these cognitive and volitive mental attitudes. As acceptances must continuously be revised in the light of new evidence and arguments, and as every decision requires a new aggregation and weighting of practical reasons, political preferences cannot be regarded as exogenous to the decision-making process.

Chapter two dealt with the fundamental assumptions about the effects of communication on actors' preferences that are implied in deliberative models of democracy. These assumptions are based on speech-act theory and essentially concern *justification* and *reciprocity* as constitutive rules of communicative interaction. Given that communicative interaction has an effect on acceptances and practical reasons, motives for entering a discourse were established. The first of these is that of achieving a fit between mind and world, which is required for instrumental action and can be pursued in theoretical discourses. The second motive is that of finding out what action eventually is to be instrumental for, i.e. what one actually wants, that can be pursued in practical discourses. Like political preferences, political discourses and decisions have both theoretical and practical aspects. They therefore require the assessment and co-ordination of both acceptances and practical reasons through different modes of communicative political interaction.

Chapter three pointed out how different modes of political interaction affect the probability of preference-transformation. Two dimensions, or properties, of interaction were argued to be of central relevance here: the *discursiveness* and the *co-ordinativeness* of interaction. A model was proposed that regards the probability of preference-transformation as depending equally on the discursive and co-ordinative qualities of interaction. Four ideal-type modes of interaction were identified: discussion, deliberation, bargaining and debate. The debate is minimally favourable for preference-transformation, as it lacks dialogical and co-ordinative qualities. Bargaining is both dialogical and co-ordinative but not public and therefore provides too few justificatory incentives to promote preference-transformation. The discussion is public and dialogical but it lacks co-ordinative incentives as its focus is on truth rather than on options for political action. Only deliberation as a mode of interaction is both fully discursive (public and dialogical) and co-ordinative and thus maximally favourable for preference-transformation. Ideal-typically, it is a mode of interaction in which citizens address a conflict of value with the goal of reaching understanding about the evaluation of alternative options for political action, about 'what we ought to do'.

The particular focus of the chapter, however, was on the relationship between actors and institutions and on the institutional properties that serve to bring about different modes of interaction in forums where individual political preference-formation takes place. For each mode of interaction, examples of forums in which it was more or less successfully institutionalised were discussed. Finally, it was pointed out that all four modes of interaction play an important role in democratic politics, and a cyclical model of policy-making which includes them all was advocated.

Chapters four and five were devoted to an empirical case study that sought to illustrate the value of the theoretical framework and was expected to yield inferences on how different institutional settings enable different modes of interaction and promote or prevent preference-transformation: the German decision whether to allow importing of embryonic stem cells. While chapter four outlined the history and the dimensions of the conflict and discussed the methods of analysis, chapter five described interaction and preference-formation in different forums that addressed the stem-cell conflict: two expert commissions, a much-noted parliamentary debate, a bargaining round behind closed doors and a citizen conference.

The results of this analysis were largely in keeping with the hypotheses derived from the theory. In the National Ethics Council, antagonistic logics of interaction and a focus on moral consistency and corollary lead to a quick polarisation and prevented co-ordination and preference-transformation. In the parliamentary Study Commission, the focus was shifted to constitutionality and feasibility, so that although participants did not change their attitudes towards ES-cell research, the way towards a compromise could be paved. The much-praised Bundestag debate on importing stem cells was, it seems, as favourable for preference-transformation as a plenary debate in a majoritarian, parliamentary political system can be. Nonetheless, there is nothing to suggest that a significant number of parliamentarians changed their preferences during the debate. The subsequent drafting of the eventual law on importing stem-cell lines by four leaders of the compromise motion to allow strictly limited importing qualifies as an instance of distributive bargaining. The participants describe the decision-making process in this informal circle as one of reaching understanding. However, there is evidence to suggest that each indeed maximised his or her own preferences under the constraints constituted by the other players' preferences. Substantial preference-transformation occurred only in the citizen conference. While there are drawbacks both with regard to its democratic legitimacy and with regard to the realisation of citizen deliberation as a mode of interaction, the example of the citizen conference also shows the potential of institutionalised citizen participation in politics.

Although *inside* the forums immediately involved in the decision on importing stem cells no preference-transformation could be observed, the way in which each of them aggregated reasons and initiated discussions has significantly contributed to the decision-making process. In sum, the way in which this fundamental conflict, which comprised both factual and moral disagreements as well as clashing interests, was dealt with is indeed exemplary: it shows how the different dimensions of a controversy can be disentangled and how an original political compromise can be found to a conflict that is in moral terms irresolvable and in terms of interest irreducible. While the decision has been criticised for being morally inconsistent and contradictory, the compromise illustrates how political decisions taken on the basis of a broad public and institutionalised debate can accommodate social conflicts.

The most important conclusion for the theory of deliberative democracy that can be drawn from the empirical theory developed in the first part of the book and from the analysis of the stem-cell conflict in the second part of the book is that deliberative democracy so far focuses too much on the cognitive-informational aspects of decision-making. It thereby neglects the need to weigh and aggregate to some extent incommensurable practical reasons and to co-ordinate conflicting interests and values. While communication and the interactive assessment of acceptances and practical reasons are important for political decisions, they will never yield a sufficient justification for any one option for political action. At the same time, actors cannot be reduced to predetermined interests, and political decision-making processes entail not only the space for, but also the necessity of preference-formation and -transformation, which cannot be captured in narrow economic models.

For any far-reaching political decision, co-ordination and compromise have to be accomplished anew by means of different modes of interaction. Although the majoritarian decision of a legislature elected by free and equal citizens is normatively and practically indispensable, modes of interaction that are important in political decision-making cannot be realised in the parliamentary plenum and must be institutionalised elsewhere. It is essential that forums in which these modes of interaction are realised provide decision-makers (representatives and citizens) with the opportunity to form rational preferences over alternatives and revise them where necessary.

Citizen deliberation, as the mode of interaction that is maximally favourable for rational preference-transformation, remains of course notoriously difficult to institutionalise. Some, including Habermas himself, hope for a broad public discourse and for the media to exert communicative power by means of laying siege to the political system (Habermas 1994: 626). A vivid public sphere and independent and critical media are obviously essential for the functioning and vitality of democratic politics. In addition to this, however, citizen deliberation can and should be institutionalised and encouraged in new types of forums.

Despite the central problem that they lack democratic legitimacy (a problem they share with expert commissions and interest-group bargaining rounds), I believe that participatory procedures in the consensus conference style have some promise. They not only engage participants in political deliberation but serve to carry discussions beyond the forum and show non-participants that lay citizens can fruitfully deal with complex matters and form justified preferences on them. If, in contrast to the citizen conference discussed here, the citizen forum meets and passes a vote before the political decision is taken and not afterwards, politicians could also show that they take this evaluation seriously. As the other three modes of political interaction appear to be easier to realise and, in most countries, are already sufficiently institutionalised, the focus of deliberative theory and deliberative politics should be on the realisation and institutionalisation of citizen deliberation in a way that enables the rational formation and transformation of political preferences.

appendix

LIST OF DATA AND DOCUMENTS USED FOR ANALYSIS

National Ethics Council and Study Commission:
- Interviews with Wolfgang van den Daele (23.01.2006 in Berlin), Ingrid Schneider (15.08.05 in Hamburg) and Margot von Renesse (14.11.2005 in Bochum)
- First motion passed on stem-cell research on July 5, 2001 (BT-Drs. 14/655)
- Report of the Study Commission on the EU-directive on patents in biotechnology (BT-Drs. 14/5157)
- Intermediate report of the Study Commission (BT-Drs. 14/7546)
- Final report of the Study Commission on work in fourteenth legislative period (BT-Drs. 14/9020)
- Report of the National Ethics Council
- Newspaper articles Jan. 2001 – Dec. 2001

Parliamentary Debate and Decision
- Motions discussed on Jan. 30, 2002 (BT-Drs. 14/8101, 14/8102, 14/8103)
- Transcripts of debate, including results of open ballot (Plenarprotokoll 14/214)
- Results of author's survey (questionnaires sent out to parliamentarians who had not signed one of the motions)

Bargaining Round (drafting of bill)
- Interviews with Margot von Renesse (14.11.2005 in Bochum), Andrea Fischer (26.02.2006 in Berlin) and Wolf-Michael Catenhusen (24.07.2006 in Berlin), report by Maria Böhmer on her experiences in the stem cell conflict and the drafting of the bill (Böhmer 2005)
- Transcript of first Bundestag debate on stem cell research on July 5, 2001 (Plenarprotokoll 14/182)
- Newspaper articles Jan. 2001 – April 2002
- Bill on stem-cell importation passed 25 April 2002 (BT-Drs. 14/8394)
- Amendment to bill on stem-cell importation passed 25 April 2002 (BT-Drs. 14/8876)

Citizen Conference
- Transcripts of plenary meetings on all three weekends, ca. 20 hours / 800 pages / 16,000 words (kindly made available by MDC, Berlin), transcripts of speeches given on the inaugural evening
- Evaluation by external observers of conference, including qualitative description

and evaluation and results of questionings after and before the meetings, as well as questionings of a control group (Henning/Erdwien 2004)
- Citizen Vote
- Book published by organisers of the conference (Tannert &Wiedemann 2004), including reports on the preparation and organisation of the conference and qualitative assessments by external observers

LIST OF SPEECH ACTS USED FOR SAA

Speaker:

Arguing
claim/assert
establish
assume
report
justify
evaluate
infer
agree
contradict
concede
insist
take back
ascertain agreement
ascertain disagreement
ask

Role:

Bargaining
demand
promote (an offer)
appeal to sth.
offer
suggest
suggest a compromise
accept (offer, proposal)
reject
make a concession
rate (an offer)
uphold (a demand)
promise
threaten
ascertain consensus / non-consensus

Rhetorical Means
ask (rhetorically)
quote
other rhet. means

Discourse Structurers
define question
define own position
greet

define topic
refer to
other disc. structurers

Others
Expressives
others

Declaratives

LIST OF ARGUMENTS USED FOR ARGUMENTATION ANALYSIS

FACTUAL

1.1 Embryonic stem cells are pluripotent → embryonic stem cells are not embryos

1.2 Embryonic stem cells are totipotent → embryonic stem cells are embryos

2.1 The clinical potential of ES-cells is low or uncertain → research should focus on adult stem cells

2.2 The epistemic potential of ES-cells is low or uncertain → research should focus on animal ES-cells

2.3 The potential of ES-cells is uncertain → importing should be allowed to enable pure research to compare different cell types

2.4 The clinical and/or epistemic potential of ES-cells is high → research with ES-cells should be supported

3.1 Quality of existing ES-cells is sufficient → importing of existing lines will fulfil requirements for pure research, no additional ones need to be produced or imported

3.2 Quality of existing ES-cells is insufficient → new ones will need to be produced inside Germany or be imported

3.3 Quality of existing ES-cells is insufficient → demand for new ones will grow and become impossible to control

LEGAL

4.1 Surplus embryos enjoy rights to life and dignity → they may not be killed or employed for research purposes

4.2 Surplus embryos enjoy only limited rights to life and dignity → they may be killed and employed for high-ranking research purposes

4.3 Rights to life and dignity are not directly affected by importing → importing must be allowed (cannot be forbidden) to ensure freedom of research

4.4 Right to life applies, but must be weighed against freedom of research → importing can and should be allowed conditionally

4.5 Right to dignity applies (and cannot be weighed) → importing must be forbidden

5.1 Researchers must fear prosecution → permission to import resolves legal uncertainty, protects researchers and prevents emigration

5.2 Researchers must not fear prosecution → interdiction does not result in legal uncertainty

6.1 EU law does not permit restrictions → Germany cannot forbid importing by national law

6.2 EU law does permit restrictions → Germany can restrict importing

7.1   Human individuality begins with fertilisation → embryos at any developmental stage possess full rights to life and dignity

7.2   Human individuality begins with nidation → embryos at earlier stages do not yet possess full rights to life and dignity

7.3   We allow abortion and intrauterine devices → we thus acknowledge that embryos do not yet possess full rights to life and dignity

8.1   We have the duty to save lives and ES-cell research promises new cures → we have the duty to support research with ES-cells ("ethics of healing")

8.2   Embryos do possess full dignity → embryos may not be killed and instrumentalized for any purpose

8.3   Clinical potential of ES-cells is low or uncertain → duty to save lives does not justify instrumentalisation

8.4   We will benefit from ES-cell research → we should contribute to research by allowing (conditional) importing

8.5   Ethically uncontroversial and clinically promising alternative of adult stem cells exists → we should support AS-cell research instead of allowing ES-cell importing

9.1   Parents are 'selfless donors' providing a resource with the potential to save lives → we can and should make use of this resource (surplus embryos/stem-cell lines)

9.2   Women become 'commodity providers', which violates their dignity → we must protect women by disallowing production and importing of ES-cells

10.1   Supply follows demand and death of embryos must be prevented → importing must be forbidden

10.2   Supply follows demand and death of embryos must be prevented → importing must be restricted to existing lines

10.3   Importing constitutes retrospective approval → importing must be forbidden

10.4   Importing constitutes retrospective approval → not only importing, but production should be allowed

11.1   Regulation of importing cannot be effective → we must permit importing to enable supervision

11.2   Complete ban cannot be effective → we must enable controlled importing to reduce pressure

11.3   (Self-) Control can only be ensured by complete ban → we must completely rule out importing (= "slippery slope")

12.1   Other countries are more liberal → we must allow importing in order to remain economically and academically competitive

12.2   Other countries are equally (or more) restrictive → we can ban (restrict) importing without inflicting competitive disadvantages on the country

OTHERS

0.1   Back-up arguments
0.2   Other arguments

CITIZEN CONFERENCE: PARTICIPANTS AND TRANSCRIPTION SCHEME

List of Participants

Role	Sex	Occupation	Age	Religion	Code	History
Citizen	f	A-level student	18	none	Bw1	completed
Citizen	f	Web designer	51	Protestant - Lutheran	Bw2	completed
Citizen	f	Assistant medical technician	30	none	Bw3	completed
Citizen	f	Lawyer	39	Protestant	Bw4	completed
Citizen	f	Deputy manager of a building centre	23	none	Bw5	completed
Citizen	f	University student in biotechnology	24	Catholic	Bw6	drop out
Citizen	f	Alternative practitioner in training	52	Christian - Protestant	Bw7	completed
Citizen	f	Learning therapist	54	Protestant	Bw8	drop out[1]

Role	Sex	Occupation	Age	Religion	Code	History
Citizen	m	University student in economics	21	Protestant	Bm1	completed
Citizen	m	Tradesman	40	Protestant	Bm2	completed
Citizen	m	Retired police superintendent	62	Protestant	Bm3	completed
Citizen	m	Self-employed sales representative	42	none	Bm4	completed
Citizen	m	Lawyer	35	Protestant	Bm5	completed
Citizen	m	Civil servant, mathematician	48	none	Bm6	completed
Citizen	m	Retired engineer	54	Catholic	Bm7	drop out
Citizen	m	Medical technician in training	19	Muslim	Bm8	drop out[2]
Citizen	m	Unemployed former painter	43	none	Bm9	drop out

Role	Sex	Occupation	Age	Religion	Code	History
Moderator	m				M1m	
Moderator	f				M2w	
Organizer	m				O1m	
Organizer	f				O2w	
Organizer	m				O3m	

NOTES

1   could not take part because of illness

2   was drafted for military service

bibliography

Altenhof, Ralf 2002 *Die Enquete-Kommissionen des Bundestages,* Wiesbaden: Westdeutscher Verlag

Ackerman, Bruce and Larry Fishkin 2008 'Deliberation Day' in James Fishkin in Laslett, Peter (eds) *Debating Deliberative Democracy,* Malden, MA: Blackwell, 7–30

Arrow, Kenneth (ed.) 1995 *Barriers to Conflict Resolution,* New York: Norton

Arrow, Kenneth 1995 'Information Acquisition and the Resolution of Conflict' in Kenneth Arrow *et al.* (eds) *Barriers to Conflict Resolution,* New York: Norton, 258–72

Arrow, Kenneth 1963 *Social Choice and Individual Values,* New York, Wiley

Austen-Smith, David 1992 'Strategic Models of Talk in Political Decision Making' *International Political Science Review* 13: 1, 48–58

Austin, John L 2002 [1962] *Zur Theorie der Sprechakte* (How to do things with Words) Leipzig: Reclam

Bächtiger, Andre 2005 *The Real World of Deliberation. A Comparative Study of its Favorable Conditions in Legislatures,* Bern: Haupt

Becker, Gary S. 1996 *Accounting for Tastes,* Cambridge, MA: Harvard University Press

Beier, Henning M. 2002 'Totipotenz und Pluripotenz: Von der klassischen Embryologie zu neuen Therapiestrategien' in Fuat S. Oduncu, Ulrich Schroth & Wilhelm Vossenkuhl (eds) *Stammzellforschung und therapeutisches Klonen,* Göttingen: Vandenhoek & Ruprecht, 36–54

ben Salem, Ali & Christof Tannert 2004 'Planung und Organisation der Bürgerkonferenz' in Christof Tannert & Peter Wiedemann (eds) *Stammzellen im Diskurs,* München: Oekom, 106–116

Benz, Arthur 2002 'Vertrauensbildung in Mehrebenensystemen' in Rainer Schmalz-Bruns & Reinhard Zintl (eds) *Politisches Vertrauen Soziale Grundlagen reflexiver Kooperation,* Baden-Baden: Nomos, 275–91

Bessette, Joseph M. 1980 'Deliberative Democracy: The Majority Principle in Republican Government' in Robert A. Schambra & William A. Goldwin (eds) *How Democratic is the Constitution?* Washington: AEI

Bogner, Alexander & Wolfgang Menz 2002 'Wissenschaftliche Politikberatung? Der Dissens der Experten und die Autorität der Politik' *Leviathan* 30: 3, 384–99

Bogner, Alexander & Wolfgang Menz 2005 'Alternative Rationalitäten? Technikbewertung durch Laien und Experten am Beispiel der Biomedizin' in Alfons Bora *et al.* (eds) *Technik in einer fragilen Welt Die Rolle der*

Technikfolgenabschätzung, Berlin: Edition Sigma, S, 383–91

Bohman, James 1996 *Public Deliberation Pluralism, Complexity, and Democracy*, Cambridge, MA: MIT Press

Bohman, James 1998 'Survey Article: The Coming of Age of Deliberative Democracy' *The Journal of Political Philosophy* 6: 4, 400–25

Bohman, James & William Rehg 1997 *Deliberative Democracy*, Cambridge, MA: MIT Press

Böhmer, Maria 2005 'Als wir Parlamentsgeschichte schrieben' in Susann Bräcklein, Jürgen Meyer & Henning Scherf (eds) *Politisches Denken ist Festschrift für Margot von Renesse*, Frankfurt am Main: Peter Lang, 157–66

Brandom, Robert B. 1994 *Making it Explicit: Reasoning, Representing, and Discursive Commitment*, Cambridge, MA: Harvard University Press

Brandom, Robert B. 2000 'Facts, Norms and Normative Facts: a Reply to Habermas' *European Journal of Philosophy* 8: 3, 356–74

Brennan, Geoffrey & Philip Pettit 2004 *The Economy of Esteem*, Oxford: Oxford University Press

Broome, John 1991 'The Structure of Good: Decision Theory and Ethics' in Michael Bacharach & Susan L. Hurley (eds) *Foundations of Decision Theory*, Oxford: Basil Blackwell, 123–46

Buchstein, Hubertus & Dirk Jörke 2003 'Das Unbehagen an der Demokratietheorie' *Leviathan* 31: 4, 470–95

Bühler, Karl 1999 [1934] *Sprachtheorie*, Stuttgart: Lucius & Lucius

Burow, Olaf-Axel & Kathrin Kühnemuth 2004 'Brauchen Wissenschaft und Politik Bürgerberatung? Möglichkeiten und Grenzen der Bürgerkonferenz' in Christof Tannert & Peter Wiedemann (eds) *Stammzellen im Diskurs*, Müchen: Oekom, 117–29

Chambers, Simone 1995 'Discourse and Democratic Practices' in Stephen K. White (ed.) T*he Cambridge Companion to Habermas*, Cambridge: Cambridge University Press

Chambers, Simone 2004 'Behind Closed Doors: Publicity, Secrecy, and the Quality of Deliberation' *The Journal of Political Philosophy* 12: 4, 389–10

Cohen, L. Jonathan 1989 'Belief and Acceptance' *Mind* xcviii: 391 (July), 367–89

Cohen, L. Jonathan 1992 *An Essay on Belief and Acceptance*, Oxford: Clarendon Press

Coleman, James S. 1990, Foundations of Social Theory, Cambridge: Belknap Press

Daniels, Norman 1996 'Is the Oregon Rationing Plan Fair?' in Thomas A. Mappes & David De Grazia (eds) *Biomedical Ethics*, New York: McGraw-Hill, 592–98

De Leon, Peter 1999 'The Stages Approach to the Policy Process: What Has It Done? Where Is It Going?' in Paul A. Sabatier (ed.) *Theories of the Policy Process*, Boulder: Westview, 19–32

De Sousa, Ronald 1998 'Modeling Rationality' in Peter A. Danielson (ed.) *Modelling Rational and Moral Agents*, Oxford: OUP, 119–34

Dienel, Peter C. 1978 *Die Planungszelle: der Bürger plant seine Umwelt Eine Alternative zur Establishment-Demokratie*, Opladen: Westdeutscher Verlag

Dienel, Peter C. 2002 *Die Planungszelle Der Bürger als Chance*, Wiesbaden: Westdeutscher Verlag

Dilling, Anne 2002 *Die Willensbildung der Bundestagsabgeordneten unter Aufhebung der Fraktionsdisziplin - untersucht am Beispiel der Entscheidung über den Import embryonaler Stammzellen*, Unpublished thesis, Universität Hamburg

Döhler, Marian & Philip Manow-Borgwaldt 1992 'Gesundheitspolitische Steuerung zwischen Hierarchie und Verwaltung' *Politische Vierteljahresschrift* 4, 571–96

Döhler, Marian & Philip Manow-Borgwaldt 1993 'Kontinuität durch Wandel: Zur Institutionengeschichte des Bundesausschusses der Ärzte und Krankenkassen' in Dietrich Milles (ed.) *Gesundheitsrisiken, Industriegesellschaft und soziale Sicherung in der Geschichte*, Bremerhaven: Wirtschaftsverlag NW, 119–42

Dowding, Keith 2002 'Revealed Preference and External Reference' *Rationality and Society*, 14: 3, 259–84

Downs, Anthony 1957 *An Economic Theory of Democracy*, New York: Harper & Row

Dryzek, John S. 2000 *Deliberative Democracy and Beyond*, Oxford: OUP

Dryzek, John S. & Christian List 2003 'Social Choice and Deliberative Democracy: a Reconciliation' *British Journal of Political Science* 33: 1, 1–28

Elster, Jon 1983 *Sour Grapes*, Cambridge: CUP

Elster, Jon 1986 'Introduction' in Jon Elster (ed.) *Rational Choice*, Oxford: Blackwell

Elster, Jon 1989 *Nuts and Bolts for the Social Sciences*, Cambridge: CUP

Elster, Jon 1990 'When Rationality Fails' in Karen S. Cook & Margaret Levi (eds) *The Limits of Rationality*, Chicago: The University of Chicago Press, 19–51

Elster, Jon 1995 'Strategic Uses of Argument' in Kenneth Arrow (ed.) *Barriers to Conflict Resolution*, New York: WW Norton and Co., 236–57

Elster, Jon 1997 [1986] 'The Market and the Forum: Three Varieties of Political Theory' in James Bohman & William Rehg (eds) *Deliberative Democracy*, Cambridge, Massachusetts: MIT Press, 3–34

Elster, Jon 1998 'Deliberation and Constitution Making' in Jon Elster (ed.) *Deliberative Democracy*, Cambridge: Cambridge University Press, 97–122

Erdwien, Birgitt 2004 'Burgerpartizipation als Gruppenpruzess: Ergebnisse der begleitenden Evaluation' in C. Tannert & P. Wiedmann (eds) *Stammzellen im Diskurs* Munchen: Oekom, 130

Eriksen, Erik Oddvar 2007 'Deliberation und demokratische Legitimität in der EU – Zwischen Konkens und Kompromiss' in Peter Niesen & Benjamin Herborth (eds) *Anarchie der kommunikativen Freiheit*, Frankfurt: Suhrkamp, 294–320

Estlund, David 1990 'Democracy Without Preference' *The Philosophical Review*

XCIX: 3, 376–424

Estlund, David 1997 'Beyond Fairness and Deliberation' in James Bohman & William Rehg (eds) *Deliberative Democracy*, Cambridge, MA: MIT Press, 173–204

Fehige, Christoph & Ulla Wessels 1998 *Preferences Perspektiven der Analytischen Philosophie*, Berlin and New York: de Gruyter

Fehige, Christoph & Ulla Wessels 1998 'Preferences – an Introduction' in Christoph Fehige & Ulla Wessels (eds) *Preferences*, Berlin: de Gruyter, xx–xliii

Feldman, Allan 1980 *Welfare Economics and Social Choice Theory*, Boston: Martinus Nijhoff Publishing

Ferejohn, John 1993 'Must Preferences Be Respected in a Democracy?' in David Copp, Jean Hampton & John E. Roemer (eds) *The Idea of Democracy*, Cambridge: CUP, 231–44

Ferejohn, John & Debra Satz 1996 'Unification, Universalism, and Rational Choice Theory' in Jeffrey Friedman (ed.) *The Rational Choice Controversy*, New Haven: Yale University Press, 71–84

Fleck, L. M. 1994 'Just Caring – Oregon, Health-Care Rationing, and Informed Democratic Deliberation' *Journal Of Medicine And Philosophy* 19: 4, 367–88

Fishkin, James 1991 *The Voice of the People: Public Opinion and Democracy*, New Haven: Yale University Press

Fishkin, James & Cynthia Farrar 2005 'Deliberative Polling: From Experiment to Community Resource' in John Gastil & Peter Levine (eds) *The Deliberative Democracy Handbook*, San Francisco: Jossey-Bass, 68–79

Fishkin, James S. & Peter Laslett (eds) 2003 *Debating Deliberative Democracy*, Malden, MA: Blackwell

Forst, Rainer 2003 *Toleranz im Konflikt Geschichte, Gehalt und Gegenwart eines umstrittenen Begriffs*, Frankfurt am Main: Suhrkamp

Forst, Rainer 2007a 'Praktische Vernunft und rechtfertigende Gründe Zur Begründung der Moral' in *Das Recht auf Rechtfertigung*, Frankfurt am Main: Suhrkamp, 23–73

Forst, Rainer 2007b 'Die Herrschaft der Gründe Drei Modelle deliberativer Demokratie' in *Das Recht auf Rechtfertigung*, Frankfurt am Main: Suhrkamp 224–69

Freeman, James B. 1991 *Dialectics and the Macrostructure of Arguments: A Theory of Argument Structure*, Berlin and New York: Foris

Friedman, Jeffrey 1996 'Introduction: Economic Approaches to Politics' in Jeffrey Friedman (ed.) *The Rational Choice Controversy: Economic Models of Politics Reconsidered*, New Haven, CT: Yale University Press

Fung, Archon 2005 'Deliberation Before the Revolution: Towards an Ethics of Deliberative Democracy in an Unjust World' *Political Theory* 33:3, 397–419

Gallhofer, Irmtraud N. & Willem E. Saris 1996 *Foreign Policy Decision-Making A Qualitative and Quantitative Analysis of Political Argumentation*

Westport, CT: Praeger

Gambetta, Diego 1998 ' "Claro!" An Essay on Discursive Machismo', in Jon Elster (ed.) *Deliberative Democracy* Cambridge: Cambridge University Press, 19–43

Gastil, John 1992 'Undemocratic Discourse: a Review Of Theory and Research on Political Discourse' *Discourse & Society* 3: 4, 469–500

Gastil, John & Peter Levine (eds) 2005 *The Deliberative Democracy Handbook*, San Francisco: Jossey-Bass

Gaus, Gerald F. 1996 *Justificatory Liberalism: An Essay on Epistemology and Political Theory*, Oxford: Oxford University Press

Gauthier, David 1986 *Morals by Agreement*, Oxford: Clarendon Press

Gigerenzer, Gerd & Reinhard Selten (eds) 2002 *Bounded Rationality: The Adaptive Toolbox*, Cambridge, MA: MIT Press

Goodin, Robert E. 1986 'Laundering Preferences', in Jon Elster (ed.) *Foundations of Social Choice Theory*, Cambridge: CUP, 75–102

Goodin, Robert E. 2000 'Democratic Deliberation Within' *Philosophy & Public Affairs*, 29: 1, 79–107

Goodin, Robert E. 2003 *Reflective Democracy*, Oxford: Oxford University Press

Goodin, Robert E. 2005 'Sequencing Deliberative Moments' *Acta Politica* 40, 182–96

Goodin, Robert E. & Geoffrey Brennan 2004 'Bargaining over Beliefs' in Anne van Aaken, Christian List & Christoph Luetge (eds) *Deliberation and Decision*, Aldershot: Ashgate

Goodin, Robert E. & David Estlund 2004 'The Persuasiveness of Democratic Majorities' *Politics, Philosophy & Economics* 3: 2, 131–42

Green, Donald P. & Ian Shapiro 1994 *Pathologies of Rational Choice Theory: A Critique of Applications in Political Science*, New Haven, CT: Yale University Press

Greven, Michael Th. 1991 'Macht und Politik in der "Theorie kommunikativen Handelns" von Jürgen Habermas' in Michael Th. Greven (ed.) *Macht in der Demokratie* Baden-Baden: NOMOS, 213–38

Greven, Michael Th. 1999 *Die politische Gesellschaft Kontingenz und Dezision als Probleme des Regierens in der Demokratie*, Opladen: Leske+Budrich

Greven, Michael Th. 2000 *Kontingenz und Dezision*, Opladen: Leske+Budrich

Greven, Michael Th. 2000 'Über demokratischen Dezisionismus: Kann es, sollte es gar einen demokratischen Dezisionismus geben?' in Michael Th. Greven *Kontingenz und Dezision*, Opladen: Leske+Budrich, 51–62

Greven, Michael Th. 2003 'Die Entscheidung zum Krieg als politische Innovation Überlegungen und Beobachtungen zu den öffentlichen Begründungsmustern "Interesse" und "Moral" in Ulrich Willems (ed.) *Interesse und Moral als Orientierungen politischen Handelns*, Baden-Baden: NOMOS, 293–314

Greven, Michael Th. 2005 'The Informalization of Transnational Governance: a Threat to Democratic Government' in Edgar Grande & Louis W Pauly (eds) *Complex Sovereignty: Reconstituting Political Authority in the Twenty-first Century*, Toronto: University of Toronto Press, 261–84

Grice, Herbert Paul 1979 'Logik und Konversation' in Georg Meggle (ed.) *Handlung, Kommunikation, Bedeutung*, Frankfurt am Main: Suhrkamp, 243–65

Grofman, Bernard & Guillermo Owen (eds) 1986 *Information Pooling and Group Decision Making*, Greenwich, CT: Jai Press

Grundahl, Johs 1995 'The Danish Consensus Conference Model' in Simon Joss & John Durant (eds) *Public Participation in Science: the Role of Consensus Conferences in Europe*, London: Science Museum, 31–40

Grüne, Till 2005 'Why Don't You Want To Be Rich? Preference Explanation on the Basis of Causal Structure' in J.K. Campbell & M. O'Rourke (eds) *Topics in Contemporary Philosophy: Explanation and Causation*, Cambridge, MA: MIT Press

Gutmann, Amy & Dennis Thompson 1996 *Democracy and Disagreement*, Cambridge, MA: Belknap Press

Haas, Peter M. 1992 'Introduction: Epistemic Communities And International Policy Coordination' *International Organization* 46: 1, 1–36

Habermas, Jürgen 1976 *Legitimation Crisis*, London: Heinemann Educational Books

Habermas, Jürgen 1984 *The Theory of Communicative Action*, Boston: Beacon Press

Habermas, Jürgen 1994 [1992] *Between Facts and Norms*, Cambridge, MA: MIT Press

Habermas, Jürgen 2000 'From Kant to Hegel: on Robert Brandom's Pragmatic Philosophy of Language' *European Journal of Philosophy* 8: 3, 322–55

Hall, Peter A. and C. R. Taylor 1996 'Political Science and the Three New Institutionalisms' *Political Studies* 44:5, 936

Hampel, Jürgen, Georg Ruhrmann, Matthias Kohring & Alexander Goerke 1998 'Germany' in John Durant, Martin W. Bauer & George Gaskell (eds) *Biotechnology in the Public Sphere*, London: Science Museum, 68–76

Hansen, Kasper Moller 2004 *Deliberative Democracy and Opinion Formation*, Odense: University Press of Southern Denmark

Hansen, Kasper Moller 2007 *Deliberative Democracy and Opinion Formation*, Presentation at the Australian National University

Hardin, Russell 1999 'Deliberation – Method, not Theory' in Stephen Macedo (ed.) *Deliberative Politics Essays on 'Democracy and Disagreement*, Oxford: Oxford University Press, 103–19

Harsanyi, John C. 1955 'Cardinal Welfare, Individualistic Ethics, and Interpersonal Comparisons of Utility' *Journal of Political Economy* 63: 4, 309–21

Hendriks, Carolyn M. 2005 'Consensus Conferences and Planning Cells: Lay Citizen Deliberation' in John Gastil & Peter Levine (eds) *The Deliberative Democracy Handbook*, San Fransisco: Jossey-Bass

Henning, H. Jörg & Birgitt Erdwien 2004 *Bürgerkonferenz zur Stammzellforschung 2003/2004* (final report) Bremen: Universität Bremen, Institut für Psychologie

Holzinger, Katharina 2001 'Verhandeln statt Argumentieren oder Verhandeln durch Argumentieren? Eine empirische Analyse auf der Basis der Sprechakttheorie' *Politische Vierteljahresschrift* 42: 3, 414–46

Holzinger, Katharina 2003 'Common Goods, Matrix Games, and Institutional Solutions' *European Journal of International Relations* 9: 173–12

Holzinger, Katharina 2004 'Bargaining Through Arguing: an Empirical Analysis Based on Speech Act Theory' *Political Communication* 21, 195–22

Holzinger, Katharina 2005 'Context or Conflict Types: Which Determines the Selection of Communication Mode?' *Acta Politica* 40: 2, 239–54

Husserl, Edmund 1980 [1920] *Ideen zu einer reinen Phänomenologie und phänomenologischen Philosophie 4*, Tübingen: Niemeyer

Jorgensen, Torben 1995 'Consensus Conferences in the Health Care Sector' in Joss Simon & John Durant (eds) *Public Participation in Science*, London: Science Museum, 17–30

Joss, Simon & John Durant (eds) 1995 *Public Participation in Science: The Role of Consensus Conferences in Europe*, London: Science Museum

Kahnemann, Daniel & Amos Tversky 2000 *Choices, Values and Frames*, Cambridge: CUP

Keck, Otto 1995 'Rationales kommunikatives Handeln in den internationalen Beziehungen' *Zeitschrift für Internationale Beziehungen* 2: 1, 5–48

King, Gary, Robert O. Keohane & Sidney Verba 1994 *Designing Social Inquiry Scientific Inference in Qualitative Research*, Princeton: Princeton University Press

Kirchgässner, Gebhard 2000 *Homo Oeconomicus* 2nd edn, Tübingen: Mohr Siebeck

Kirsch, Werner 1977 *Einführung in die Theorie der Entscheidungsprozesse* 2nd edn, Wiesbaden: Th. Gabler

Klein, Wolfgang 1980 'Argumentation und Argument' *Zeitschrift für Literaturwissenschaft und Linguistik* 38/39, 9–57

Klüver, Lars 1995 'Consensus Conferences at the Danish Board of Technology' in Simon Joss & John Durant (eds) *Public Participation in Science*, London: Science Museum, 41–52

Knudsen, Christian 2004 'Alfred Schutz, Austrian Economists and the Knowledge Problem' *Rationality and Society* 16: 1, 45–89

Landwehr, Claudia 2006 'Kann über die Verteilung von Gesundheitsgütern demokratisch entschieden werden? *Forschungsjournal Neue Soziale Bewegungen* 19: 4, 84–97

Lehmbruch, Gerhard 1999 'Verhandlungsdemokratie, Entscheidungsblockaden und Arenenverflechtung' in Wolfgang Merkel (ed.) *Demokratie in Ost und West (Festschrift für Klaus von Beyme)*, Frankfurt am Main: Suhrkamp, 402–24

Lehrer, Keith 1981 'Self-Profile' in Radu J. Bogdan (ed.) *Keith Lehrer*, Dordrecht: D. Reidel Publishing

Lehrer, Keith 1990 *Metamind*, Oxford: Clarendon

Lehrer, Keith 1997 *Self-Trust: A Study of Reason, Knowledge, and Autonomy*, Oxford: Clarendon Press

Lehrer, Keith 2000 *Theory of Knowledge* 2nd edn, Boulder, CO: Westview

Leib, Ethan J. & Baogang He 2006 *The Search For Deliberative Democracy in China*, New York: Palgrave Macmillan

Levi, Isaac 1991 *The Fixation of Belief and Its Undoing*, Cambridge: CUP

List, Christian 2002 'Intradimensional Single-Peakedness and the Multi-dimensional Arrow Problem' *Theory and Decision* 52: 3, 287–301

List, Christian 2004 'Substantive and Meta-Agreement' in Anne van Aaken, Christian List & Christoph Luetge (eds) *Deliberation and Decision*, Aldershot: Ashgate, 119–34

List, Christian & Robert E. Goodin 2001 'Epistemic Democracy: Generalizing the Condorcet Jury Theorem' *The Journal of Political Philosophy* 9: 3, 277–306

Macedo, Stephen (ed.) 1999 *Deliberative Politics: Essays on 'Democracy and Disagreement'*, New York: Oxford University Press

MacIntosh, Duncan 1998 'Categorically Rational Preferences and the Structure of Morality' in Peter A. Danielson (ed.) *Modelling Rationality, Morality, and Evolution, Vancouver Studies in Cognitive Science*, Oxford: Oxford University Press, 282–301

MacKay, A. F. 1980 *Arrow's Theorem: The Paradox of Social Choice*, Yale: Yale University Press

Mackie, Gerry 1998 'All Men Are Liars: Is Democracy Meaningless?' in Jon Elster (ed.) *Deliberative Democracy*, Cambridge: Cambridge University Press, 69–96

Majone, Giandomenico 1989 *Evidence, Argument and Persuasion in the Policy Process*, New Haven and London: Yale University Press

March, J. G. & J. P. Olsen 1989 *Rediscovering Institutions: The Organizational Basis of Politics*, New York: Free Press

McLean, Iain 1991 'Forms of Representation and Systems of Voting' in David Held (ed.) *Political Theory Today*, Cambridge: Cambridge University Press, 172–96

Miller, David 1991 'Deliberative Democracy and Social Choice' *Political Studies* 40, 54–67

Millgram, Elijah 1998 'Deciding to Desire' in Christoph Fehige & Ulla Wessels (eds) *Preferences*, Berlin: De Gruyter, 3–25

Moravcsik, Andrew 1991 'Negotiating the Single European Act: National Interests and Conventional Statecraft in the European Community' *International Organization*, 44: 4, 19–56

Moravcsik, Andrew 1999 'Explaining the Treaty of Amsterdam' *Journal of Common Market Studies* 37: 1, 59–85

Müller, Harald 1994 'Internationale Beziehungen als kommunikatives Handeln

Zur Kritik der utilitaristischen Handlungstheorien' *Zeitschrift für Internationale Beziehungen* 1: 1, 15–44

Mutz, Diana 2006, *Hearing the Other Side: Deliberative versus Participatory Democracy*, Cambridge: Cambridge University Press

Niewöhner, Jörg 2004 'Integration von Bürgerbeteiligung als politische Aufgabe?' in Christof Tannert & Peter Wiedemann (eds) *Stammzellen im Diskurs*, München: Oekom, 67–74

Niemeyer, Simon 2002 *Deliberation in the Wilderness: Transforming Policy Preferences Through Discourse,* Unpublished thesis, Australian National University

Nozick, Robert 1974 *Anarchy, State and Utopia*, New York: Basic Books

Nozick, Robert 1993 *The Nature of Rationality*, Princeton, New Jersey: Princeton University Press

Nullmeier, Frank 2003 'Sprechakttheorie und Textanalyse' in Matthias Leonhard Maier, Achim Hurrelmann, Frank Nullmeier, Tanja Pritzlaff & Achim Wiesner (eds) *Politik als Lernprozess?* Opladen: Leske+Budrich, 211–23

O'Flynn, Ian 2006 *Deliberative Democracy in Divided Societies*, Edinburgh: Edinburgh University Press

Offe, Claus 1992 'Wider scheinradikale Gesten - Die Verfassungspolitik auf der Suche nach dem "Volkswillen" in Gunter Hofman & Werner A. Perger (ed.) *Die Kontroverse: Weizsäckers Parteienkritik in der Diskussion* Frankfurt am Main: Eichboin Verlag 126–42

Offe, Claus 1998 'Vox Populi und Verfassungsökonomik Anmerkungen zum Beitrag von Feld und Savioz' in Gerd Grözinger & Stephan Panther (eds) *Konstitutionelle Politische Ökonomie: sind unsere gesellschaftlichen Regelsysteme in guter Verfassung?* Marburg: Metropolis, 81–88

Offe, Claus 2001 'Wessen Wohl ist das Gemeinwohl?' in Lutz Wingert & Klaus Günther (eds) *Die Öffentlichkeit der Vernunft und die Vernunft der Öffentlichkeit*, Frankfurt am Main: Suhrkamp

Parkinson, John 2003 'Legitimacy Problems in Deliberative Democracy' *Political Studies* 51, 180–96

Pettit, Philip 1991 'Decision Theory and Folk Psychology' in Michael Bacharach & Susan Hurley (eds) *Foundations of Decision Theory*, Oxford: Basil Blackwell, 147–75

Pettit, Philip 1997 *Republicanism: A Theory of Freedom and Government,* Oxford: Oxford University Press

Przeworski, Adam 1998 'Deliberation and Ideological Domination' in Jon Elster (ed.) *Deliberative Democracy*, New York: Cambridge University Press, 140–160

Rawls, John 1971 *A Theory of Justice*, Cambridge, MA: Belknap

Revel, Saul W. 1994 *Tarifverhandlungen in der Bundesrepublik Deutschland Eine Untersuchung der Bedeutung verschiedener Verhandlungsebenen für die sozialökonomische Forschung*, Baden-Baden: Nomos

Richardson, Henry S. 1994 *Practical Reasoning about Final Ends*, Cambridge: Cambridge University Press

Richardson, Henry S. 2002 *Democratic Autonomy: Public Reasoning about the Ends of Policy Oxford Political Theory*, Oxford: Oxford University Press

Riker, William H. 1982 *Liberalism against Populism: A Confrontation Between the Theory of Democracy and the Theory of Social Choice*, San Francisco: Freeman

Risse, Thomas 2000 '"Let's Argue!" Communicative Action in World Politics' *International Organization* 54, 1–39

Rostbøll, Christian F. 2005 'Preferences and Paternalism: On Freedom and Deliberative Democracy' *Political Theory* 33: 3, 370–96

Rüb, Friedbert W. 2003 'Vom Wohlfahrtsstaat zum "manageriellen Staat"? Zum Wandel des Verhältnisses von Markt und Staat in der deutschen Sozialpolitik' in Roland Czada & Reinhard Zintl (eds) *Politik und Markt* (PVS-Sonderheft 34) Wiesbaden: VS Verlag, 256–99

Russell, Bertrand 1954 *Human Society in Ethics and Politics*, London: Allen and Unwin

Rutschmann, Frank 2002 *Der europäische Vermittlungsausschuss Eine organisationsrechtliche Untersuchung der interinstitutionellen Vermittlungseinheit im Rechtsetzungsverfahren*, Berlin: Duncker & Humblot

Samuelson, Paul A. 1938 'A Note on the Pure Theory of Consumer Behaviour' *Economica* 5: 61–71

Sanders, Lynn M. 1997 'Against Deliberation' *Political Theory* 25: 3, 347–76

Saretzki, Thomas 1996 'Wie unterscheiden sich Argumentieren und Verhandeln? Definitionsprobleme, funktionale Bezüge und strukturelle Differenzen von zwei verschiedenen Kommunikationsmodi' in Ker von Prittwitz (ed.) *Verhandeln und Argumentieren Dialog, Interessen und Macht in der Umweltpolitik*, Opladen: Leske+Budrich, 19–39

Scharpf, Fritz W. 1997 *Games Real Actors Play: Actor-Centered Institutionalism in Policy Research*, Boulder, CO: Westview Press

Schindler, Peter 1999 *Datenhandbuch zur Geschichte des Deutschen Bundestages 1949–1999* (3 volumes) Baden-Baden: Nomos

Schütz, Alfred 1993 *Der sinnhafte Aufbau der sozialen Welt: eine Einleitung in die verstehende Soziologie* 6th edn, Frankfurt am Main: Suhrkamp

Searle, John R 1979 'A Taxonomy of Illocutionary Acts' in John R. Searle *Expression and Meaning Studies in the Theory of Speech Acts*, Cambridge: Cambridge University Press, 1–39

Searle, John R. 1983 *Intentionality: An Essay in the Philosophy of Mind*, Cambridge: Cambridge University Press

Searle, John R. 1995 *The Construction of Social Reality*, New York: Free Press

Searle, John R. 2001 *Rationality in Action*, The Jean Nicod Lectures, Cambridge, MA: MIT Press

Selten, Reinhard 2002 'What is Bounded Rationality?' in Gerd Gigerenzer & Reinhard Selten (eds) *Bounded Rationality: The Adaptive Toolbox*, Cambridge, MA: MIT Press, 13–36

Sen, Amartya 1982 *Choice, Welfare and Measurement*, Oxford: Basil Blackwell

Sen, Amartya 1982 'Rational Fools: a Critique of the Behavioural Foundations of Economic Theory' in Amartya Sen *Choice, Welfare and Measurement*, Oxford: Basil Blackwell, 84–106

Sen, Amartya 2002 *Rationality and Freedom*, Cambridge, Massachusetts: Belknap Press

Shafir, Eldar; Itamar Simonson & Amos Tversky 2000 'Reason-Based Choice' in Daniel Kahnemann & Adam Tversky (eds) *Choices, Values and Frames*, Cambridge: Cambridge University Press, 597–619

Shapiro, Ian 1999 'Enough of Deliberation Politics is about Interests and Power' in Stephen Macedo (ed.) *Deliberative Politics: Essays on Democracy and Disagreement*, New York and Oxford: Oxford University Press, 28–38

Shapiro, Ian 2003 'Optimal Deliberation?' in James S. Fishkin & Peter Laslett (eds) *Debating Deliberative Democracy* Oxford: Blackwell, 121–137

Sidgwick, Henry 1907 [1874] *The Method of Ethics* 7th edn. London: Macmillan

Simon, Herbert 1983 *Reason in Human Affairs*, Stanford: Stanford University Press

Slovic, Paul 2000 'The Construction of Preference' in Kahnemann & Tversky (eds) *Choices, Values and Frames*, Cambridge: Cambridge University Press, 489–502

Solomon, G. B. H. & D. R. Wolfensberger 1994 'The Decline of Deliberative Democracy in the House and Proposals for Reform' *Harvard Journal On Legislation* 31: 2 (Summer), 321–70

Spörndli, Markus 2004 *Diskurs und Entscheidung*, Wiesbaden: VS Verlag

Steedman, Ian & Ulrich Krause 1986 'Goethe's Faust and Arrow's Possibility Theorem' in Jon Elster (ed.) *The Multiple Self*, Cambridge: Cambridge University Press, 179–231

Steiner, Jürg, Andre Bächtiger, Markus Spörndli & Marco R Steenbergen 2004 *Deliberative Politics in Action*, Cambridge: Cambridge University Press

Stokes, Susan S. 1998 'Pathologies of Deliberation' in Jon Elster (ed.) *Deliberative Democracy*, Cambridge: Cambridge University Press, 123–39

Sunstein, Cass R. 1990 'Preferences and Politics' *Philosophy and Public Affairs* 20: 1, 3–34

Sunstein, Cass R. 1993 'Democracy and Shifting Preferences' in David Copp, Jean Hampton & John E. Roemer (eds) *The Idea of Democracy*, Cambridge: Cambridge University Press, 196–230

Sunstein, Cass R. 2003 'The Law of Group Polarization' in James S. Fishkin & Peter Laslett (eds) *Debating Deliberative Democracy*, Malden, MA: Blackwell, 80–101

Svejnar, J. 1986 'Bargaining Power, Fear of Disagreement, and Wage Settlements – Theory and Evidence from United-States Industry' *Econometrica* 54: 5 (September), 1055–78

Tannert, Christof & Peter Wiedemann (eds) 2004 *Stammzellen im Diskurs Ein Lese- und Arbeitsbuch zu einer Bürgerkonferenz*, München: Oekom

Todd, Peter M. 2002 'Fast and Frugal Heuristics for Environmentally Bounded

Minds' in Gerd Gigerenzer & Reinhard Selten (eds) *Bounded Rationality: The Adaptive Toolbox*, Cambridge, MA: MIT Press, 51–70

Toulmin, Stephen Edelston 1958 *The Uses of Argument*, Cambridge: Cambridge University Press

Tsebelis, George 1990 *Nested Games: Rational Choice in Comparative Politics*, Berkeley: University of California Press

Tugendhat, E. 1979 *Selbstbewußtsein und Selbstbestimmung*, Frankfurt am Main: Sulrkamp

Tversky, Amos & Daniel Kahnemann 1974 'Judgment under Uncertainty: Heuristics and Biases' *Science* 185, 1124–31

Tversky, Amos & Daniel Kahnemann 2000 'Rational Choice and the Framing of Decisions' in Amos Tversky & Daniel Kahnemann (eds) *Choices, Values and Frames*, Cambridge: Cambridge University Press, 209–23

Urban, Hans-Jürgen 2001 *Wettbewerbskorporatistische Regulierung im Politikfeld Gesundheit Der Bundesausschuss der Ärzte und Krankenkassen und die gesundheitspolitische Wende*, Berlin: Wissenschaftszentrum Berlin für Sozialforschung

van den Daele, Wolfgang 2005 'Einleitung: Soziologische Aufklärung zur Biopolitik' in Wolfgang van den Daele (ed.) *Biopolitik Wiesbaden: Leviathan*, Sonderheft:VS Verlag, 7–44

van Eemeren, Frans H. Rob Grootendorst, J. Anthony Blair & Charles A. Willard (eds) 1987 *Argumentation: Perspectives and Approaches*, Dordrecht: Foris

van Thiel, Sandra 2004 'Trends in the Public Sector: Why Politicians Prefer Quasi-Autonomous Organizations' *Journal of Theoretical Politics* 16: 2, 175–201

van Wright, Georg Henrik 1974 *Erklären und Verstehen*, Frankfurt am Main: Athenäum

Vanberg, Victor & James M. Buchanan 1994 'Interests and Theories in Constitutional Choice' in Victor Vanberg (ed.) *Rules and Choice in Economics*, London and New York: Routledge, 167–77

von Kutschera, Franz 1973 *Einführung in die Logik der Normen, Werte und Entscheidungen*, Freiburg: Karl Alber

Weber, Max 1985 [1922] *Wirtschaft und Gesellschaft: Grundriß der verstehenden Soziologie* 5th edn, Tübingen: Mohr

Windhoff-Heretier, Adrienne 1991 'Institutions, Interests and Political Choice' in Roland Czada (ed.) *Political Choice*, Frankfurt am Main: Campus / Westview, 27–52

Young, Iris Marion 2003 'Activist Challenges to Deliberative Democracy' in James S. Fishkin & Peter Laslett (eds) *Debating Deliberative Democracy*, Malden, MA: Blackwell

Zintl, Reinhard 1994 'Kooperation kollektiver Akteure: Zum Informationsgehalt angewandter Spieltheorie' in Nida-Rümelin, Julian (ed.) *Praktische Rationalität*, Berlin: Walter de Gruyter, 239–57

Zintl, Reinhard 2002 'Politisches Wissen und Wissen in der Politik' in Christoph

Engel, Jost Halfmann & Martin Schulte (eds) *Wissen – Nichtwissen – Unsicheres Wissen*, Baden-Baden: Nomos, 93–112

Zintl, Reinhard 2006 'Der ökonomische Ansatz in der politischen Theorie – nützliches Instrument oder Prokustesbett?' in Thomas Bräuninger & Joachim Behnke (eds) *Jahrbuch für Handlungs- und Entscheidungstheorie,* Wiesbaden: VS Verlag, 215–30

index

abortion debate 81, 82, 157 n.3
academic debate 62-3, 66, 68, 71, 102
acceptance(s) 36-7, 38, 43-4
    as a cognitive premise 39, 43, 46,
    47, 55, 60, 117, 222
    assertions and 57, 58
    belief and 36, 49 n.15, 50 n.20, 21,
    59, 85, 87 n.7
    discursive co-ordination of see co-
    ordination, discursive
    information pooling and 73, 74
    outcomes and 40-1
    political decision-making and 47-8
    preference formation and see pref-
    erence-formation and transformation
    transformability of 50 n.22, 72
        expert discourses and 72, 117
    volition and 37-8, 43-4
Ackermann, B. 105, 129 n.2, 130 n.23
Acta Politica 8 n.2
action
    collective 61, 103, 105, 123
    definition of 12
    instrumental 222
    intention and 20
    judgement and 87 n.7
    justification of 34, 87 n.7
    preference and 38
    moral reasons for 50 n.24
    rational 9, 12, 91
        as rational choice 29
        classical model of 23, 38

    see also rationality and rational
    action
    solidaristic 73
    theories of 9, 12-13
        descriptive/prescriptive 14, 17
    utility and 5, 49 n.12
    welfare and 22
Aigner, I. 218 n.49
akrasia 28
Altenhof, R. 160
altruism 27, 49 n.14
argument and arguing 5, 55, 93, 101, 125
    bargaining, difference with 122,
    141, 147, 149
    'force of the better' 101
    purpose of 134
    religious and conscientious 179
    speech acts 149
argumentation 134-5, 158 n.18
    analysis 147-8, 151-5, 157, 173
        see also German stem-cell
        debate, case study
    conflict of interests and 141
    open and closed quaestios 134
    speech act analysis and 152, 173-4
Arrow, K. 4, 32-3, 71, 74, 75, 79
    impossibility theorem 32-3, 45, 50
    n.18, 78, 80, 83, 85
assertions/assertives 54-5, 56-9, 174,
    217 n.32
    acceptance and 58
    deontic status of 56, 65

Printed in the United Kingdom by
Lightning Source UK Ltd., Milton Keynes
141089UK00002BA/1/P

Peacekeeping is a creation of practice rather than law, and it has gone through many transformations since its creation. As conflicts go through a profound mutation, so should peacekeeping. This volume offers important recommendations that should help peacekeeping reinvent itself, going beyond principles that are no more adapted to the realities of contemporary conflict.

Jean-Marie Guéhenno, *the former UN Under Secretary-General for Peacekeeping and currently the President & CEO of the International Crisis Group (ICG)*

Aoi, Karlsrud and de Coning have produced a timely and relevant study on the changing nature of UN peacekeeping, focusing on the widening gap between principles and practice, and the need to upgrade doctrine to include key concepts such as stabilization. The authors not only focus on the current challenges posed by the latest generation of lethal non-state actors, but they also offer direction for how UN peacekeeping doctrine and political realties can be reconciled.

Karin von Hippel, *Director General, Royal United Service Institute*

Realistic. Timely. Objective. Extremely necessary. Touches the key points: principles, doctrine and practice; the most important question in UN peacekeeping. All the peacekeepers, from New York to the field should read this book, fundamental to protect civilians and UN itself.

Lt.Gen. Carlos Alberto Santos Cruz, *former Force Commander of the UN mission in the Congo (MONUSCO)*

At a time when peace operations are confronting increasingly complex and dangerous challenges, the United Nations' High Level Panel could only begin a much-needed attempt to bring doctrine and practice closer together. This thoughtful volume significantly advances this essential task: both practitioners and analysts should read it and be provoked to engage in a debate which is vital for the UN and its partners.

Ian Martin, Executive Director, *Security Council Report and member of the UN High Level Panel on Peace Operations*

The security architecture of the 21st century places an increasing reliance on the use of force in peacekeeping. The Security Council has crafted mandates, which in some cases go beyond the existing norms of peacekeeping and this has resulted in situations where existing physical and doctrinal deficiencies leaves peacekeepers vulnerable and unsuitable for the task. This book works towards identifying the gaps between international ambitions, present doctrine, principles, operational procedures and actual practice, reappraises the doctrinal deficit and presents options for a UN doctrine for future missions. Undoubtedly a valuable literary addition to the UN Peacekeeping reform process that is presently underway.

Lt.Gen. Abhijit Guha, *former Deputy Military Advisor to the UN and member of the UN High-level Independent Panel on Peace Operations*